Database Sockets and Web Application Development

Papers and Presentations

Second Edition

A collection of the database socket and web application design and management papers and presentations, 1997-1999, with examples of how n-tier web systems were first designed and operationalized.

Patrick Benson

Database Sockets and Web Application Development Papers and Presentations

Second Edition

Print Version: ISBN-13: 978-0-9979215-1-9

Print and eBook Published by GO *-1, Flagstaff, Arizona, USA

Address inquiries about these materials to Patrick M. Benson via pbenson@uw.edu or patrickmbenson@gmail.com.

DEDICATION

This book is dedicated to all the geeks who dreamed of what the web could be and made it so, and to those developers who will make it better, faster, cheaper and more useable in the future.

CONTENTS

The University of Washington financial administrative systems. The first problem area addressed by the socket technology described by these papers and presentations.

The UW had an extensive suite of legacy financial applications developed over a twenty-year span by different vendors and teams. Each application had unique development techniques, several different technologies incorporated and business needs addressed.

The only common thing among the applications was that all were mission critical.

Figure 1 Abbreviations

Ariba Buyer - eCommerce System
ASTRA - User Authorization Service
Enterprise Repository - Data Warehouse(s)
FAS - Financial Accounting System
FAST - FAS Transaction Transfer (Download) System
FASTRANS - Financial Transaction Input (Upload) System
HEPPS - Higher Education Payroll and Personnel System
JDE - JD Edwards Warehouse Mgmt and Inventory System
OASIS - Online Asset Information System
PAS - Purchasing Accounting System
Person Registry - Authentication System

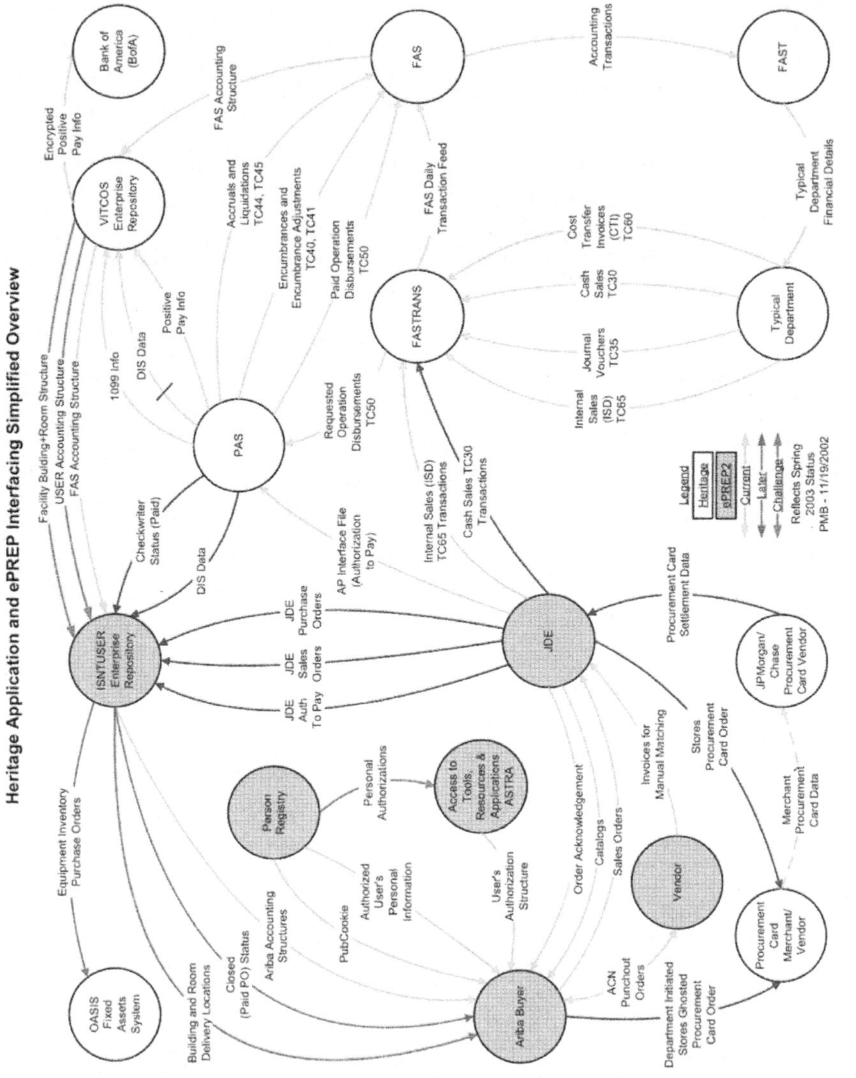

Figure 1 – A graphical overview of the financial application suite at the University of Washington during the 1995-2005 period. This is the environment the author first addressed with socket technology, and that are the subject of the papers and presentations in this book.

ACKNOWLEDGMENTS

The support of the University of Washington during development of socket technology is gratefully acknowledged. I would especially like to acknowledge the contributions of Edith Shen, Ping Lo, the late Dan Groves, and Rita Johnson – thanks guys.

I also appreciate the University giving me the copyrights to these works in 2005 when I moved from the UW to Northern Arizona University.

Patrick M. Benson, PMP
Flagstaff, Arizona – June 2012

Preface and Introduction to the First Edition

I developed sockets technology during the mid-1990s. I don't know that I can take full credit for the basic idea of n-tier technology in a patent-it sort of way. I really don't know who came up with that idea first. What I can take credit for are the initial successful and enterprise-scale web implementations with true n-tier architecture, external high-capacity databases, and external authorization and authentication systems.

The papers and presentations included in this collection were prepared and presented during the mid-1990s. After the initial public presentation, at the 1997 O'Reilly Perl Conference in Santa Clara, my works describing how to implement database socket technology were presented to support software design and development in the public, higher education sector.

The materials, designs and technology described here were put in the public domain by myself and my employer at that time, the University of Washington. Although sockets in general, and database sockets specifically, have broad application, and the technology is in widespread use today (2012), and colleagues still chide me for placing database socket technology in the public domain – it is intended that it remain available equally to all, forever.

Today you may find these papers and presentations bootlegged for sale across the Internet. Couple this theft with my retirement from active IT responsibilities and multiple emerging patents that are derivatives of this public domain technology – and I feel it just made sense to update and publish this collection. In addition, the bootlegged versions are usually just the PowerPoint slides without the speaker notes, and certainly without my at-the-moment updates included in this collection.

I hope that readers will find these documents helpful and educational, or at least historical. I also hope readers recognize the contributions of the University of Washington staff noted in the various papers and presentations. Although the concept and ideas of application and database socket technology are fairly mainstream today, and I have generally retired, I welcome reader's comments.

Preface to the Second Edition

At this point in time the technology described in this book is firmly established. I took the opportunity in this second edition to address numerous misspellings, to update the document so it may easily be converted for download to various versions of e-Readers, and to update the 'About the Author' section, especially the various email addresses I now use.

Shortly after the first edition was published, I wrote to various software firms advising them that it was my intention that this technology was in the public domain. These letters were dated June 6, 2012. The body of these letters is as follows:

> To Whom It May Concern:
>
> First off - I do not seek to sell, give or do business, threaten legal action, etc., with any of the firms addressed in this letter. I am providing a warning about a recent patent application by an IBM employee that might affect products and services the addressees offer. I am resorting to this snail mail because it is difficult to find corporate intellectual property email addresses.
>
> During the mid-1990's I worked as a software developer and manager with the University of Washington. I developed and put into the public domain the technology popularly known today as "database sockets". It continues to be my intention, as well as that of the University of Washington as of May 2012, that this technology remains in the public domain.
>
> Recently, a colleague brought to my attention that an employee of IBM has filed a US Patent Application based upon a derivative of the original database socket technology – one applying to virtual machine database sockets. An electronic version of this application may be found at http://www.google.com/patents/US20110153581. Given the emergence of cloud computing, the general application and expansion of database socket technology, and use of virtual machines, this patent might adversely affect your business. A web search for keywords " 'database sockets' patent" indicates

that there are various other efforts by individuals and firms to split the technology threads and patent derivatives of the original work. I believe these efforts and patent applications are flawed because of prior art.

The original public presentation of the technology was in 1997, as "Perl as a System Glue" at one of the main sessions of the first O'Reilly Perl Conference. The PowerPoint used for that conference presentation is widely available on the web under that same title. The supporting paper with the same title is less widely distributed.

There were three follow-up presentations where I explored and discussed and presented the technology.

- Indiana University 1998 WebDevShare Conference (presentation titled "OASIS, A Web Based Fixed Assets System")
- CAUSE (now Educause) 1998 Conference (presentation titled "OASIS A Web Based Fixed Assets System"
- Indiana University 1999 WebDevShare Conference (presentation titled "Performance Driven Design Issues in Web Development")

At this last presentation the name "database sockets" was applied to the technology, apparently for the first time, during explorations of applications-specific uses for sockets. At the 1998 WebDevShare conference I also provided a version of the web and database server-side C-code to implement database sockets.

These presentations and code are available from my web sites and should still be available from the specific conference web sites. My original versions (generally updated to more current releases of MS-PowerPoint and MS-Word) may be found at sites I maintain. See: http://oak.ucc.nau.edu/pmb38/ or http://sites.google.com/site/patrickmbenson/

I am unsure how to proceed to address this or if it is even appropriate to move in any direction at all since this technology is to be in the public domain. However, I do understand the difficulty in reversing a granted patent. For that reason, I am raising red flags to firms I believe, know or suspect are using this technology and might be adversely affected by this patent application so they might act in their best interest.

Sincerely:

As of the date of this writing, January 22, 2020, all indications are that the patent application is still in process.

From the google patent web site https://patents.google.com/patent/US20110153581 I extracted the following:

Application US12/970,513 events

2009-12-23 Priority to DEEP09180651.3
2009-12-23 Priority to EP09180651
2010-12-16 Application filed by International Business Machines Corp
2010-12-16 Assigned to INTERNATIONAL BUSINESS MACHINES CORPORATION
2011-06-23 Publication of US20110153581A1
2014-11-25 Application granted
2014-11-25 Publication of US8898191B2
2020-01-22 Application status is Expired - Fee Related
2032-05-10 Adjusted expiration

So, the ability to use this technology may eventually be compromised.

As I noted in the first edition comments, feedback from readers is welcome.

How Database Sockets Came To Be

During the 1990's the world wide web emerged as the preeminent way of doing electronic business. In short order, open source web applications, common and open specifications, and user expectations blew away the legacy mainframe and proprietary Electronic Data Interchange, EDI, based systems. From the point of view of a participant in the information technology side of this revolution this was an incredibly exciting time. It seemed new technology emerged daily. Information technology folks, the geeks of the world, were pushed onto the world stage by the media. Some survived and prospered, some just survived.

From a web commerce perspective, the initial limitations of doing business on the web were not all technologically based. Computers capable of handling the loads generated by e-commerce systems were mid-range and mainframes, while developers had desktops and hand-me-down UNIX boxes. It was difficult to get access to the systems and database programmers who were management's gatekeepers. Absent the profit motive and backed by executives with the flexibility to "fiddle" in this new technology, higher education emerged as a key source for innovation. I have asked students to compute and consider the value brought to the world beyond information technology from the University of Illinois Champaign-Urbana release of the NCSA Mosaic browser version 1.0 in November 1993.

In late 1994 my financial applications customers and teams at the University of Washington were facing challenges with software that ran on dissimilar operating systems and platforms. Oftentimes the OS and platform combinations did not match in-house technical resources, university or IT management strategic direction, or plain common sense. (Note – do NOT get me started on elected officials selecting software packages based on low-cost bids!) This various disconnects resulted in the teams having to support different small, midsize and large applications running different operating systems with different data formats and languages. Oftentimes support was catch-as-catch-can. It was a world of expensive incompatibility benefiting the vendors far more than customers.

At the UW I had the distinct pleasure to work with Edith Shen and Dan Groves, two of the best programmers with whom I've ever worked. This is not to take away from Nghia Do, Suantin Mach, Larry Burns, Sharon Erwin, Jan Sullivan or the rest of the financial programmers with whom I worked. Edith and Dan were just really, really good programmers. I also had a super-supportive customer representative, Rita Johnson.

Edith was hired as a general programmer, and she was a generalist in the same way that Steve Wosniak was a general programmer with Apple. We were challenged to support a VAX/VMS mid-range used only for hosting a fixed assets package from a vendor described as the "slumlord of packaged software" by our IT Director. The application development tool was awful and rigid, there was no meaningful vendor support, and the application only used about 5% of a machine that nobody else wanted or needed.

I had hired Dan some years earlier when he left the Air Force. He was primarily hired to maintain and extend the early-style CRM package that the late Dick Phillips and I wrote (Dick wrote most of it, I just made it work better). The Graduate Records System, GRS, was the tool used at the UW for fund development – Burroughs mainframe COBOL, DMS-II and MCP. When Dan had spare cycles he studied and learned, at heart becoming a systems programmer who truly "understood" Unix. Like many talented geeks he did not suffer fools easily, and clashes with management eventually drove him from the UW.

A programmer developing an editor behind a new email system, the precursor to the Pico editor and Pine email systems, put on a demo of this new Mosaic "web service" on the one and only X-Terminal that UW Information Technology Services owned. Edith, Dan and I realized quickly that the most significant problem with the solution was that it was throughput limited. It was a one-tier solution – the web browser, server and database (such as it was back then) resided on the same box. We "appropriated" time and user permissions on an older Unix box that Ping Lo had configured as an independent web server. Experimentation led to a two-tier setup – where the user's desktop computer, with its distinct OS and browser (Windows NT and Netscape by then) was one-tier and the web/data server (AIX/Unix and Perl) was the second-tier.

The two-tier setup was much better, but it also was challenged. We found that it required constant tweaking of the web and data server services. It could be made more responsive to either the input-output side of the problem (the web server) or to the data access and formatting side of the problem (the data server) – but never both.

Unhappy with the level of effort needed to keep the two-tier configuration operational and balanced, I tasked Edith focused on tweaking the application code base, Perl and C-code; and I tasked Dan Groves to help build a Unix network that would allow us to split the web server from the data server running our Informix SQL DBMS.

In one of those "ah ha" afternoons he showed me how to use remote shell commands to control another Unix box to save the time and energy of additional logging in and authentication yourself - and the idea of three tier jumped out at me.

Quickly, the three of us constructed a Perl-based connection process using Unix fork processes to keep the database server up and answering data requests without the need to reinitialize the DBMS for each and every request. By having the web server second-tier always communicate with the database server third-tier as the same named user, our license with our database engine vendor, Informix, was only burdened by one user license fee – a situation that caused issues later on, but those were financial not technical.

Being able to independently tweak the web-server and data-server put us on the path to having enterprise scale web applications. Ping Lo, a systems guy responsible for most of the C-code used in later releases of database sockets, pointed out that the O'Reilly Publishing folks were going to hold a Perl conference. He suggested they might be interested in what we had done. I wrote a proposal, they accepted.

At the First Annual Perl Developers Conference, 1997 in Santa Clara, I had the honor of sharing a stage with Randle Schwartz and presenting the concept. This presentation was titled "Perl as a System Glue" and the paper, PowerPoint and background materials are included as Section 1 of this collection.

The attention the technology garnered at the UW led to a presentation at the Indiana University 1998 WebDevShare Conference. The interest at this conference was from higher education sector technical people and I added explanations and extensions of the socket concepts. In addition to actually naming the technology "database sockets", I included socket level connection concepts and provided a single-instance version of Ping's C-code to implement them. This presentation was titled "OASIS, A Web Based Fixed Assets System" and the paper and PowerPoint are included here as Section 2.

WebDevShare conference leaders talked up the presentation and I was invited to make a similar one at the international 1998 EduComm/CAUSE (now Educause) Conference. This presentation was for a more-management focused audience. I skewed the presentation on how applications worked in a web environment and the costs differences between web and traditional mainframe systems. Here, too, there were some extensions of the database sockets concepts. This presentation is included as Section 3 – there was no presentation paper.

The WebDevShare committee invited me to speak again at the 1999 program. Here, in a program titled "Performance Driven Design Issues in Web Development" I was able to present to a technical audience a review of the EduComm/CAUSE program. I gave a review the status of our socket-based systems first two-years of production. Then explained the ins and outs of n-tier technology and seriously frustrated the pre-Oracle acquisition PeopleSoft team.

Although I've been asked to speak about sockets several times, the 1999 WebDevShare Conference would be my last presentation or paper on the subject. I had been promoted to a management role and passed the baton to others. Soon I was pulled into the morass that was a multiple-system, multiple OS, multiple language, multiple everything, Y2K conversion. And then implementing e-commerce applications to replace some of the UW's more risky legacy applications.

Section 1 – (1997 O'Reilly Perl Conference) Perl as a System Glue

As noted in the Introduction, database sockets emerged quite rapidly as a result of the benefits of separating workstations from application/web servers from data servers. The primary benefit is resolving the fundamental and conflicting tuning needs.

The paper, additional materials and slides that follow are from my "Perl as a System Glue" presentation the First O'Reilly Perl Conference held in Santa Clara in 1997. Included here are:

- Practical Examples of Perl as Cross-Platform Glue – The abstract - This is the document I originally submitted to the O'Reilly team. It has been reformatted to meet the needs of e-publishing and e-books but it contains all the original text.
- Practical Examples of Perl as a System Glue – The Paper – This document was included with the conference materials. It has been reformatted to meet the needs of e-publishing and e-books but it contains all the original text, foibles and all. Later in this book, I've added the errata and after-the-fact information; see the 'Summary Notes and Materials Section'.
- Perl as a System Glue – The Slides – This section includes the slides and my notes used during the presentation. I've included updates from audience questions and comments from the conference – this portion also has been reformatted to meet the needs of e-publishing and e-books.
- Supplementary Notes and Materials – Here is various background and follow-up materials sent out – this portion also has been reformatted to meet the needs of e-publishing and e-books.

A personal note from the 2012 review for publication of these papers and presentations - In some of the documents in this book I refer to the First Perl Conference as having been held in San Jose. This error, and it most certainly is one, worked its way into my various documents almost immediately and I have no idea why or when this first happened. It was held in Santa Clara.

Today, 2012, this conference is held annually, and known as the Open Source Conference. The O'Reilly folks still host it.

ABSTRACT
PRACTICAL EXAMPLES OF PERL AS CROSS-PLATFORM GLUE

Practical Examples of Perl as Cross-Platform Glue
By Patrick M. Benson
Senior Computing Specialist
University of Washington
Seattle, Washington, USA

Abstract:

The paper will describe two examples of using Perl to link diverse platforms and operating systems. Two examples will be presented, a file forward and verification utility and an example of Perl used in CGI generation of dynamic web HTML.

First: a file forward and verification utility. In this application, an insecure platform initiates a Perl script that copies, forwards and echoes a data file between two different, secured platforms.

Second: a Perl web dynamic HTML CGI example. Here, Perl code accepts web parameters, constructs and issues SQL commands through a firewall, accepts data results and generates dynamic HTML results for end user review.

Example One

This Perl is simple. The code serves as an introduction to Perl scripting. It shows the language's ease of use, its form and readability, and the broad scope of operations (cross platform, operating system and language) in which it may be used.

In this example, two trusted host relationships exist. A remote login ("rlogin") and remote shell ("rshell") agreement links Platform A, a VAX/VMS system residing outside the organization's firewall, and Platform B, an IBM RS-6000 running AIX, inside the firewall. A similar relationship exists between Platform B and Platform C, an IBM-309x mainframe running VM that resides inside the firewall of a different organization.

The platform outside the institution's firewall, Platform A, uses the Digital Command Language (DCL) Remote Shell command (rsh) call to command Platform B to pass a file to Platform C. The guts of the process reside on Platform B, where a Perl script first captures the file from Platform A, pulling it through the institution's firewall. The script then forwards the file to Platform C. To verify file integrity, Platform B then pulls a copy of the file back from Platform C, then returns it to Platform A where a DCL "DIFF" command verifies the data returned matches the data sent.

Example Two

This is a more complex example, using a methodology called "Half-a-Perl" for security. Here a fixed HTML script running outside the firewall calls a Perl script CGI that formulates and completes an SQL inquiry then returns a dynamic HTML with results. The example provides a sample Perl script that completes web-to-database connections; tests general access authorizations; generates compliant HMTL; and presents dynamically sized two-dimensional result tables back to the web browser.

In this example, a "thinnest" client (a web browser only) input has an ACTION of a Perl script. A "trusted host" relationship exists between the web server and a database server, similar to that described in Example One, above. A script resident on the web server first accepts the parameters from the client, then constructs an SQL command in the form of a partially completed "rsh" command. This command is the first "half-a-Perl". The script verifies the database server will respond to an "rcp" command; and then issues the "rcp" to send the partially completed SQL command through the firewall. Once through the firewall a remote shell command is executed by the other "half-a-Perl", where it is automatically submitted for execution. When the SQL has completed on the data server, the results are returned and reformatted by the web server Perl script into an HTML friendly format. The number of rows and columns are counted, the data is split apart, a dynamically sized HTML Table is constructed, and a web page is returned to the client browser.

This example shows the string handling capabilities of Perl in a real-world application. Parameter handling, associative and direct array processing, string splitting and concatenation are shown. Examples of loop processing and interception within loops are included. The character handling capabilities and limitations of Perl inside and outside of web applications are addressed, as are security issues surrounding the application of the technology in the web environment. The practical use of the dynamic table approach in light of proposed enhancements to the management of browser cached-memory tables is reviewed. Additionally, the splitting of Perl scripts into discrete objects for improved development times is noted and examples provided.

PAPER - PRACTICAL EXAMPLES OF PERL AS CROSS-PLATFORM GLUE

(1997 PERL CONFERENCE)

Patrick M. Benson

Senior Computing Specialist
University of Washington
Seattle, Washington, USA

Perl As A System Glue

This paper will describe examples of using Perl (the Practical Extraction and Report Language) to link diverse platforms and operating systems. Two examples will be presented, a file forwarding and verification utility and an example of Perl used in CGI generation of dynamic web HTML.

First: a file forwarding and verification utility. In this basic application, an insecure platform initiates a Perl script that copies, forwards and echoes a data file between two different, secured platforms.

Second: a Perl CGI example. Here, Perl code accepts web parameters, constructs and issues SQL commands through a firewall, accepts data results and generates dynamic HTML results for end user review.

Example One, A File Forwarding and Verification Utility

This Perl program is simple. The code serves as an introduction to Perl scripting. It shows the language's ease of use, its form and readability, and the broad scope of operations (cross platform, operating system and language) in which it may be used.

Overview: the Physical Network and Software Environment

Refer to Figure 1, Overview. In this example, the user application runs on a VAX/VMS system. Here they run a FOCUS script to enter parameters that call a Digital Command Language (DCL) command file that initiates the process. This VAX host is considered "untrusted" since there is direct access to the platform without full security controls. However, a trusted host relationship exists between this platform and a routing server inside the firewall, specifically to an IBM RS-6000 running AIX. This platform, in turn, has a trusted relationship to another platform, an IBM-309x mainframe running VM, residing inside the firewall of another remote host.

2012 NOTE – The following are four footnotes in the original document and the printed version in my print version of the same name. These notes are reproduced here due to the inconsistent rendering on various web browsers.

1. FOCUS, in this context, is a registered trademark of Information Builders, Inc. The product is used at our site as a data extraction and report writer.

2. Digital Command Language, DCL, VAX, VMS and DEC, in this context, are registered trademarks of Digital Equipment Corporation.

3. IBM, AIX and VM, RS-6000, in this context, are registered trademarks of International Business Machines, Inc.

4. All the talk of remote this and remote that, trusted this and untrusted that, can be confusing. The remote host (rhost), remote shell (rsh) and network resource (netrc) commands allow untrusted commands to be processed on a trusted platform. "Untrusted" here means the command is issued by or on another platform, and therefore should be treated cautiously. The philosophy behind the operation is that a user who is trusted may indicate that account AAA with password MMM on host XXX is trusted to issue commands on account BBB with password NNN on host YYY. Because this was done the untrusted is process

allowed. I liken it to getting the advice of a trusted friend about an auto mechanic with whom you have never dealt; only because they say the mechanic may be trusted do you take your car to the mechanic. Here is an explanation from Figure 1. The RS-6000 platform has a file in the target account named ".rhost". This file contains a single entry listing the domain name of the VAX remote host with the trusted account name from which the FTP commands will come. For this application it resembles "bronte.u.washington.edu oasisdev", allowing user "oasisdev" to pass data files through to the IBM-309x (assuming all the other security measures are in place, see below). I was trusted to enter the target account and build the ".rhost" file, therefore the process I send is trusted. Between the RS-6000 and the IBM-309x another, similar, relationship exists. This one requires a network resource file (".netrc") on the RS-6000 to indicate the domain, account and password where data may be sent. Entries in this file are restrictive and structured, containing the keywords "machine", "login" and "password". Providing this key is the IBM-309x portion of the trust relationship. For this application the entry resembles "machine bronte.u.washington.edu login $usr42 password Okd0k3y"

Graphically the application may be represented as follows:

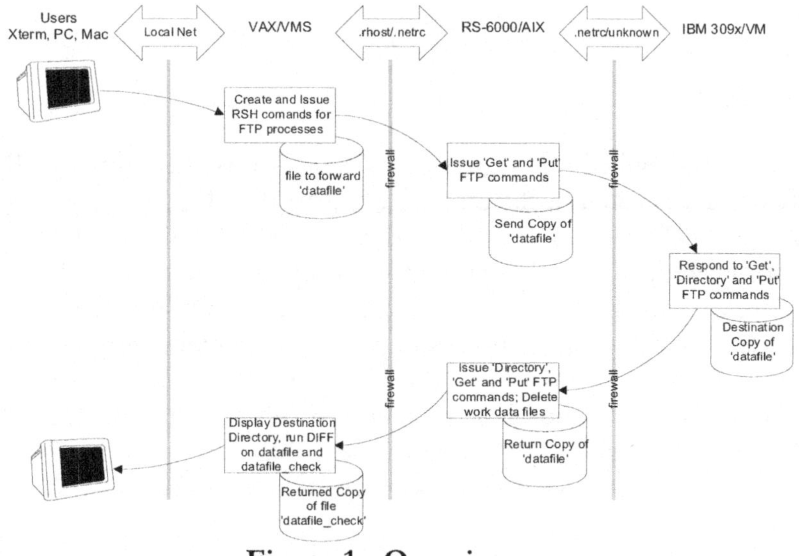

Figure 1 - Overview

Details of the RSH Store, Forward and Loop-Back Process

Step 1

The user accesses software on the VAX/VMS platform outside the institution's firewall, using FOCUS and DCL. This DCL, see Listing 1, VAX/VMS DCL Script, after housekeeping in lines 10-24, issues a Remote Shell (rsh) command call to pass parts of the necessary command to the RS-6000/AIX platform, see lines 26, 27 and 28. After issuance of the rsh the DCL waits patiently for the Perl script to complete, see Step 5 below.

Step 2

This DCL rsh command tells the RS6000 the specific Perl script to run and the arguments it should receive. In this Perl, see Listing 2, RS-6000/AIX Perl Listing, lines 16-25 assign the passed filename arguments to local variables and prints a housekeeping display. Line 27 is the command that pulls the file from the insecure VAX/VMS platform through the firewall and saves it locally. On lines 29-33, the security is changed to read only and a directory of the file is displayed. This is so the user will see that something is happening. Since the commands are being executed under a remote shell, all output that would normally be displayed on the RS-6000 system will be passed back to the VAX/VMS. It appears to the user as if the VAX is executing the commands.

Step 3

The file pulled through the firewall is pushed from the RS-6000/AIX through a different firewall to the IBM-309x/VM; see Listing 2, RS-6000/AIX Perl Listing, lines 34-35. Once the FTP put is completed, another FTP directory command is issued so the user will have some proof that the file got where it was supposed to go. Again, since the function is being executed under a remote shell, now under an FTP shell on the IBM-309x/VM platform, all the output that would be displayed there is relayed back through the RS-6000/AIX, and from there to the VAX/VMS. To the user, it still appears as if the commands are being executed locally.

Step 4

A final step in the rsh process is to pass a copy of the file as it now resides on the final destination back to the VAX/VMS for an integrity test. See Listing 2, RS-6000/AIX Perl Listing, lines 42-46. This is an unnecessary step intended to provide the end user with a local verification that what was received was what was supposed to be received. Once this step finishes, the Perl script removes both the incoming and returned loop-back test files. These are only temporary files on the RS-6000. Then the Perl script terminates and control is passed back to the VAX/VMS DCL script.

Step 5

The VAX/VMS DCL scrip completes a "differences" test on the file sent and the copy returned. See Listing 1, VAX/VMS DCL Script, lines 29-31. When this completes the loop-back check file is deleted from the system, line 32, and a routine "process completed" message is displayed to the user, see line 33.

Start of Listing 1 - VAX/VMS DCL Script

```
1.  $! FTP_THRUSTER.COM
2.  $!
3.  $! This DCL takes a user supplied filename and initiates a remote shell
4.  $! command on the trusted host "thruster.u.washington.edu". This is the
5.  $! start of the store-and-forward and return-for-comparison command
6.  $! script.
7.  $!
8.  $! Set up and load local values for passed parameters
9.  $!
10. $ bronte_filename  = "nofilename"   ! initialization needed
11. $ remote_filename  = "nofilename"   ! initialization needed
12. $ if (P1 .nes. "") then bronte_filename = P1
13. $ if (P2 .nes. "")
14. $ then
15. $   remote_filename = P2
16. $ else
17. $   remote_filename = bronte_filename
18. $ endif
```

```
19. $!
20. $ post_ftp_filename =
    "PGM$ROOT:"bronte_filename'_check"
21. $ ftp_filename    = "PGM$ROOT:"bronte_filename'"
22. $ secure_host     = "thruster.u.washington.edu"
23. $ secure_host_user = "oasisdev"
24. $ secure_script    = "ftp_driver.pl"
25. $!
26. $ write sys$output "Process initiated"
27. $ rsh 'secure_host /username='secure_host_user -
28. "~/"secure_script' "bronte_filename' "remote_filename'"
29. $ write sys$output "Process completed, checking file echo for
    errors."
30. $ diff 'bronte_filename 'post_ftp_filename
31. $ set noverify
32. $ delete 'post_ftp_filename;*
33. $ write sys$output "Process completed"
```

End of Listing 1 - VAX/VMS DCL Script

Start of Listing 2 - RS6000/AIX Perl Script

```
1.  !#/usr/local/bin/Perl
2.  ##############################
3.  # FTP_DRIVER.PL
4.  $|=1;          # turn off Perl's buffering
5.  #
6.  # This script gets the user supplied file name from calling
    host. The
7.  # .netrc file must contain the machine name and password
    combination.
8.  #
9.  # sample DCL calling command: rsh
    thruster.u.washington.edu
10. # /username=oasisdev "nfs/oasis/code/ftp_driver.pl
    infilename outfilename"
11. #
12. print '\nRemote Host contacted, starting FTP processes \n';
13.
14. # Check the number of parameters supplied, must be exactly 2
    (#0 and #1)
```

```
if ($#ARGV != 1) {
  print '\n\n ********************************************';
  print '\n * ARGUMENT MISMATCH ERROR #", $#ARGV, " CONTACT I.S. *';
  print '\n ******************************************\n';
  exit -1;}

$infile = $ARGV[0];
$outfile = $ARGV[1];
$chkfile = $infile . '_check';
print $infile, ' ', $outfile, '\n';

system ("echo \"get $infile\" | ftp bronte.u.washington.edu");

# set security then forward to next box

$set_security = `/bin/chmod 400 $infile`;
$dir_ectory  = `/bin/ls -al $infile`;
print $dir_ectory;
print "\nSending ", $infile, " as ", $outfile, " to Thruster\n";
$send_file = `echo "put $infile $outfile" | ftp vsvm.dis.wa.gov`;

print "Forward complete. Gathering file statistics. \n";
$dir_ectory  = `echo "dir $outfile" | ftp vsvm.dis.wa.gov`;
print $dir_ectory;
print " ... Retain above for reference ... \n\n";

print "Echoing file back for integrity test. \n";
$get_file  = `echo "get $outfile $chkfile" | ftp vsvm.dis.wa.gov`;
$dir_ectory = `ls -al $chkfile`;
print $dir_ectory, "\n";
$send_file  = `echo "put $chkfile" | ftp bronte.u.washington.edu`;

$del_ete = `rm -f $infile`;
$del_ete = `rm -f $chkfile`;

exit 0;
```

End of Listing 2 - RS6000/AIX Perl Script

Note: the paths to UNIX commands that are not build in functions of the shell, in this example ls, rm and ftp, should be fully qualified to the specific code desired. This improves security and reliability.

Example Two, a Perl CGI

This is a more complex example. It uses a methodology locally referred to as "Half-a-Perl" for added operational security. A fixed Hypertext Markup Language (HTML) script running outside the firewall calls a Perl Common Gateway Interface (CGI) that formulates and completes a Structured Query Language (SQL) inquiry, and then creates dynamic HTML with the results.

Overview: the Physical Architecture and Software Concept

Refer to Figure 2, Physical Architecture. In this example, a "thinnest" client HTML script uses a Perl CGI script as an input ACTION. A "trusted host" relationship exists between the web server and a database server, similar to that described earlier in Example One. This Perl CGI script, resident on the web server, first accepts the parameters from the client, then constructs an SQL command in the form of a partially completed remote shell (rsh) command. This command is the first Half-a-Perl. The script verifies the database server will respond to a remote copy (rcp) command and then issues the rcp to send the partially completed SQL command through the firewall. Once allowed through the firewall, the other Half-a-Perl executes the rsh command. When the SQL completes on the data server the results are returned and reformatted by the web server Perl CGI script into an HTML friendly format. The number of rows and columns are counted, the data are split apart, a dynamically sized two-dimensional HTML Table is constructed, and a web page is returned to the client browser.

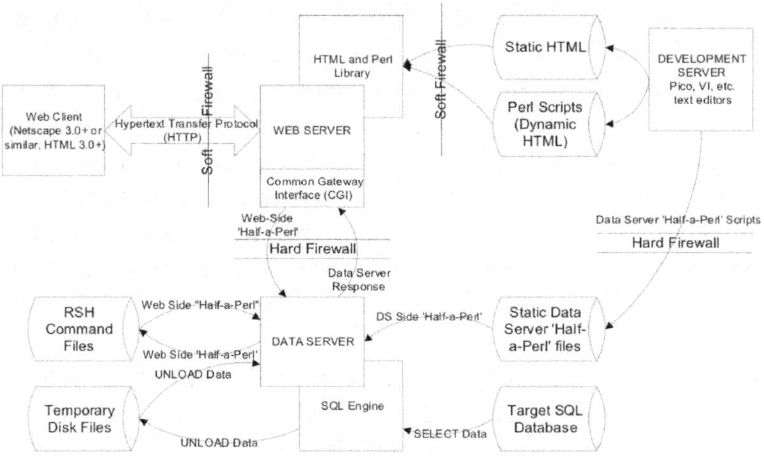

Figure 2 – Physical Architecture

(2012 NOTE – This is the first drawing showing how the n-tier architecture would be implemented. The "Hard Firewall" initially was resolved with the rsh/rcp (later ssh/scp) and later C-Code to provide security. See the text below.)

2012 NOTE – The following is a footnote in the original document and the printed version in my print version of the same name. The note is reproduced here due to the inconsistent rendering on various web browsers.

> [1] The term "thinnest client" is used to indicate that it is a web browser only; there are no plug-ins, Java, Java-Script, Active-X or other tools needed. The term "thin client" has been broadening, and this approach uses a bare-bones web client to promote cross client functional equivalence.

The Half-a-Perl concept provides security by splitting the web data request construction from the database engine meeting the request. It is a logical extension of the classical three-tier data warehouse architecture. There is no direct or logical contact between the web and the data. It enforces a condition where the right hand does not know what the left hand is doing, but the two must work together to meet the user's request.

The web side knows what it wants done, but not what database engine will do the work. The database side knows what engine to use and that all requests must be processed only by a limited set of scripts, but not what requests will be performed. The name and location of the database server and engine are hidden in the web side Perl CGI, reducing the opportunity for unauthorized activities. Any unrecognized command mimics the failure of the SQL command to find matching data. A null string is returned and the web perceives this as a "no rows found" search result.

In this example, the Web Perl CGI is written to prepare an SQL statement and process a returned string (which is delimited with an ISQL dependent character). It sends the SQL statement out and does nothing until a return string is provided. The data server is programmed to funnel whatever command string is provided to a specific ISQL processor and to return a resulting file as a string to the calling web Perl CGI application. It is not programmed to operate at a shell level and does not accept control characters.

Description of Figure 2, Physical Architecture

A Web Client user passes HTML transactions through standard (Hyper Text Transfer Protocol (HTTP). The Web Server has a "Soft Firewall" requiring a system specific userid and password before granting a connection to the application pages. This is a stateless one-time-per-session verification. A "Soft Firewall" is a point where a general-purpose security algorithm is in place, for example, htaccess. This filters out most unauthorized access.

Static HTML pages meet many of the application's needs. These functions include general "Introduction", "Help", "Send Us Email" and "Who is Responsible" type pages. Construction and operation of these functional pages are covered in various reference manuals. See "Further Reading" later in this paper.

When an access to the Data Server must be made, a static HTML calls a Perl script that constructs half of a command, for example, an SQL SELECT statement with all parameters and embedded punctuation. This command is passed through a "Hard Firewall" and stored in temporary space on the Data Server. This is where a Data Server Perl process provides the current machine timestamp to the Web Client browser session. A "Hard Firewall", in this context, is the point where some user identification and access permissions are required. See the discussion of trust relationships in Example One.

To improve security, software development creates a set of Unix commands that are manually placed through the hard firewall as one line data files labeled in Figure 2 as the Static Data Server "Half-a-Perl" files. The composition of such files might be:

/bin/date (Returns the data server timestamp when called)

/Informix/isql oasisdev $1 $2 (Returns a string in $2 meeting SQL request of $1)

By expressly limiting the names and types of commands that user "NOBODY" (the web default set on the Data Server) may perform, the use of these files limits the functions that may be performed. This limiting reduces the opportunity for Trojan Horse and Web Client manipulated HTML GET code hacking.

The access to the Data Server is more restrictive than to the Web Server because of the special nature of these files, they and their permissions are critical. Local software release and management procedures should be developed so these files have execute permissions only. This is an essential portion of the Half-a-Perl concept security.

Details of Dynamic HTML CGI Example

Refer to Listing 3, Perl CGI Listing. For the specific application being discussed, all data is handled by SQL UNLOAD … SELECT type commands. The results are sent back through the Hard Firewall with the "cat -e -v" portion of the rsh command for parsing and display by the Perl CGI that originated the request. For this discussion, the Perl script is broken into five sections.

1. Initializations – Lines 1 through 35
2. Main Driver – Lines 36 through 45
3. SQL Development and Execution – Lines 46 through 105
4. HTML Output Control – Lines 106 through 141
5. HTML Output – Lines 142 through 250

Both Perl's great strength and great weakness are based in the language's flexibility. From the viewpoint of a software developer the strength is there are ten ways to meet any need. From the viewpoint of a software maintainer these same ten ways force you to figure out how and why the (idiotic (?)) developer used one over another. In Listing 3 different ways to do things are presented to show Perl's flexibility, the inconsistent approach is on purpose.

1. Initializations – Lines 1 through 35

The HTML Header Section – Lines 1 through 10

Lines 1 through 10 are the most basic initialization. In 1, the shell bang (shebang) indicates that this is a Perl script. The directory path used follows a standard practice. Line 9, the Content-Type, is an HTML directive telling both browser and server that what follows is HTML. This allows use of Perl block printing of HTML commands rather than requiring line by line "print" statements. At line 10, is the browser command that forces reloading of the HTML, rather than retrieving from local cache, when the page is processed on the Client. This is not needed in static HTML, but since this is the entry point to the table's update and delete functions, it is necessary here. Otherwise a user could delete a table entry and hit the browser's <Back> button and it would seem that nothing had happened. The old table would be retrieved from their local cache rather than having a refreshed table look-up completed. Here, in 10, the print of two carriage returns, the "\n\n", signals the browser that this is the end of the HTML Header section.

Local Variables – Lines 11 through 35

This block of code could be, and perhaps should be, contained in a copy library since all the Perl scripts of the application should use the same text. Here it is included as a part of the mainline since Perl "packages" are beyond the scope of this document. It also shows the differences in visibility between internal and external Perl script fragments.

Line 12 is a standard linkage to an external code library. Here, reference is made to a library of Perl routines, but any external script may be called.

Next, in lines 14 through 23, is a set of commands with critical formats for this application. These are the commands that will set up the rsh and rcp userid and database host names. In a real world this information may be sensitive, and therefore it should be placed in an external code library subroutine where execution will return the variables but exactly what is in those variables may be hidden from the casual observer.

In Lines 27 and 28 variables are constructed containing some of the userid and host name variables discussed above. These commands must be built with careful attention to spacing and special character construction.

The Local Variable section ends with some debug code that has been commented out. During development, these four lines helped during troubleshooting, so they are included here. Notice that the carriage control characters used are HTML not Perl. Due to the Context-Type, and that this code is in the HTML body rather than the header, this is allowed.

2. Main Driver – Lines 36 through 45

This short section is the real guts of the Perl Script. Line 37 calls an external script in the library listed above in the description of line 12. Perl works rationally, meaning it looks for called subroutines or code blocks locally then in all identified external libraries in order of appearance, before ending. An end without finding a called subroutine is abnormal and is completed by return of a negative code such as a -1.

In this example the subroutine ReadParse scans all parameters passed to this Perl script from the HTML script and builds an associative array of them (by default $in{..} is the name of the input array). This allows line 39 to set a local variable "table_name" to be whatever followed the text "table_name=" in the HTML that called this Perl. The position in the calling sequence is not important, allowing new HTML to supply parameters in a different order or to supply more or less parameters than this Perl requires. Unlike some other languages, Perl may be written without concern for parameter reference. Any parameter may be referenced once, twice, not at all, or even referenced when not passed.

The three subroutine calls on lines 41, 42 and 43 drive construction of the SQL statement, issue that command to the data server, accept the returned string and display the results.

Line 45 terminates execution.

3. SQL Development and Execution – Lines 46 through 105

Creation of foreign programming language commands is where Perl really shines.

Lines 49 through 59 make up a short local subroutine. Note the inclusion in squiggly brackets, this is how blocks of code are segmented in Perl. Here the script constructs an SQL statement to unload all occurrences of two data elements from a data table whose name is passed as a parameter. The Half-a-Perl construction technique presupposes that the calling HTML, Perl or shell knows what it is doing. If an improper calling sequence is used the Data Server will return an empty string which the CGI will interpret as "no rows found". For example, if a rogue user passes "rm –fr /*" rather than supplying a correct string such as "table_name=bldg_id", the script will fail and return a null string because this is not a valid SQL command.

Next, lines 62 through 71, this SQL statement is copied to a working file with a known, fixed name on the web server. In a large scale application, where dozens of hits per second occur, it would be a good idea to dynamically name these files by adding the hostname and id variables from the debug stuff in lines 34 and 35. Consideration should be given to using the Perl Global Special Variable "$$" to attach the process number of the Perl running the script to the file name. Since Perl, unlike HTML, has state, each instance of the script is allowed to control specific files from creation to deletion. In 71, the permissions of the working file are changed so that the remote copy service can read the file. This file is the web server's half of the "Half-a-Perl".

In 72 through 80, the permission of the web server to access the data server is tested. The remote shell command to return the data server time will work only if a proper .rhost relationship between the two machines has been constructed. If it has then the time data block will be returned as $info_time. If it has not or if the data server is not available for any reason, a null will be returned. This null is interpreted in 77, where failure results in a generic display and immediate exit from the process.

If the remote host relationship is sound, the SQL command file built in 62 through 71 is copied across the firewall to the data server by line 86. Here, too, security is maintained if there is no write permission on the data server for the userid of the calling web server this remote copy command will fail. This failure is trapped during execution of the command.

Line 94 commands execution of the SQL statement. It is a remote shell command that passes specifically formatted text to the specifically named SQL engine through a specifically named data file. In the example being discussed, an explosion of the variables would yield the following:

$info = `rsh equip –l oasis "oasis_rsh_1 oasisdev@equipdev isql_tables.sql; cat -e -v TEMPTBL; rm TEMPTABLE"`

This command is named and is "back ticked" with the ` character. This has the effect of saying the following.

Return as a string of undefined length into the "$info" variable the contents of file TEMPTBL. This string has carriage returns replaced by " | $" and is removed after passing. The contents of the file are the results of passing the text "equip –l oasis" to a command file named "oasis_rsh_1" that needs the parameters "oasisdev@equipdev" and "isql_tables.sql". The script contents of this file are the data server "Half_a_Perl".

Whew! Perl is terse where it needs to be terse. This command does point to a pitfall for novice writers, and that is the need for rcp and rsh commands to occupy a single line. Continuation and concatenation may be done in print and variable constructions, but not in execution. This limitation is because the receiving Unix server doesn't know when the command ends, so the carriage return is assumed to be that end.

The result of the SQL are returned in string $info. Line 100 splits that string into data table rows and 101 gives us the depth of the output table needed. Line 102 splits the first returned record and 103 counts the number of columns in row 1, giving us the width.

A sharp Perl writer will quickly jump on a potential problem with this logic. This sample presupposes that the first or only record returned will have something other than nulls in the second returned variable. This is because this script is written for system tables where another Perl script assures that the contents of name_value and name_full_text both are present (these are the database element names from the SQL statement construction in line 53). If you are returning 50, 60 or more columns (I've returned over 80 in other parts of this system) it is better to count the columns to return by counting the number of input cells requested. If you expect 20 columns and the first record has nulls after column 12 then the variable $col_count will be set to 12. If records after number 1 have entries in columns 13 through 20, those data will not be displayed. Later, below when setting the table size during creation of the dynamic table, there are comments addressing this issue. A better method is to test for every element that might be returned up near line 39. Testing each possible column name passed (use the same name for the SQL data element and the local data element) for a not null value and incrementing the variable $col_count back there would do the trick. This technique is used in scripts that are more complex; the not null test is used as an opportunity to build an array of column headings, too.

4. HTML Output Control – Lines 106 through 141

In this example, the output is arranged into subroutines under the control of a master subroutine. The master is the short subroutine in lines 106 through 114. This code first calls another short subroutine that sets up the table headers depending upon the name of the table being displayed. This code section, lines 116 to 141, is an example of nested "if" statements in Perl.

5. HTML Output – Lines 142 through 250

This last area for discussion contains the Perl that creates the HTML returned to the client browser. It is broken into three sections, header, body and footer. The header and footer are Perl "copy through tag" blocks. Since HTML ignores carriage returns, it is acceptable to split Perl commands across lines when generating code in this manner.

The Web Page header, all the text that appears at the top of the dynamic table, is in lines 142 through 163.

The body of the HTML contains the dynamic table logic. It may appear daunting but is fairly easy to walk through. The initial TABLE tag is printed by line 175. This uses the variable $col_count to set the number of columns. Also here is an example of backslash control of Perl editing. The BORDER tag has double quotation marks preceded by backslashes around the value. These tell the Perl interpreter to consider it as a special character. This allows the quotation mark to be passed from Perl to HTML, where it is correctly processed. For example, "\n" tells Perl to substitute a carriage return while "\"" resolves into a single double quote. The Perl script fragment (from line 183) "<TD ALIGN=\"CENTER\"> resolves into "<TD ALIGN="CENTER"> when it finally reaches the web browser. You will note extensive use of backslashes when Perl is used to create HTML. It is difficult, at times, to tell them from single quotes. They are a newer variation of the "0" and "O" problem.

The "for" statement in line 176 uses the variable $row_count that was set during the initial splitting of our returned data stream. This statement prints both the Table Header columns and the Table Body containing the returned results. See lines 180 through 185 for the Header and lines 188 through 207 for the Table Body.

The Table Body sets column 1 to be a form, allowing click and jump access to that specific record. If a wide and deep table is displayed, over 200 lines of 10 columns (although I have seen up to 500 displayed this way), it takes a measurable amount of time to build this number of FORM tags and pass the data to the browser for display. Some thought should be given to constructing an inner loop for 20 to 40 entries. Additionally, when off-the-shelf web browser print functions are used the user may face substantial challenges trying to get a many column report to fit onto one page. There also are web browser inconsistencies in printing buttons and anchors.

A solution to his problem is to have the Static Web HTML post a radio box allowing the user to request the CGI to format the output for "point-and-click" or "send to printer". The Perl CGI then creates buttons (or anchors) for the "point-and-click" requests (as in this example) and can use the HTML "<PRE> formatted line text </PRE>" command for "send to printer" type requests.

After the dynamic portion of the table, an "Add New" form is constructed by lines 209 through 217. The HTML end-of-table tags are printed here, too.

The footer is made up of lines 218 through the end of Listing 3. It concludes with an "End of data" message, an HTML FORM providing an anchor to the system email page and displays a copyright label block. In this final block of code you find the </BODY> and </HTML> ending commands.

Start of Listing 3, Perl CGI

```
1. #!/usr/local/bin/Perl
2. ###################################
3. # EQUIP/UTIL/TRANSTABLE.CGI
4. $|=1;          # turn off Perl's buffering
5. #
6. # This Perl script receives the table name and returns a
   formatted list
7. # of the contents
8. #
9. print "CONTENT-TYPE: text/html","\n";
10. print "Pragma: no-cache","\n\n";
11.
12. require "/www/world/cgi-bin/cgi-lib.pl";
13.
14. $rcp_user  = 'oasis';
15. $rcp_cmd   = '/usr/ucb/rcp';
16. $rcp_host  = 'equip.u.washington.edu';
17.
18.
19. $rsh_user  = 'oasis';
20. $rsh_cmd   = '/usr/ucb/rsh';
21.
22. $sql_host  = 'equip.u.washington.edu';
```

```
$sql_db   = ‘oasisdev@equipdev’;
$rsh_file  = ‘oasis_rsh_1’;

# Local commands built from global definitions spaces are critical

$rcp_destination = $rcp_user . ‘\@’ . $rcp_host . ‘:.’;
$sql_user = $sql_host . ‘ -l ‘ . $rsh_user . ‘ ‘;

# some debug stuff that comes in handy

# print "<p>", `whoami`;
# print "<p>", `pwd`;
# print "<p>", `hostname`;
# print "<p>", `id`;

&ReadParse;

$table_name = $in{'table_name'};

&set_extract;
&run_extract;
&write_report;

exit;
#
# *************** subroutines ***************
#
sub set_extract {

# Set up extraction parameters

 $sellist  = ‘name_value, name_full_text’;
 $passlist  = “‘$table_name’”;
 $sql_tables = ‘UNLOAD TO TEMPTBL SELECT ‘ . $sellist
   . ‘ FROM names’
   . ‘ WHERE name_type = ‘ . $passlist
   . ‘\n’;
}
# ***************
```

(See Note on Listing 2, RS6000/AIX Perl Scrip about UNIX command path specification.)

```

sub run_extract {

# Copy the sql string to the pass-file name, the z, y and z are
# for troubleshooting

 $v = `rm $isql_tables.sql`;
 $w = open(isql_tables_dummy, ">isql_tables.sql");
 $x = print isql_tables_dummy $sql_tables;
 $y = close(isql_tables_dummy);
 $z = `chmod 755 isql_tables.sql`;

# Hit target with time request to verify access permissions
# and server presence

 $info_time = `$rsh_cmd $sql_user "/bin/date "`;
 if ($info_time eq '') {
  print "<P>Database Server not responding ... try again later.";
  exit;
 }

# Remote copy the sql command pass-file to the sql server
# e.g. rcp isql_tables.sql oasis@equip.u.washington.edu:.

 $d = `rcp isql_tables.sql $rcp_destination`;

# Issue the rhost command to initiate the sql, file TEMPTBL
# contains the results, the 'cat -e -v' is used to facilitate
# the split command catching each returned row. NOTE: The rsh
# command must be on one line, even if it extends past the margin
# or Perl will split it and put in a <CR>. That will end execution
# (probably prematurely) of the command.

 $info = `rsh $sql_user "$rsh_file $sql_db isql_tables.sql; cat -e -v TEMPTBL ; rm TEMPTBL"`;
```

```

# Set up size of output table, the $#row_data + 1 is needed
# because there is no trailing delimiter (was stripped out by
# initial table split command)

 @table_data = split('\|\$',$info);
 $row_count = $#table_data;
 @row_data = split('\|',$table_data[0]);
 $col_count = $#row_data + 1;
}

# ***************

sub write_report {

 &build_headers;
 &write_header;
 &write_body;
 &write_footers;
}

# ***************

sub build_headers {

# Construct the HTML result column headers, defaults first, then real

 $table_title[0] = 'Column 1';
 $table_title[1] = 'Column 2';
#
if ($table_name eq "class") {
  $table_title[0] = 'Class Code';
  $table_title[1] = 'Class of Equipment';}
elsif ($table_name eq "cond") {
  $table_title[0] = 'Condition Code';
  $table_title[1] = 'Asset's Present Condition';}
 elsif ($table_name eq "bldg") {
  $table_title[0] = 'Building Number';
  $table_title[1] = 'Building Name';}
 elsif ($table_name eq "owner") {
  $table_title[0] = 'Ownership Code';
```

```
 $table_title[1] = 'Asset Ownership'; }
elsif ($table_name eq "org") {
 $table_title[0] = 'Org Code';
 $table_title[1] = 'Organization Description';}
}

# ***************

sub write_header {

# page header printed here

print <<end_of_header;
 <HTML>
 <HEAD><TITLE>
 Table Contents Inquiry
 </TITLE></HEAD>
 <BODY>
 <P>
 <H2>
 $table_title[0] Table as of : $info_time
 </H2>
 <P>
 <B>$table_title[0] Table Contents Inquiry</B> Click on the highlighted
 $table_title[0] to be taken to the Table Update for that item.
end_of_header
}

# ***************

sub write_body {

# Dynamic table creation and print. For each returned row split the
# results into the correct column positions. Only thing not dynamic is
# creation of column headers. That part is process dependent and must
# be tailored, and the addition of a 'Add New' last entry. The Column
```

```
# 1 entries (after the header) are stand alone forms to allow point-
# and-click selection and execution of the table update CGI.

print "<P> <TABLE COL=$col_count BORDER=\"1\" ";
for ($i = 0; $i < $row_count; $i++) {

# print the column headers from the table_title array

if ($i == 0) {
 print "<THEAD><TR>";
 for ($j = 0; $j < $col_count; $j++) {
  print "<TD ALIGN=\"CENTER\"> $table_title[$j] </TD>";
 }
 print "</THEAD><TBODY>";
}

#
# dynamic print, one for each returned record, the real data, column 1
# is a form for the click-to-jump to the udpate CGI.

# The $row_data[0] =~ s/\xA//g; command is to drop the linefeeds
# (interprets as replace $row_data[0] with $row_data[0] less the hex A
# linefeed character)

@row_data = split('\|',$table_data[$i]);
for ($j = 0; $j < $col_count; $j++) {
 if ($j == 0) {
  $row_data[0] =~ s/\xA//g;
print "<TR><TD><FORM METHOD=\"GET\"ACTION=\"./update_table.cgi\">
  <INPUT TYPE=\"hidden\" NAME=\"$table_name\"
  VALUE=\"$row_data[0]\">
  <INPUT TYPE=\"SUBMIT\" VALUE=\"$row_data[0]\"></FORM></TD>";
 } else {
  print "<TD> $row_data[$j] </TD>";
```

```
  }
 }
}

# Add-a-New last entry

 print "<TR><TD><FORM METHOD=\"GET\" ACTION=\"./add_table_cell.cgi\">
 <INPUT TYPE=\"HIDDEN\" NAME=\"$table_name\" VALUE=\"addanew\">
 <INPUT TYPE=\"SUBMIT\" VALUE=\"Add New\"> </FORM></TD> ";
 print "<TD> Add a New $table_title[0] </TD>";
 print "</TBODY></TABLE>";
}

# ***************

sub write_footers {

# standard HTML footer

print <<end_of_footer;
 <BR>
 End of data returned from inquiry.
 <BR>
end_of_footer

# put up the quit box

print <<end_of_form_quit;
 <FORM METHOD=\"GET\" ACTION="../os_tables.html">
 <INPUT TYPE="SUBMIT" VALUE="Quit back to Table Selection Page" </FORM>
 <HR>
Contact EIO or IS via the email interface. Click here,
 <A HREF="../os_mail.html">Email</A>, for the Oasis Emailer
end_of_form_quit

# standard copyright stuff
```

```
print <<end_copyright;
<HR>
<P>
&copy; University of Washington, 1997
Last Update: (Under Development)
</BODY>
</HTML>
end_copyright
}
```

End of Listing 3, Perl CGI

Security and the Half-a-Perl Concept

The Half-a-Perl concept shown here is based on the behavior of Perl and ISQL interpreters. All commands passed through from the web server to the data server must go through one of the predefined scripts. These scripts are untouchable by the web, since they reside behind a hard firewall on the data server and only have execute permission. In this case, bogus commands, like submitting the HTML form after replacing the usual parameter string with "rm *", are not recognized since only valid ISQL commands will yield any results. In addition, if a determined rogue user sent a bogus but properly formed escape sequence, ISQL will terminate with control returning immediately to the calling Perl script.

The example presented is not complex but intended to show a methodology. The concept may be extended by putting Perl (or shell scripts) in the Data Server Half-a-Perl files. This will allow calls to other processes and domains or platforms as needed to fulfill the web-initiated request. The essential point is the Perl CGI on the Web Server only prepares a parameter string for the Data Server. It does not act directly upon the data. The Perl on the Data Server only acts on the data, leaving the input and output formatting to the Web Server. Protecting the Data Server code elements, with the special installation and management policies as noted earlier, provides a level of security for the data.

One piece of processing should be considered for all Perl scripts accepting web input, that is an escape character pre-process. These act to scan all inputs and place backslashes ahead of escapable characters, like the single quote that may appear in a person's name. A good meta-character scan routine may be built around the samples provided by Tracy Monaghan, University of Washington, that is an extension of one available at www.cerf.net. These subroutines should be inserted and called when necessary.

```
#
# Escape meta-characters, remove new lines
# $_[0] is the user-supplied data
#
sub DropEscapeChar {
 $_[0] =~ s/%(..)/pack("c",hex($1))/ge;
# Escape the nasty metacharacters
# (List courtesy of http://www.cerf.net/~paulp/cgi-
security/safe-cgi.txt)
 $_[0] =~ s/([;<>\*\|`&\$!#\(\)\[\]\{\}:'"\n])/\\$1/g;
# SECURITY FIX: REMOVE NEWLINES
 $_[0] =~ tr/\n//d;
 return $_[0];
}

#
# Unescape meta-characters (see above)
# $_[0] is the user-supplied data
#
sub AddbackUnescapeChar {
# Unescape previously escaped nasty metacharacters
# (List courtesy of http://www.cerf.net/~paulp/cgi-
security/safe-cgi.txt)
 $_[0] =~ s/\\([;<>\*\|`&\$!#\(\)\[\]\{\}:'"\n])/$1/g;
 return $_[0];
}
```

Summary

These two examples show the usability, readability and flexibility of using Perl to glue different platforms and operating environments together. The Store-and-Forward example works in a complex environment of three different platform types and operating systems, where the type of network management software at the end of the process is not even known. The Perl CGI example shows how Perl may be used to construct SQL commands, issue them for execution and return results in a form resulting in consistent web displays. The "Half-a-Perl" concept outlined in this example also provides a measure of security since only those commands that are acceptable by the untouchable half will successfully complete.

Acknowledgements and Further Reading

Daniel Groves, Tracy Monaghan and Rick Anglin, all fellow C&C Staff at the University of Washington, helped, harassed, reviewed and encouraged me during the development of the Perl concepts outlined in this paper. I would like to thank Jerry Luiten and Mike Pingree for allowing me professional development time to complete the work.

My library includes the following volumes I consider required reading for Perl and HTML.

"Programming Perl", Larry Wall and Randal L. Schwartz, O'Reilly & Associates, 103 Morris Street, Suite A, Sebastopol, CA 95472, 1991-3

"UNIX in a Nutshell", Daniel Gilly and the staff of O'Reilly & Associates, 1986-94

"CGI Programming on the World Wide Web", Shishir Gundavaram, O'Reilly & Associates, 1996

"HTML Sourcebook", Ian S. Graham, John Wiley & Sons, 1996

SOME PRESENTATION BACKGROUND – FEAR IN SANTA CLARA

This presentation, my first in a commercial setting, was an exciting event. The O'Reilly team had told me to plan for 50 attendees. I brought that many copies of the paper with me. I checked into the Speaker's Room when I arrived the day before the conference. Hit by a bit of stage fright, I thought I'd check out the aura of the room where I'd be speaking and asked which it was and how to get there.

The nice fellow (and in my experience all of Tim O'Reilly's conference people are nice - really, they all are!), looked at his sheet and said, ominously. "You're in … (dramatic pause … really dramatic pause)…. the big room."

This was followed with a nervous laugh. Although from this distance of time I cannot remember now which of us laughed more nervously. Him at the look on my face or me at the way he pronounced "the big room."

He had a young lady to lead me to the speakers' entrance of "the Big Room." True to its name it looked the size of four football fields.

I asked the young lady how many it sat.

"1,200 … more or less."

And how many folks do you think will really be here?

"You're sharing the stage with Randle (Schwarz) so it probably will be standing room only."

What about copies of the paper and …

"Tim had all your material included in the conference binder. Oh, I need you to sign a video recording release and distribution form, too."

Yikes! If I went down in flames it would be very public.

I didn't sleep well that night. The next morning, I shared the elevator with Tim Brenners-Lee and he asked if I'd have breakfast with him. There is nothing, nothing, nothing in this world like breaking bread with God to calm the nerves – yeah, right! For the record he was very gracious. It ended up that he was called away by a reporter for *PC World* or *Information Week* or one of the trade publications shortly after we started eating so my panic was short-lived.

A word of advice to those who share a platform with Randle. God bless him, but he has a lot to say (most of it better than good) and can burn through a lot of time. I ended up with about half the time I'd planned for and cut the first part of my presentation completely on the fly. If memory serves me, I said something like, "If this is too complex for you then you're at the wrong conference."

In any event, things went well. Here are the presentation slides.

Search as I might, I cannot find my original copy of the presentation, the one upon which I'd have written notes. My memory is that there were only three questions. Two having to do with using 'ssh' instead of 'rsh' for security, and one having to do with support resources needed. I worked both those topics into the 1998 WebDevShare paper and presentation.

For what is worth, over the years and in a couple other places in this book, I've noted that I let an error creep into various later presentations – I placed this conference in San Jose rather than Santa Clara. Oops.

PRESENTATION - PERL AS A SYSTEM GLUE

Slide 1

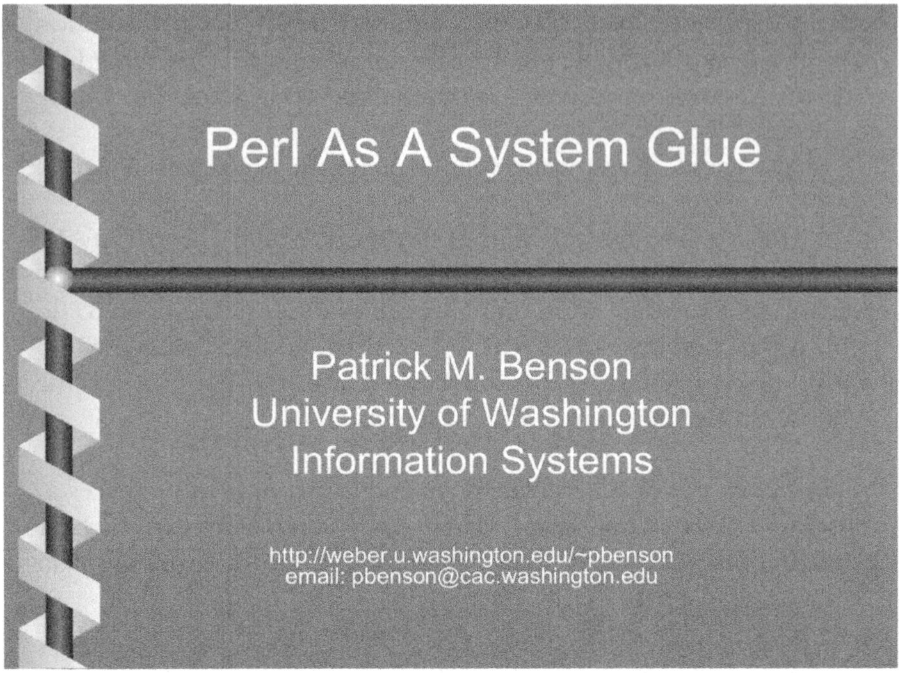

(2012 Note - The original presentation was in an early version of PowerPoint, about the 94 one – and there was a neat little animation where the white ball at the intersection of the horizontal and vertical lines moved up from the bottom, hooked a right at the intersection, then continued off the right side of the display. It was cool, but useless, and it doesn't work any longer.)

(2020 Note – The web and email information on this slide is incorrect. I've moved on from the University of Washington. See later in the 'About the Author' section.)

Slide 2

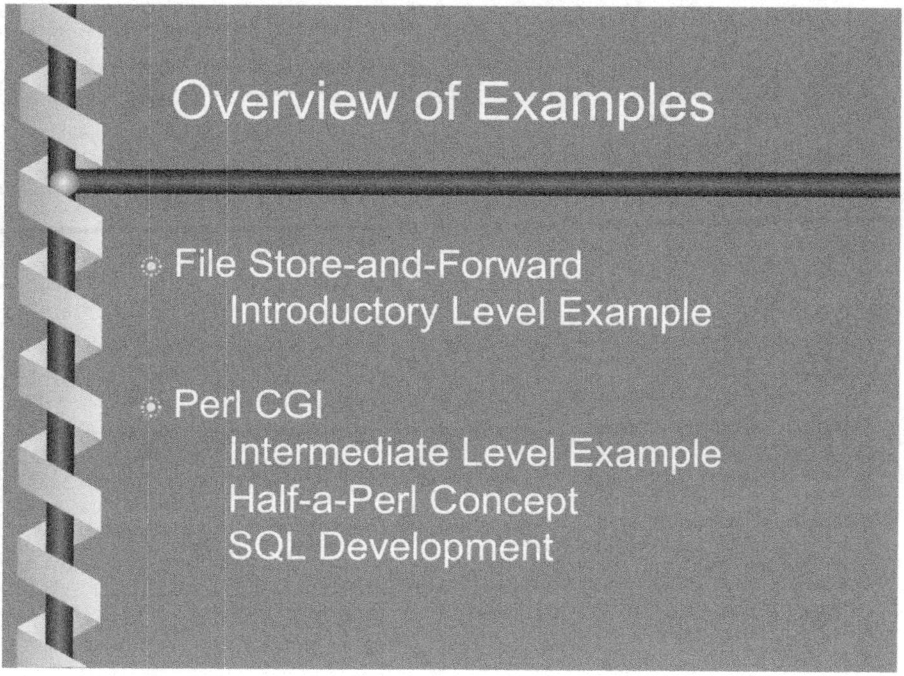

(2012 Note – Before reaching the podium I knew I wouldn't have enough time to get through everything so at this slide I told folks I'd be skipping the first section.)

(2020 Note – By "first section" I meant the File Store-and-Forward section. That was very platform centric. At the time I thought it was superfluous to the web-centric nature of the conference.)

Slide 3

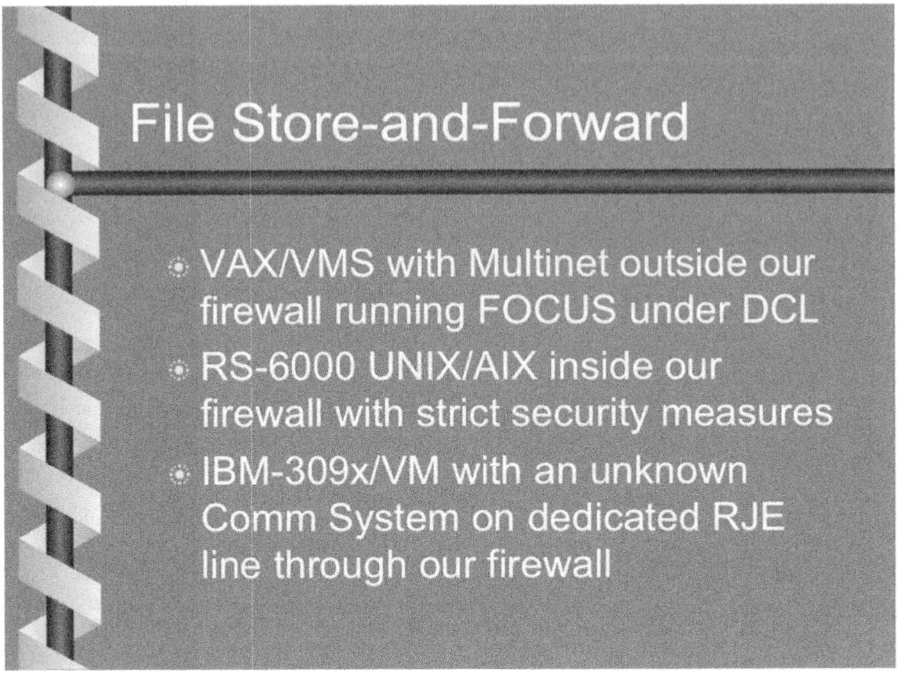

(2012 Note – At this slide I said something to the effect of, "If you don't understand this, you're at the wrong conference." It was greeted with a laugh at the time but later in the conference I was asked about this several times.)

Slide 4
(2012 Note - This slide was one of those skipped)

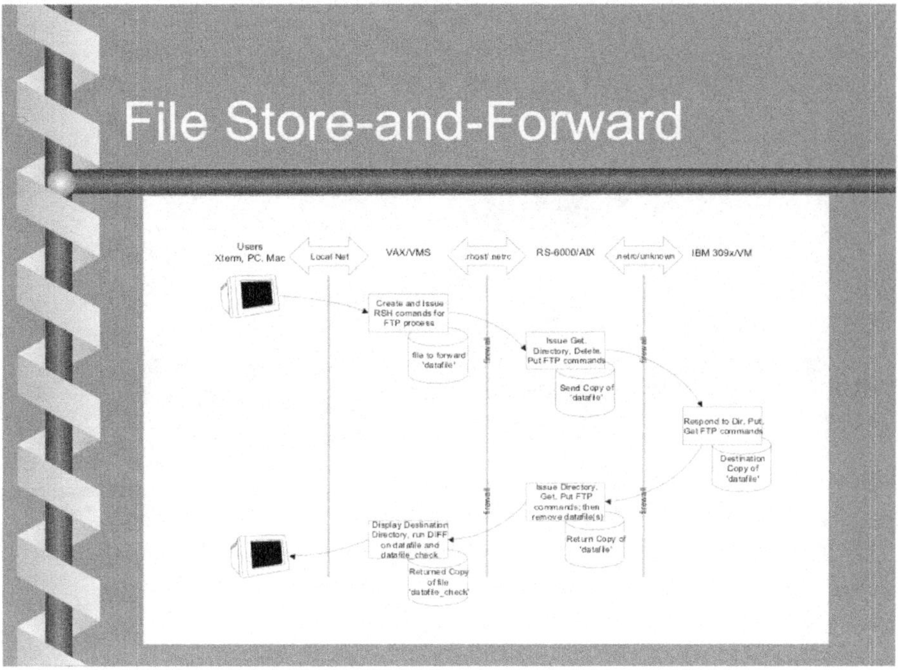

Slide 5
(2012 Note - This slide was one of those skipped)

Slide 6
(2012 Note - This slide was one of those skipped)

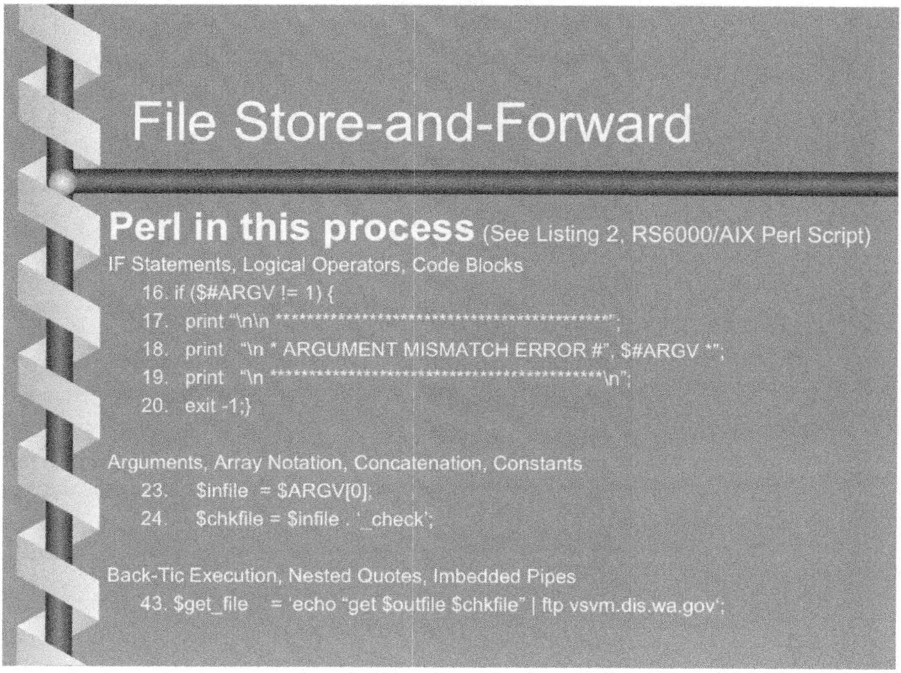

Slide 7
(2012 Note - This is where I started the presentation.)

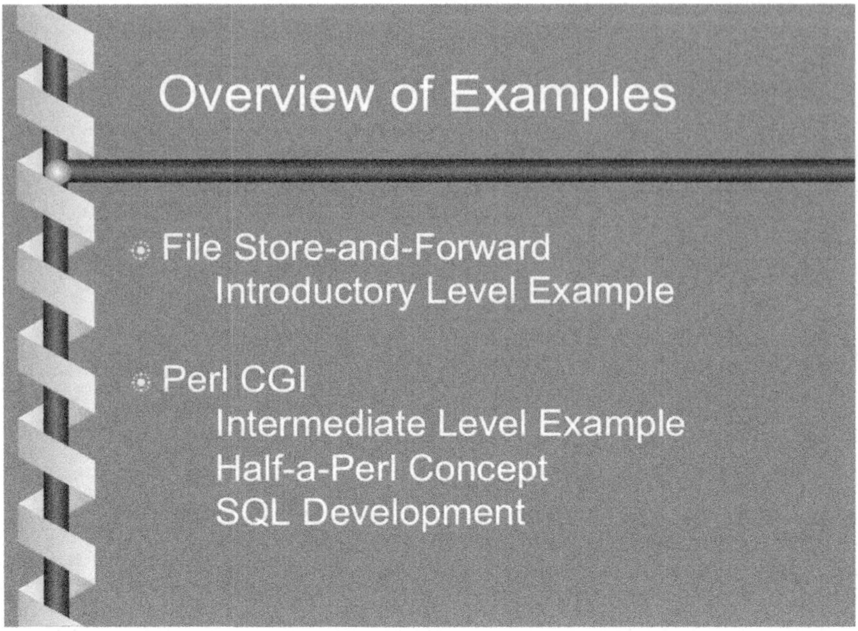

Slide 8

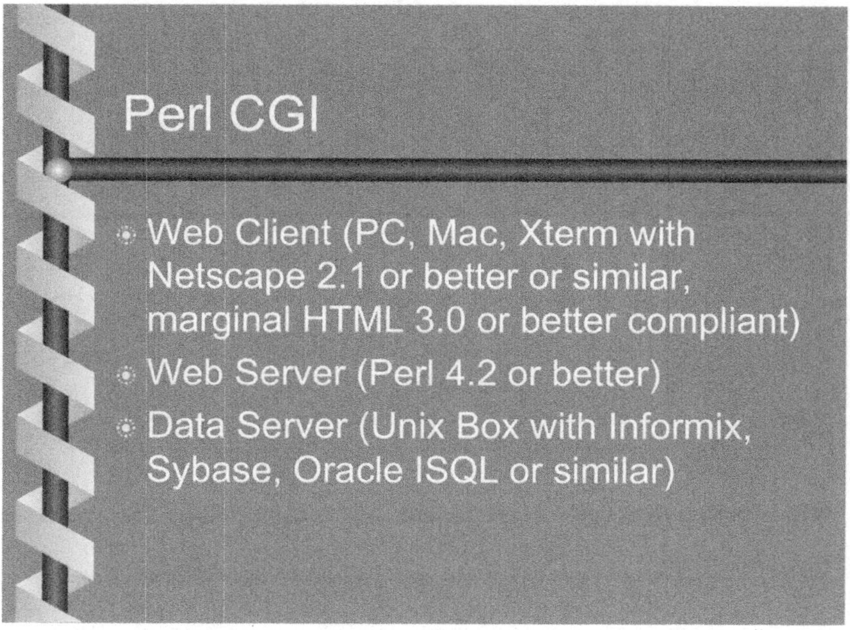

- Stress various browsers.
- Stress enterprise-scale databases

Slide 9

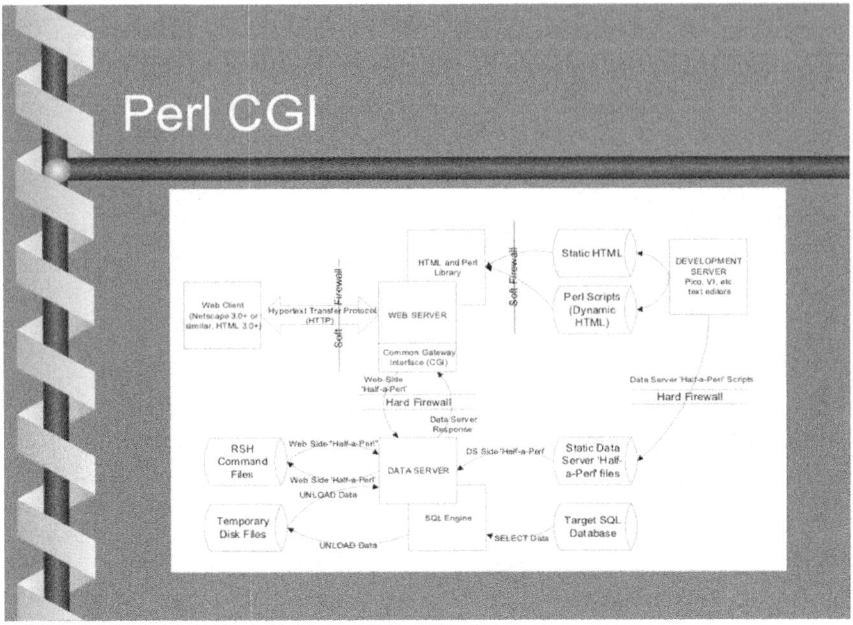

Stress the "trusted" relationships

(2012 Note – I was asked about this slide at SeaTac Airport after the conference. After we spoke and I reminded the fellows that this was all in the public domain the fellow suggested I call his boss at a new company, Amazon.Com, because he would be taking the technology there and they might need someone with my skills and experience. I made a half-hearted effort and spoke with a guy named Jeff. I hear he's done quite well for himself and his firm. Darn it.

The core of this slide is included at the end of this section in a more readable format.

Slide 10

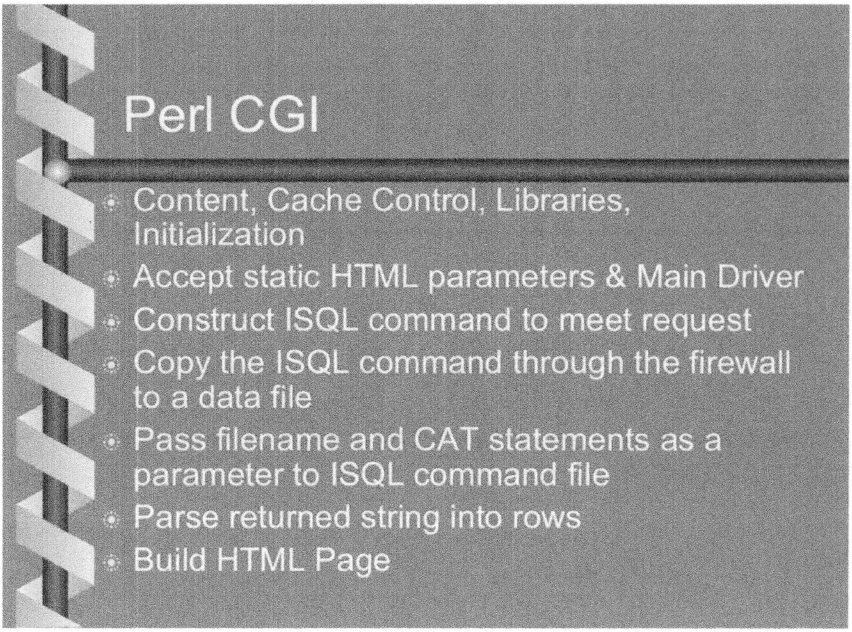

(2012 and 2020 Notes – I spent a fair amount of time on this slide but, as noted in above, my original notes have gone missing. For the life of me, I cannot remember why.)

Slide 11

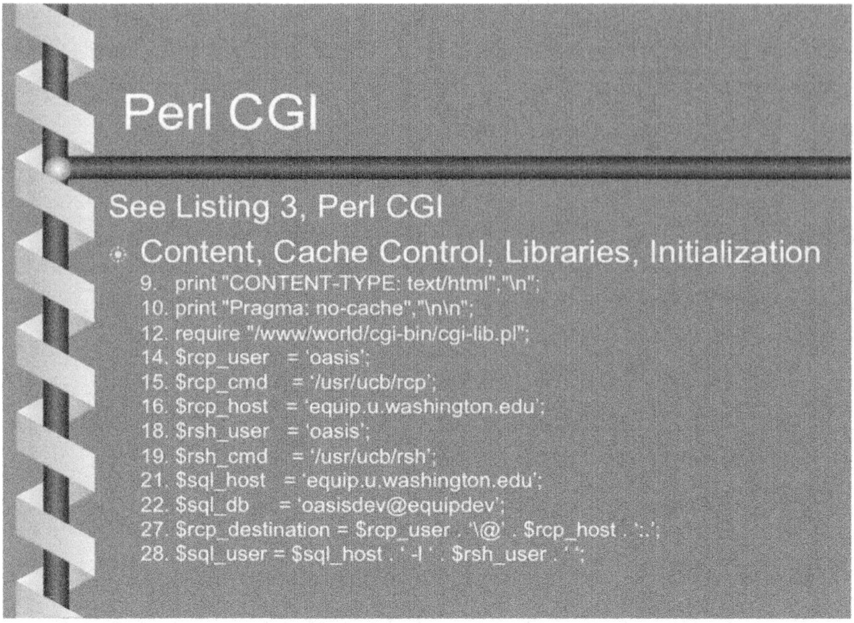

I went through this slide quickly.

Slide 12

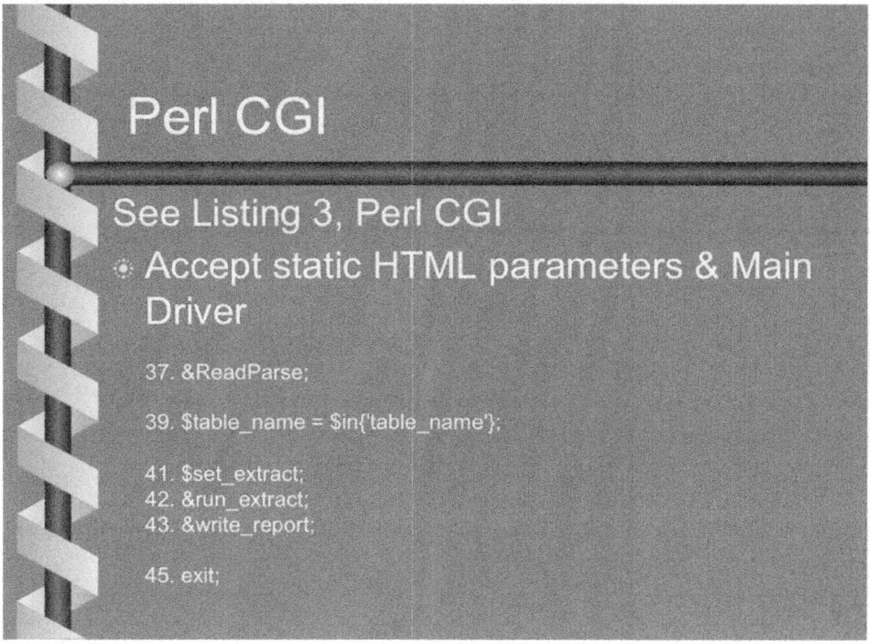

Typical of Unix parameter passing techniques.

Slide 13

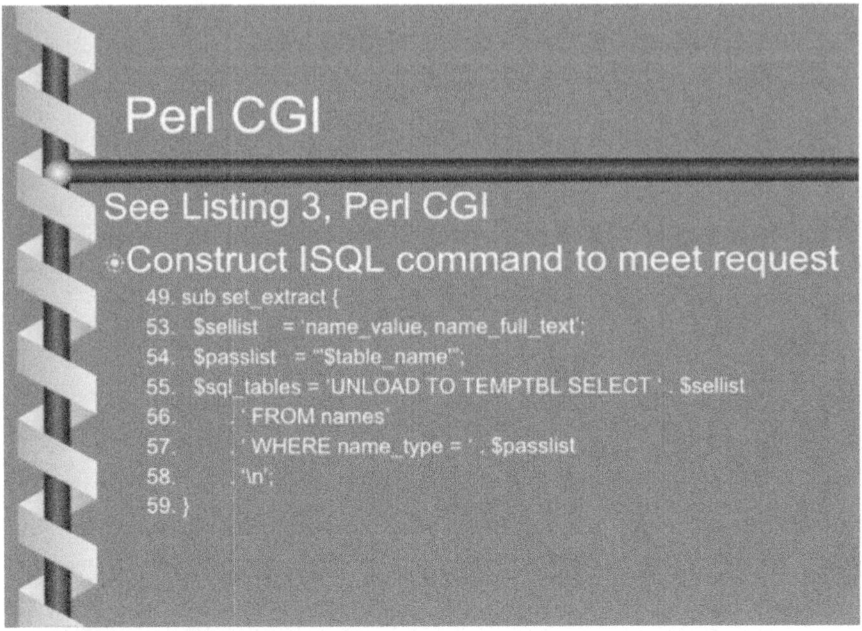

Example of string constructing power of Perl.

Slide 14

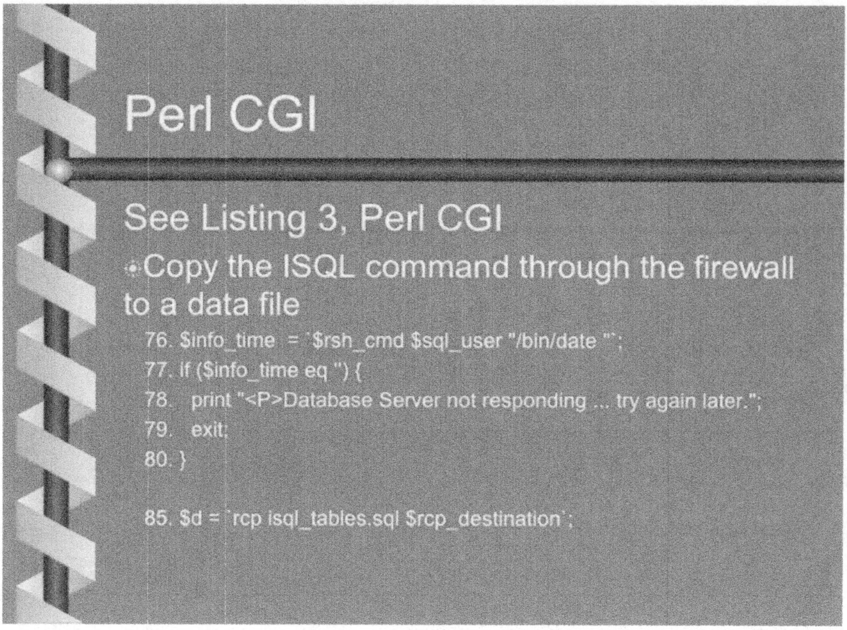

(2012 Note – this attracted questions about security.)

Slide 15

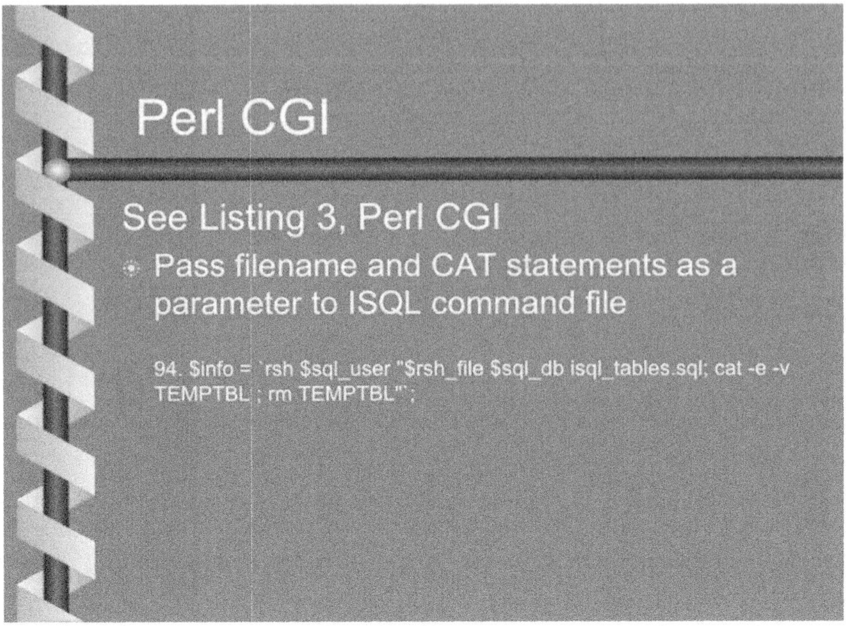

(2012 Note – This is how a Perl socket passes info.)

Slide 16

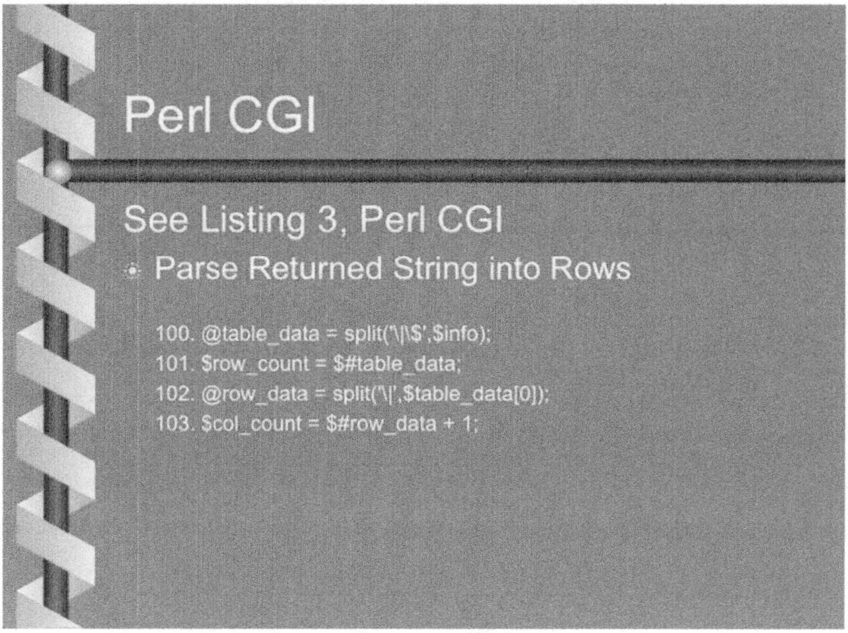

More strength of Perl in handling strings!

Slide 17

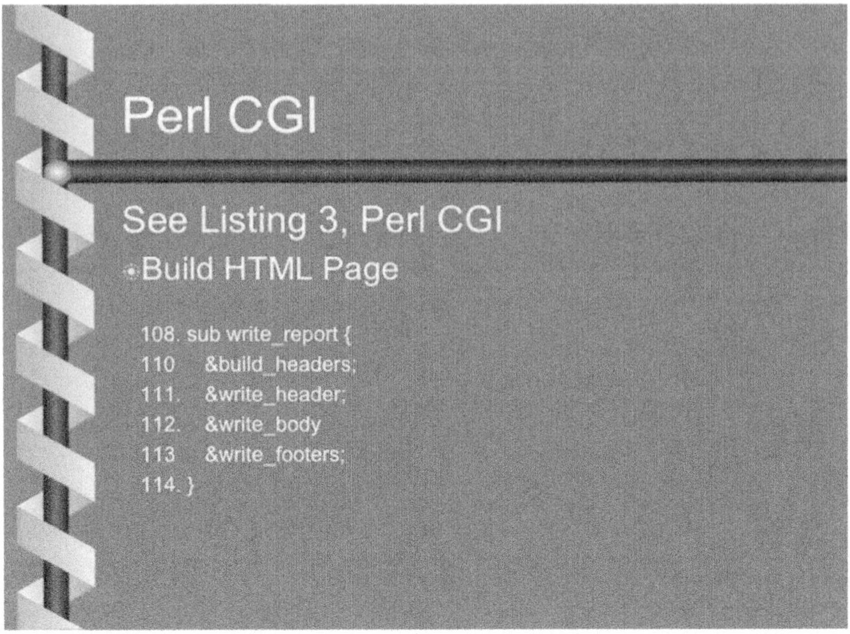
Perl CGI
See Listing 3, Perl CGI
Build HTML Page
108. sub write_report {
110 &build_headers;
111. &write_header;
112. &write_body
113 &write_footers;
114. }

Slide 18

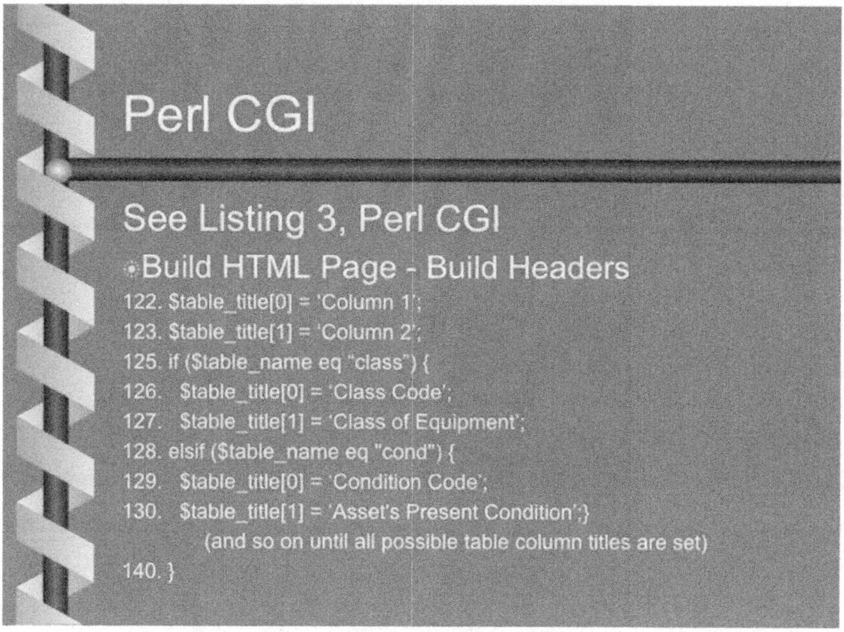

Look at the paper for more details on this.

Slide 19

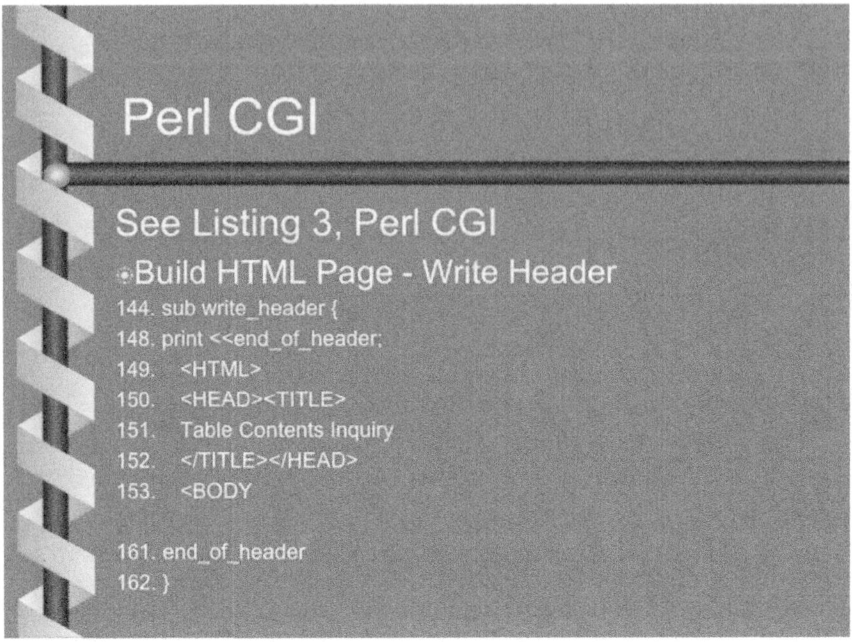
Perl CGI
See Listing 3, Perl CGI
Build HTML Page - Write Header
144. sub write_header {
148. print <<end_of_header;
149. <HTML>
150. <HEAD><TITLE>
151. Table Contents Inquiry
152. </TITLE></HEAD>
153. <BODY
161. end_of_header
162. }

Slide 20

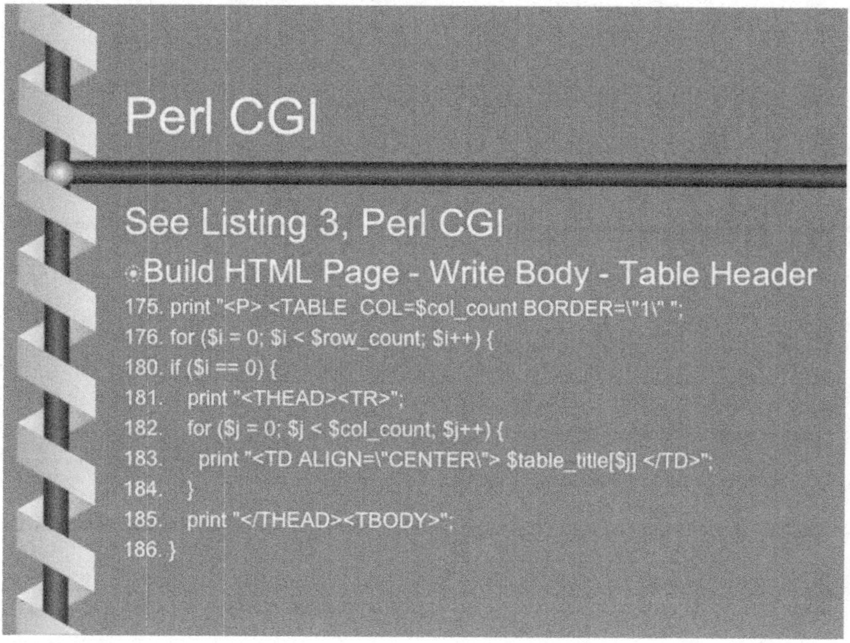
Perl CGI
See Listing 3, Perl CGI
Build HTML Page - Write Body - Table Header
175. print "<P> <TABLE COL=$col_count BORDER=\"1\" ";
176. for ($i = 0; $i < $row_count; $i++) {
180. if ($i == 0) {
181.   print "<THEAD><TR>";
182.   for ($j = 0; $j < $col_count; $j++) {
183.   print "<TD ALIGN=\"CENTER\"> $table_title[$j] </TD>";
184.   }
185.   print "</THEAD><TBODY>";
186. }

Slide 21

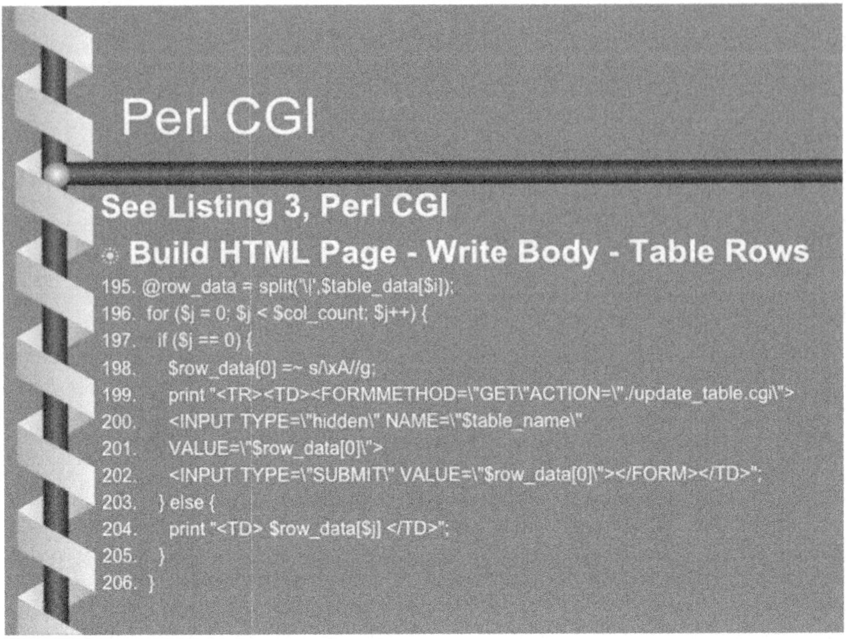

(2020 Note – Perl string processing is a language strength.)

Slide 22

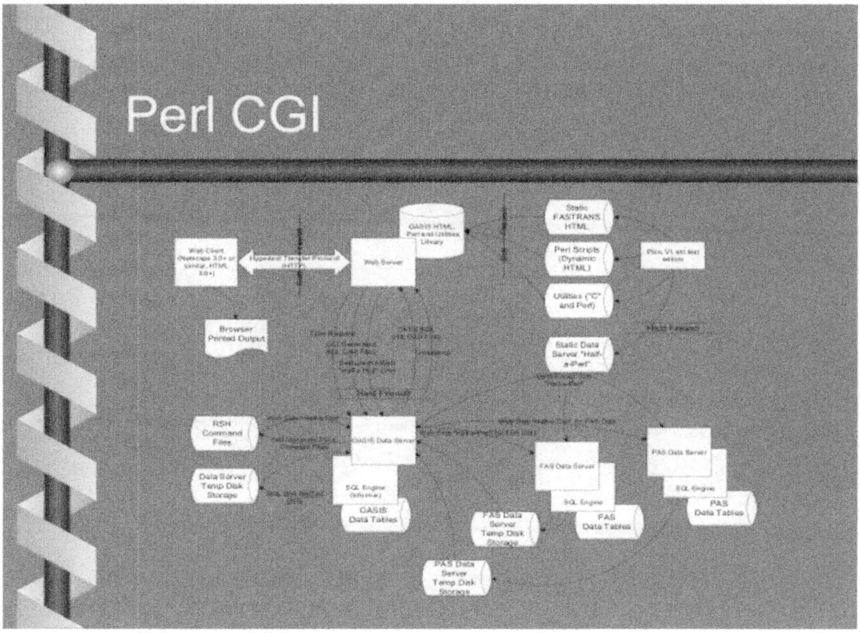

O'Reilly folks added a full-size picture of this to the conference packet. It shows much better.

(2012 Note – This picture was used extensively at the 1998 WebDevShare to show just what n-tier really meant. PeopleSoft was using the phrase, but in their case, version 7.x, 'n' was only one or two. This was not fully addressed by disabling two-tier access until Oracle pulled the plug on it in version 9.1!, in 2011-12.) The pre-Oracle PeopleSoft team was not happy when I pointed this out during a Q&A session at the conference.

(2012 Note - The core of this slide is included at the end of this section in a more readable format.)

Slide 23

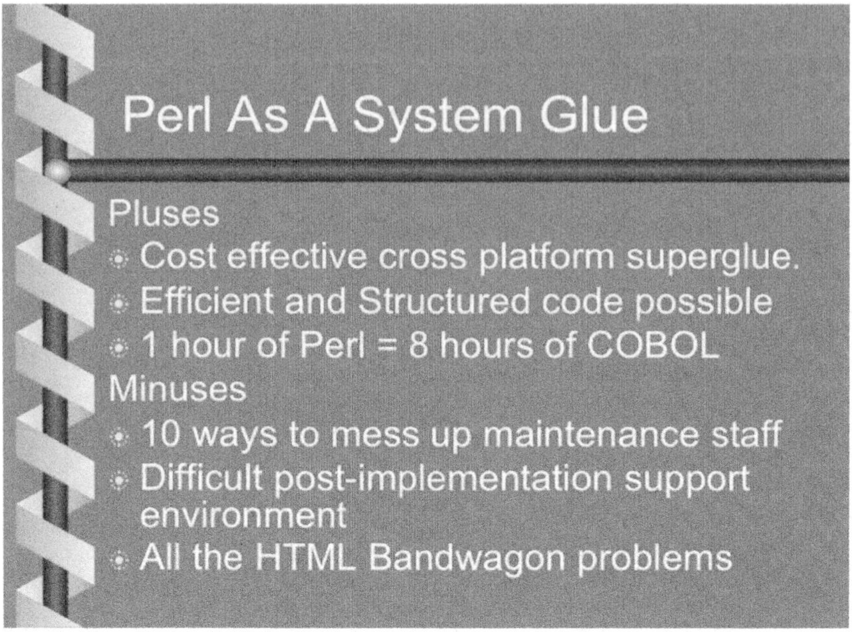

(2012 Note – This was the last slide. I didn't leave one for questions. I think it had been there but the conference team removed it because they didn't think there would be time. As it was there were only two or three questions. I noted those in the introduction to this section and on the slides where the material was covered.)

Portion of Slide 9 (for readability)

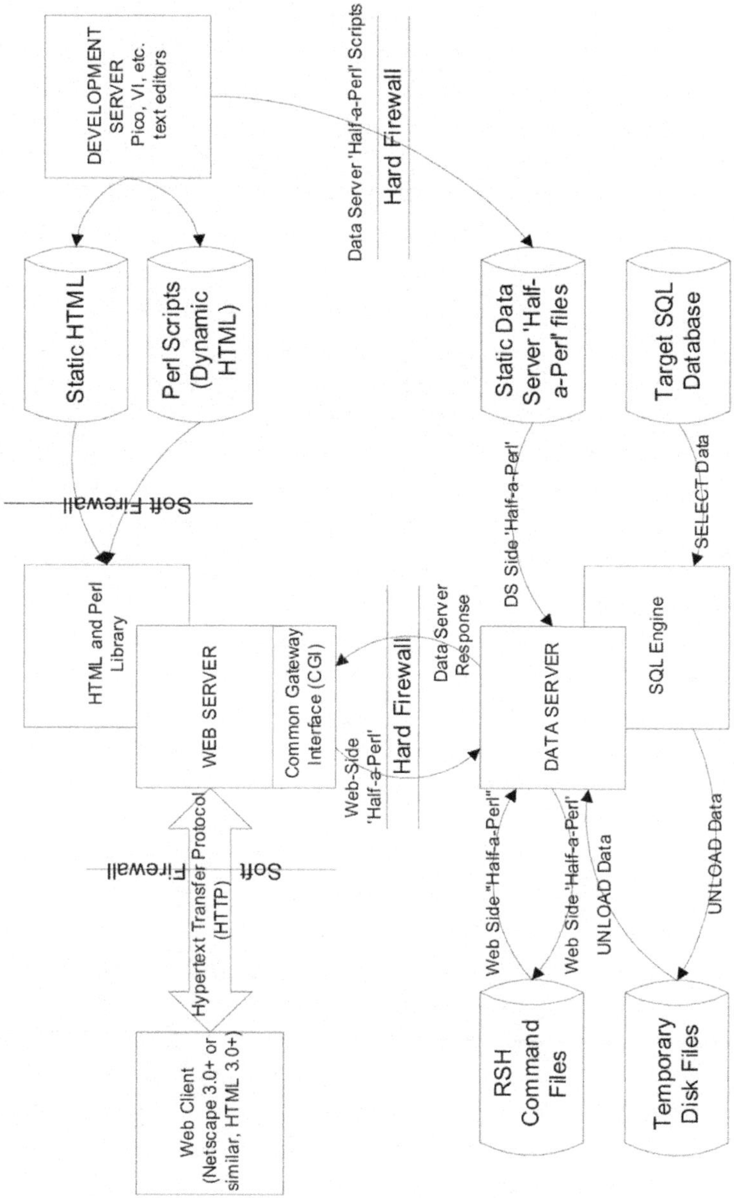

Portion of Slide 22 (for readability)

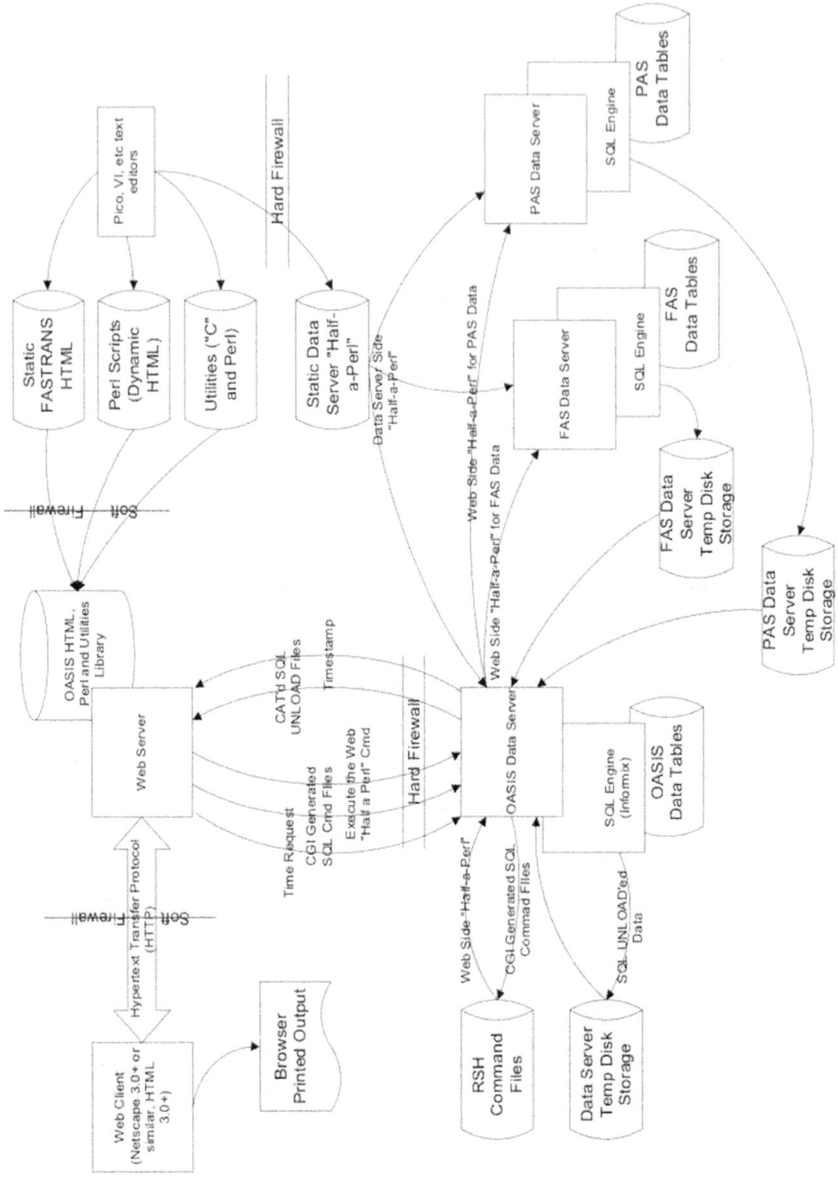

SUPPLEMENTAL MATERIALS

Patrick M. Benson - Biographical Info for O'Reilly & Associates

(2020 Note - This information was included in the conference packet. It does not appear on the O'Reilly sites.)

Patrick Benson is a Senior Computing Specialist with Information Systems of the University of Washington in Seattle.

Mr. Benson was born in Seattle in 1951 and raised in the Puget Sound area. He spent twelve years with the US Air Force. During that time, he worked as a technician on tactical fighter-bomber aircraft weapons systems, taught avionics to American and Allied Foreign students, and worked as a systems programmer with the Strategic Air Command and the US Joint Strategic Target Planning Staff. In 1981, Patrick joined CAP Gemini DASD as a Staff Analyst, specializing in personnel, payroll and materials management systems for the ship building industry. He became the Data Processing Manger with the Ernst and Whinney Telecommunications Group in 1983, where he developed cost accounting and toll separation software. Mr. Benson joined the staff of the University of Washington in 1985. His areas of work at the UW include fund raising and donor recognition support, financial accounting, equipment inventory and data entry applications. These last two applications, equipment inventory and data entry, are being migrated to the Web, and Perl will be a major component of the migration.

Patrick is a graduate of the University of Washington School of Business Administration. He lives with his family in the Seahurst area of Burien, a city just south of Seattle.

Attachments to Patrick Benson's "Perl As A System Glue" Paper

(2012 Note – These were included in a stack at the back of the main ball room, "The Big Room," where the presentation was given. As I'd only brought 50 copies per the O'Reilly team suggestion. They went quick. I suspect few copies remain.)

The paper will be available on my home page (http:/weber.u.washington.edu/ ~pbenson) in the near future.

(2012 Note – See the introduction to this book for current addresses).
(2012 Note – That web site was dropped after I left the UW in 2005.)

Given the recent agreement between Microsoft and Apple regarding Internet Explorer on Apple platforms it is likely that the final product will not include Netscape unique features such as "BORDERS" referenced on Page 20 of the MS PowerPoint display. This feature may be dropped or code added interrogating the environment variables to control generation of the most attractive and appropriate HTML.

(2020 Note – IE is no longer available on Apple products; Safair or Chrome are choices.)

Errata:

On the MS PowerPoint displays, Slide 12, Line 41 should read &set_extract. This matches the text in the paper.

On the MS PowerPoint displays, Slide 22, the text FASTRANS in the upper right portion of the flowchart should read OASIS.

Recent Run of the File Store-and-Forward Perl

This is what the user sees on their session attached to the VAX/VMS when the Perl script executes on the interim host:

```
Remote Host contacted, starting FTP processes
-r--r--r--  1 fasafrs user    87451 Aug 15 12:11
FXEI001_970630_5.SARS
Removing file at destination.
DELE fails: EXAFRS.SARS.UW9706 does not exist.
Remove complete. Gathering file statistics.
No data sets found.
Forward complete. Gathering file statistics.

   Volume Unit Referred Ext Used Recfm Lrecl BlkSz Dsorg
Dsname

PRS008 3390  08/15/97 1  15 VB   256 29000 PS
'EXAFRS.SARS.UW9706'

 ... Retain above for reference ...

Echoing file back for integrity test.
-rw-r--r--  1 fasafrs user    87451 Aug 15 12:12
'EXAFRS.SARS.UW9706'
Process completed, checking file echo for errors.
Number of difference sections found: 0
Number of difference records found: 0

DIFFERENCES /IGNORE=()/MERGED=1-
  DISK$V:[EICSCHD.FOCUS]FXEI001_970630_5.SARS;4-
  DISK$V:[EICSCHD]FXEI001_970630_5.SARS_CHECK;1
Process completed
Press ENTER to continue:
```

There are some display differences between the same in Listing 2 and the production version. The file deletion was added on the request of the end recipient to help with disk management. The display was expanded at our user's request to fill one 24-line screen.

Run of the Perl CGI example

Display of the page generated by the Perl CGI used in the example yields the following (display of the SQL Command and Raw Data have been added).

SQL Command at Line 59 ->UNLOAD TO TEMPTBL SELECT name_value, name_full_text FROM names WHERE name_type = 'class'

Raw Data Stream at Line 95 -->703707|17 IN MONITOR, COLOR|$ 701601|X-TERMINAL B/W|$ 703802|MONO. LASER PRINTER|$ 701203|486 PC/CLONE|$

Class Code Table as of : Fri Aug 15 12:57:19 PDT 1997

Class Code Table Contents Inquiry

Click on the highlighted Class Code to be taken to the Table Update for that item.

Class Code	Class of Equipment
703707	17 IN MONITOR, COLOR
701601	X-TERMINAL B/W
703802	MONO. LASER PRINTER
701203	486 PC/CLONE
Add New	Add a New Class Code

End of data returned from inquiry.

© 1997 (in development)

Section 2 - (1998 WebDevShare) OASIS, A Web Based Fixed Assets System

As noted in "How Database Sockets Came To Be" earlier in this book, my presentation at the First Perl Conference generated quite a bit of attention. This led to an invitation to present at the Indiana University 1998 WebDevShare Conference. I knew the audience would be far smaller than the 1,200 in Santa Clara, and that they and I would have more in common since we worked in the higher education sector. I added extensions of the concepts that emerged between the O'Reilly Conference and this one. In addition to actually naming the technology "database sockets", I included socket level connection concepts and provided a single-instance version of Ping's C-code to implement them. This presentation was titled "OASIS, A Web Based Fixed Assets System" and it is included in this section.

The paper, additional materials and slides that follow include:

- OASIS, The Web Based Client-Server Fixed Assets System – The Paper – This document has been reformatted to meet the needs of e-publishing and e-books, but it contains all the original text and a couple of typos. The internal table of contents has been left to reference the original document page numbers. The formatting of this size of book is different than the 8.5*11 of the original, so even though they're wrong, the page numbers there to this page number will get you close to where you want. Think of it as indirect addressing (I am still a geek at heart) to the printed page.
- OASIS, The Web Based Client-Server Fixed Assets System – The Slides – This section includes my notes used during the presentation and updates from audience questions and comments.

OASIS, THE WEB BASED CLIENT-SERVER FIXED ASSETS SYSTEM

By Patrick M. Benson
Senior Computing Specialist
University of Washington
Seattle, Washington, USA

Abstract - OASIS, The Web Based Client-Server Fixed Assets System

By Patrick M. Benson
Senior Computing Specialist
University of Washington
Seattle, Washington, USA

Abstract

The paper describes a fully functional and integrated web based fixed assets system.

Currently, the software is in Alpha release and Beta development, with full production cutover scheduled for late fall. This package uses the "Half-a-Perl" concept with a three-tier architecture separating the Netscape™/Internet Explorer™ client browser, Apache web server and Informix™ SQL data server on fully autonomous platforms.

Features discussed include: architecture and advantages of the standard three-tier model, access control for the public and private sections (the internet and the intranet), Perl CGI as a system glue, and integration techniques for assorted institution financial applications (budget index, organization index, surplus property, risk management, and fixed assets).

The paper contains the following main sections:

1. A Management Summary.
2. Functional summary of the hardware, software and environment.
3. A System Overview including descriptions of the resources necessary to support the web server, the file and system structure, software authentication and access controls, and intra-system data access control.
4. Code Samples for Conditional HTML, SQL interfaces, results parsing and display management.
5. Development cycle for the project, including extensibility of the "Half-a-" concept to different generations of Web and Data Server connectivity software.

6. SQL Data Tables, directory structures, control files and permission descriptions.
7. Observations about the role and problems of "The Steering Committee" in the web development environment, the application of "My Application" concepts to software such as this package, references to Best Practices and a Summary.

Note - At the First Perl Conference, held in San Jose in August 1997, the author introduced the "Half-a-Perl" concept. That paper first presenting the "Half-a-Perl" concept is available on my web page http://weber.u.washington.edu/~pbenson.

(2012 Note - The First Perl Conference was held in Santa Clara NOT San Jose. I am unsure how this error got in here initially - or managed to stay so long once it did!)

(2020 Note – These addresses and phone numbers are no longer accurate. Please see the introduction and 'About the Author' sections for current information.)

OASIS, The Web Based Client-Server Fixed Assets System

Management Summary

The paper describes a system developed during the migration of an enterprise wide application from a vendor VAX/VMS package to a locally developed web based client-server environment. It includes full documentation on the three-tier hardware and software environment, SQL table descriptions and an Entity Relationship Diagram (ERD) for all data tables including linked databases, security concepts and implementation plan, data handling and interchange concepts and samples, and numerous supporting documents.

The application, a Fixed Assets Package, currently is in Alpha release and Beta development, with full production cutover scheduled for late fall. This package uses the "Half-a-Perl" concept with a three-tier architecture separating the Netscape/Internet Explorer client browser, Apache web server and Informix SQL data server on fully autonomous platforms. The concept of 'My Application', where the user tailors the product to their individual needs, is included.

Both technical and managerial issues are addressed in the paper. Technical issues featured include: architecture and advantages of the standard three-tier model, access control for the public and private sections (the internet and the intranet), Perl CGI as a system glue, and integration techniques for assorted institution financial applications (budget index, organization index, surplus property, risk management, and fixed assets). The paper addresses management issues including the development lifecycle, the problems with steering committees, approaches to dealing with moving technology, post-implementation support plans and the roles of the key players during design, development and day-to-day after the fact operations. Topics that are both technical and managerial include: the distinct design differences between web systems designed for record management and those designed for record entry, and the applicability of the "Half-a" technique to the DB Connection with sockets, and J++ and Microsoft Transaction Server environment is addressed.

At the First Perl Conference, held in San Jose in August 1997, the author introduced the "Half-a-Perl" concept. This formed the basis for this second paper, being delivered at the 1998 WebDevShare conference in September 1998. The presentation paper for the "Half-a-Perl" concept is available on my web page today. The WebDevShare paper will be available soon after the conference (http://weber.u.washington.edu/~pbenson).

(2012 Note - that web site was dropped after I left the UW in 2005)

Functional Summary

This application uses a "thick" web server, and "thin" web client and data server to support what the user side management estimates are 400 customers. Statistics for the existing software indicate it should see an average of 35 concurrent users. Nearly any version of popular browsers is usable. Perl CGI scripts, resident on the web server, accept input from the client, then construct links to other Perl CGI scripts or build SQL commands in the form of a partially completed Select statement. This command is the first "Half-a-Perl". The script issues a remote copy (rcp) command to send the partially completed SQL statement through the firewall as a file with a known name. Once allowed through the firewall, the other "Half-a-Perl" is called upon to execute the contents of the file by a remote shell (rsh) command. When the SQL completes on the Data Server the results are returned by a catenate and print (cat) command and reformatted by the web server Perl CGI script; an HTML friendly format is generated. The number of rows and columns are counted, the data are split apart, a dynamically sized two-dimensional HTML Table is constructed, and a web page is returned to the client browser.

2012 NOTE – The following is a footnote in the original document and the printed version in my print version of the same name. The note is reproduced here due to the inconsistent rendering on various web browsers.

> The terms "thin" and "thick" have become muddled by academic rhetoric and advertising hype. Here, the term "thin" is used to indicate that the web client is a bare-bones web browser and the data server is accessed with generic SQL through batch mode dbaccess. There are no plug-ins, Java, Java-

Script, J++, Active-X, 4GL, stored database procedures, or other software needed. The term "thick", as used here, means an Apache Server, modified to support CHTML, that runs all the control, edit, data preparation and management, display, access and authorization controls. Future releases may break from this strict format to optimize responsiveness. See the sections titled "J++ and Microsoft MTS" and "DBConnect and Socket Connections" later in this paper.

The "Half-a-Perl" concept provides security by splitting the web data request construction from the database engine meeting the request. It is a logical extension of the classical three-tier data warehouse architecture. There is no direct or logical contact between the web and the data. It enforces a condition where the right hand does not know what the left hand is doing, but the two must work together to meet the user's request.

Both insecure (http) and secure (https) access are used; however, there is no static HTML in the system. All pages in this release are Perl CGIs. They may be accessed through an insecure server, the portion I call "Public Space", that allows open access to the homepage, bulletin board, help and email functions so visitors can explore, find out what the system is, how it works and who to contact for additional information and access. The "guts" of the system, the code where asset records are managed and reported, may only be accessed through a secure server, the portion I call "Private Space". Routinely, authorized users will pass between Public and Private Space while doing business with this system. Private Space is protected by .htaccess files that contain commands necessary to call a local authorization service.

Conditional HTML pre and post processors are used; they are controlled by switch settings at installation time. Raw development is done in an open environment, alpha and beta testing is completed with the Conditional HTML turned on or off as needed, and the final deployed output code must pass through the CHTML processors. With CHTML turned on, all output is piped to a work file, HTML for a standard header and footer are applied, and the work file is passed as a text script from the web server to the client. This allows a measure of centralized control of the overall format, assuring that all pages attached to the Homepage have a common look and feel. The web server is tweaked so that it refuses to output content that has not passed through the CHTML process.

A "trusted host" relationship exists between the web server and a database server. This relationship is extended to all remote servers that pass inquiry or update transactions. Direct access to the web and data servers requires userid authorization, specific group permissions, and acceptance of a single use SecurID card id number.

The web side knows what it wants done, but not what database engine will do the work. The database side knows what engine to use and that all requests must be processed only by a limited set of scripts, but not what requests will be performed. The name and location of the database server and engine are hidden in the web side Perl CGI, reducing the opportunity for unauthorized activities. Any unrecognized command mimics the failure of the SQL request to find matching data; the result is a null string that the software processes as a "no rows matching criteria found" search result.

System Overview

Hardware

The web servers, named "weber.u.washington.edu" as a group, is a small cluster of DEC Alpha boxes. An NFS mounted string of disks drives provides about 30 Gigabytes of storage. These two pieces of equipment are constantly being tweaked for performance, so the actual number of boxes in the cluster and disk space available changes too often to be accurately reported here. Connections on campus are through modem, commercial grade thin and thick net, departmental home-grown communications networks, and the institution's fiber optic ring network. This installation meets the general web function needs of the student body, faculty, administrative staff, and the general public. University Computing Services manages the hardware and system software. This configuration fielded 1.3 million hits during May 1998, the last month for which I have statistics, making it the 4th most active '.edu' web site in the United States.

Central administrative software development is done by Information Systems, where X-Terminals, Microsoft Windows-95 and Windows-NT are used. On the OASIS Project, the user community point of contact, the Equipment Inventory Office, will develop some content for the Help functions. This group uses desktops running Windows 95.

The Data Server is a RS6000/AIX platform with 7 Gigabytes of storage dedicated to the Informix Database Manager. This platform also hosts the budget and organization indexes that are referenced by the Fixed Assets software described in this paper.

User access authentication is handled by a connection to the payroll and personnel database on the administrative Unisys A-19 mainframe. The data there is under the control of the Unisys Data Management System (DMS-II). The Financial Accounting System, also on this platform, is the source for the budget and organization indexes used.

Two other platforms that may request data and provide updates are the Surplus Property and Risk Management Systems. Both are RS6000/AIX boxes running Informix.

2012 NOTE – The following is a footnote in the original document and the printed version in my print version of the same name.

> The full report is at:
> http://chronicle.com/free/98/06/98061701t.shtml)

Graphically, the system is as shown below in Figure 1, Physical Architecture.

Figure 1 – Physical Architecture

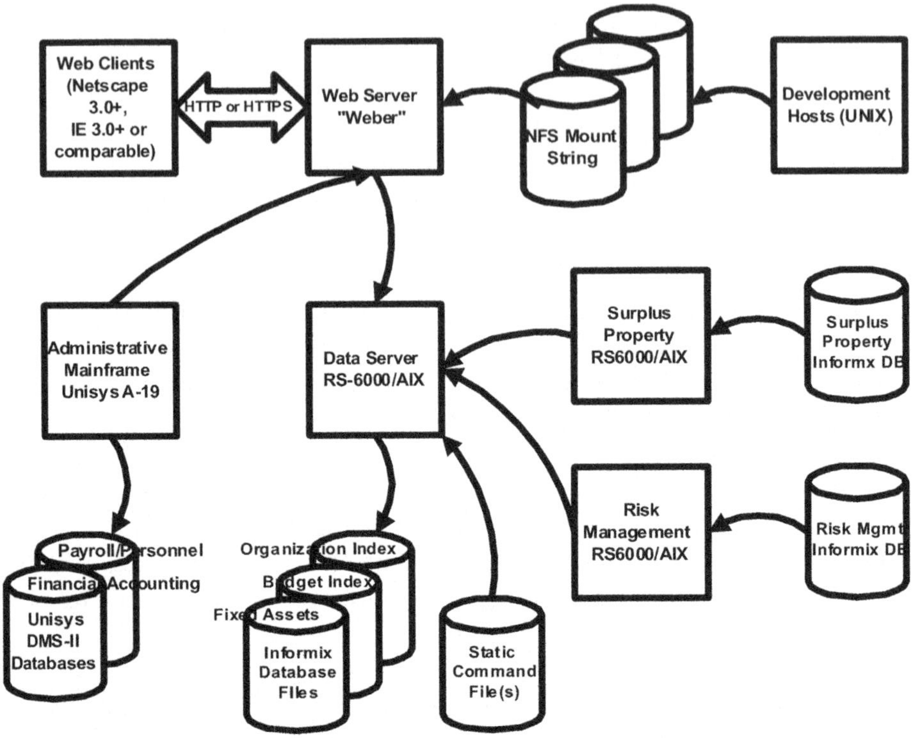

Software

A Web Client requests a named CGI, such as the homepage oasis_index.cgi. This particular Perl script, like the rest in the system, generates a working file of HTML text with Conditional HTML Pre and Post Processor commands. The filename is passed to a procedure that fleshes out the script with the institutional standard font formats, color bars, icons and images. The final output is passed as standard Hypertext Transfer Protocol commands through an open or secure channel (HTTP or HTTPS) as appropriate.

The Web Server has a "Soft Firewall" isolating itself so that anyone can call up pages from some directories, but access to others is limited to University of Washington students or faculty and staff. This is a stateless one-time-per-session verification that requires entry of an institutional specific user-id and password before granting a connection to the application pages. A "Soft Firewall" is a point where a general-purpose security algorithm is in place, in this case an application controlled by reference in the various ".htaccess" files, to filter out most unauthorized access.

When an access to the Data Server must be made, the called Perl CGI script constructs half of a command, for example, an SQL SELECT statement with all parameters and embedded punctuation. This command, the Web "Half-a-Perl" which is not executable in and of itself, is passed to the Data Server by an "rcp" command. It is stored in a temporary file.

The application causes execution of the SQL inquiry by issuing an "rsh" command for one of the Static Command Files. These are the Data Server "Half-a-Perl" files manually placed on the data server as incomplete command files, none is executable in and of itself. By passing the name of the file of the temporary file and an output file as parameters the SQL inquiry is submitted correctly as a batch mode Interactive SQL (ISQL) command, and the output is piped to another temporary file on the Data Server.

The Web Server, as a part of the "rsh" command causing the SQL inquiry to be run, also requests the data be returned by a "cat –e –v" command. This provides a stream of data with a known delimiter at the end of each record ("$|" in this case) that Perl can use to parse to construct an array of records meeting the SQL inquiry.

The composition of the Static Command Files might be:

/bin/date (Returns the data server timestamp)

/Informix/isql oasisdev $1 $2 (Returns inquiry results in file $2 meeting SQL request in the file $1)

By expressly limiting the names, permissions and types of the command files the user "nobody" (the web default set on the Data Server) may perform; the use of these files limits the functions that may be performed. This limiting reduces the opportunity for Trojan Horse and Web Client manipulated HTML GET code hacking.

The access to the Data Server is more restrictive than to the Web Server because of the special nature of these files, they and their permissions are critical. Local software release and management procedures should be developed so these Static Command Files have world execute permissions only (744). This is an essential portion of the "Half-a-Perl" concept security.

Organizational Environment

Historically and evolutionarily, all administrative data processing services for the institution have been centralized in Computing and Communications. Within C&C, support and development of administrative software, information services, web services, lab instruction and training are the responsibility of Information Systems. The management and operation of administrative computing equipment, system software, mainframes and such, are under the control of University Computing Services. As networks expanded, the many diverse roles evolved into the Communications Technology and Network and Distributed Computing groups. A newer group is emerging from these two; Video and TV Technologies. This team supports UWTV and education access cable television stations.

Financial Structure, Access and Span of Control

For three decades the University of Washington has used a six numeric position budget number chart of accounts. To identify administrative departments as separate entities from budget units, a ten position Organization Code was developed. The goal was to allow accounting roll-ups to administrative units by attaching users to organization codes and placing budgets under this organization structure. This was to simultaneously give an organization's staff access to all appropriate budgets and restrict access to information outside their organizational span of control. It should have provided a data summary structure resembling tree roots. This concept of budgets and organizations still works in a computerized batch mode. Unfortunately, after binding this concept to the University and to the security processes of the on-line Financial Accounting System, the organizational structure changed. Budgetary restrictions, departmental expansion and unit realignments caused organizational trauma; for example, moving the School of Biotechnology from the College of Arts and Sciences to the College of Engineering while reducing staff, forced the reporting tree roots to be cut from one place and grafted onto another. It became apparent that both staff and budgets will cross rigid organizational boundaries; and therefore, so must software and data access controls.

Management at the highest level of the University has directed a shift toward distributing responsibility for data development and management from the centralized functional area, such as IS, to the information end-using department. The work will be web based because there is no other way to provide the services needed at a reasonable cost given the budgetary and time constraints faced. The University Services Renewal (USER) Project is working at the cutting edge of our information technologies toward this goal.

Web System Authentication and Access

All access controls at the University of Washington is based upon the user status. A person may simultaneously be a student, alumnus, staff, faculty and friend. A set of authentication mechanisms has been constructed that allows an entry in the .htaccess file to direct which authentication server is used to verify access. Each application uses the service appropriate to the need; for example, payroll transaction entry requires a distinctly higher level of access control than asset entry. Through his process each application may expect that only authenticated users will have access to their URLs in directories protected by an appropriate .htaccess file. Each application must also contain a mechanism for restricting data and function access within itself.

The Fixed Assets System, OASIS, is split into Public and Private Space. It uses .htaccess files resembling the following to meet the authentication need; see Figure 2, Public Space .htaccess File, and Figure 3, Private Space .htaccess File.

```
redx_25:oasis% cat .htaccess
chtmlUse on
```

Figure 2, Public Space .htaccess File

This is the current .htaccess file for the OASIS home page directory. It only says that CHTML use is on. See later in this paper for a description of CHTML. There are no access restrictions here.

```
redx_28:myprofile% cat .htaccess
SSLAccess          SSL
Options       execCGI
AuthSrvService     uapasswd
AuthSrvUserkey     username
AuthSrvPasskey     uapasswd
AuthName           OASIS
AuthType           Basic
ExternalAuthorizefacstaff
<Limit GET POST>
require user xxxx
</Limit>
```

Figure 3, Private Space .htaccess File

This is a more complex .htaccess file. It resides in the directory containing the functions that allow the user to maintain their email address, preferred printer and "My Oasis" parameters. The contents specify, in order, that SSL is required so access must be through a secure server (https://). The service called to produce the login dialogue box is referenced by symbolic name uapasswd. This locally written server takes inputs, here specified as username and uapasswd. It verifies that the username/uapasswd combination maps to a facstaff entry. The access verification process uses the AuthName and AuthType commands during creation and execution of the userid, password and SecurID dialogue box processing functions. SecurID is a single use random number token presented on a credit card sized unit and entered by the user when requested. The directory can have CGI's executing programs (execCGI) and both Get and Post functions may be used by all users.

Intra-System Access Control

Users with access to OASIS generally do not have total and unrestricted access to all data. A two-path approach has been developed. Any user may see any single asset, but to update or have the asset included on a report the asset_master record must have a budget number or organization code that falls into a range approved for the user. Each user has a set of approved ranges of budget numbers and organization codes maintained by the Equipment Inventory Office. Two tables implement these controls, see Figure 4, User and Permissions Table Description.

```
CREATE TABLE oasis_user
(
user_id         CHAR(12),
user_name          VARCHAR (50,20),
user_email_addr      VARCHAR (50,20),
user_pref_printer     VARCHAR (30,12),
last_access        DATE,
access_counter      SMALLINT,
security_level      CHAR(01)
);
CREATE INDEX oasis_users ON oasis_user(user_id);


CREATE TABLE permission
(
user_id         CHAR(12),
perm_seq_nbr       SERIAL(00000001),
perm_range_type      CHAR(01),
perm_i_e_flag            CHAR(01),
perm_from_range      CHAR(12),
perm_to_range       CHAR(12)
);

CREATE INDEX permissions ON permission (user_id,
perm_seq_nbr);
```

Figure 4, User and Permissions Table Description

A user who has a specific Security Level ("Manager Access") in their oasis_user table entry can access any data on any functional page. A user who is not a Manger can see all data that falls into at least one of their Included Organization Code or Budget Number ranges … provided that the data does not fall into any one of the Excluded Organization Code or Budget Number ranges. This is Positive Include with Priority Exclude (PIPE) logic. This allows mapping individuals to disjoint ranges of both code types and provides positive restriction of ranges within both.

Note that a full set of Data Tables in included Figure 7 – Data Tables, later in this document.

The Gory Details

Conditional HTML (CHTML)
CHTML Code Location and Function

CTHML is a coding convention that is supported by modifications in the Apache Web Server. The purpose is to enforce site standards for header, body and footer formats by allowing insertion of enterprise wide HTML text and by restricting the output of web applications so they must pass through a filter. A side benefit is that the server is tweaked so that CHTML files are constructed and parsed in hardware cache, which dramatically cuts response time by allowing content no-cache and textural caching within a single document. It is not unusual to see performance improvements of seven to ten times (as in, a page that took twenty seconds to fully render taking only two or three). Files that are not passed through the filter will not display, assuring management that only content they have some measure of control over is allowed to go out over their web.

To allow system modules to work in either a CHTML or traditional HTML environment (a dual mode CGI) a global subroutine below, Listing 1, init_global_items, is executed early on by each CGI. Of special interest is Line 5 where a server specific and dynamic temporary file is created for CHTML output.

```
1. sub init_global_items {
2.  use lib '/www/lib/auth', '/www/lib';
3.  $chtml_file = 'OASIS_TMP';      # put 'STDOUT' if chtml
   not used
4.  if ($chtml_file ne 'STDOUT') {
5.   $tmpfile = ($ENV{'SERVER_TMPDIR'} || '/tmp') .
   "/oasis$$.html";
6.   die "Failed Open chtml file $tmpfile"
7.   unless open $chtml_file, ">$tmpfile";
```

```
print $chtml_file <<END_of_Text;
 <!-- DOCTYPE HTML PUBLIC "-//W3C//DTD HTML 4.0//EN"
 "http://www.w3.org/TR/REC-html40/strict.dtd" -->
END_of_Text
}
else {
 print "CONTENT-TYPE: text/html","\n\n";
}
```

Listing 1- init_global_items

Listing 2, web_page_header, shows how a standard header is written by a dual mode CGI. Note that the relative linked style sheet <LINK REL="stylesheet" HREF="/home/home.css" TYPE="text/css"> contains the description of several items, including the <FONT CLASS="navlink"> reference. This allows a central administrator to change a selection bar color and have that change become effective throughout the enterprise nearly immediately. The next loading of any page of the application causes the new format to be shown. See below, in The CTHML Pre and Post-Processor Commands, for an explanation of the text brought in by the two lines <!--chtml include "//home/incs/cheader.inc"--> and <!--chtml include "//home/incs/nav.inc"-->. Here, Lines 2-8 bring in the style sheet, 15-16 bring in the control structure and heading text, 17-33 build the part of the system specific navigation bar used for page to page jumping, and 34-50 create the static system Bulletin Board, Email and Help navigation bar entries

Start of Listing 2 - web_page_header

```
1. sub web_page_header {
2. print $chtml_file <<end_header1;
3.  <HTML>
4.  <HEAD>
5.  <TITLE>
6.  $web_page_title
7.  </TITLE>
8.  <LINK REL="stylesheet" HREF="/home/home.css"
   TYPE="text/css">
9.  </HEAD>
```

```
<BODY>
end_header1

&web_menu_java_arrows;
&check_for_message;

print $chtml_file <<end_header2;

<!--chtml include "//home/incs/cheader.inc"-->
<!--chtml include "//home/incs/nav.inc"-->

<TABLE BORDER="0" CELLPADDING="0"
CELLSPACING="0" WIDTH="100%">
<TR VALIGN="MIDDLE">
 <TD ALIGN="LEFT">
 <A HREF="$homepage_url"><FONT
CLASS="navlink">OASIS Home Page</A>
 </TD>
 <TD ALIGN="LEFT">
 <A HREF="$submenu_url"><FONT
CLASS="navlink">$submenu_name</A>
 </TD>
 <TD ALIGN="LEFT">
 <A HREF="$sub_submenu_url"><FONT
CLASS="navlink">$sub_submenu_name</A>
 </TD>
 <TD ALIGN="LEFT">
 <A HREF="$submenu_url_2"><FONT
CLASS="navlink">$submenu_name_2</A>
 </TD>
 <TD ALIGN="LEFT">
 <A HREF="$help_rtn_data"><FONT
CLASS="navlink">$help_rtn_name</A>
 </TD>
 <TD ALIGN="RIGHT">
 <TABLE BORDER="0" CELLPADDING="0"
CELLSPACING="5">
 <TR VALIGN="MIDDLE" ALIGN="RIGHT">
  <TD>
  <A HREF="$messages_data"><FONT
CLASS="navlink">$Message</A>
  </TD>
```

```
  <TD>
  <A HREF="$help_data"><FONT
CLASS="navlink">Help</A>
  </TD>
  <TD>
  <A HREF="$email_data"><FONT
CLASS="navlink">Email</A>
  </TD>
 </TR>
 </TABLE>
</TR>
</TABLE>
web_page_header
```

End of Listing 2 - web_page_header

Listing 3, web_page_footer, shows how the file directed to CHTML or STDIO is closed and passed to the CHTML post processor through a Perl system call when appropriate. As noted earlier, this system call invokes a process tweaked to provide web output. It has the "brains" to cache images but not text. See below, in The CTHML Pre and Post-Processor Commands, for an explanation of the text brought in by the line <!--chtml include "//home/incs/footer.inc"-->. Line 9 is the key to bringing in the standard footer, while 13-17 calls the post processor if CHTML is in force.

Start of Listing 3 - web_page_footer

```
1. #==================
2. # Web Page Footer
3. #
4. # This is the subroutine used by pages that want NO CACHE
   turned on.
5. # Generally, these are private update type pages.
6. sub web_page_footer {
7. print $chtml_file <<end_footer;
8.  <P>
9.  <!--chtml include "//home/incs/footer.inc"-->
10. </BODY>
11. </HTML>
12. end_footer
```

```
if ($chtml_file ne 'STDOUT') {
 close ($chtml_file);
 $cmdstring = "/nfs/info/www/lib/chtml-postproc -r -d
  `pwd` -h "
     . "\"Pragma:no_cache\" $tmpfile";
 system $cmdstring;
 }
}
```

End of Listing 3 - web_page_footer

The CTHML Pre and Post-Processor Commands

The three CHTML command lines are inserted into the output file by the CGI

```
<!--chtml include "//home/incs/cheader.inc"-->
<!--chtml include "//home/incs/nav.inc"-->
<!--chtml include "//home/incs/footer.inc"-->
```

These cause the CHTML processor to add the enterprise wide style sheets, header and footer command text to the output file. At our site this CHTML processor is called whenever the final product is to be viewable by the general public; meaning that a .htaccess file containing restrictive commands does not protect the directory of origin.

The text brought in by the first two commands defines the global navigation bar, standard graphics, the color and font scheme that management has decided will be used to represent the institution. During development of the OASIS application the specific text included as follows in Listing 4, Header and Navigation Includes. The exact information brought in, especially the initial graphic, varies between applications, based in part on the application's default directory. This allows automatic re-titling when management decides it is appropriate. In this listing, Lines 1-9 and 27-29 are inserted from the cheader.inc file, while 9-26 comes from the nav.inc file.

Start of Listing 4 - Header and Navigation Includes

```
<A HREF="/computing/"><IMG SRC="/home/graphics/hComp.gif"
  WIDTH="450" HEIGHT="35" BORDER="0" ALT="[Computing and Networking]"
  VSPACE="2"></A><BR>
<TABLE BORDER="0" CELLPADDING="0" CELLSPACING="0" WIDTH="100%" BGCOLOR="#333399">
 <TR WIDTH="100%" VALIGN="MIDDLE">
 <TD ALIGN="LEFT"><A HREF="/"><IMG BORDER="0"
  VSPACE="1" SRC="/home/graphics/navarrow.gif" WIDTH="14" HEIGHT="11"
  ALT=""><FONT COLOR="#FFCC33"
  CLASS="barlink">University of Washington</FONT></A></TD>
 <TD ALIGN="RIGHT">
  <TABLE CELLPADDING="0" CELLSPACING="0" BORDER="0">
  <TR VALIGN="MIDDLE" ALIGN="RIGHT">
   <TD><A HREF="/cgi-bin/search/home/"><IMG BORDER="0"
      VSPACE="1" WIDTH="14" HEIGHT="11" SRC="/home/graphics/navarrow.gif"
      ALT=" | "><FONT COLOR="#FFCC33"
      CLASS="barlink">Search</FONT></A></TD>
   <TD><A HREF="/home/directories.html"><IMG BORDER="0" VSPACE="1" WIDTH="14"
      HEIGHT="11" SRC="/home/graphics/navarrow.gif"
      ALT=" | "><FONT COLOR="#FFCC33"
      CLASS="barlink">Directories</FONT></A></TD>
   <TD><A HREF="/tools/"><IMG BORDER="0" VSPACE="1" WIDTH="14" HEIGHT="11"
      SRC="/home/graphics/navarrow.gif"
      ALT=" | "><FONT COLOR="#FFCC33"
      CLASS="barlink">Reference Tools</FONT></A></TD>
  </TABLE>
 </TD>
 <TD> </TD>
 </TR>
```

```
</TABLE>
```

End of Listing 4 - Header and Navigation Includes

The standard footer command adds a graphic and processes the contents of a text file named "address.inc". The contents of this file provide the address information, the point of contact email address and an indicator telling the post-processor to find the latest update in the current directory path and use that for the "Last Modified" date. The exact text brought in resembles that in Listing 5, Footer Include, below. Here the contents of Lines 8-10 are brought in by the post processor from a file named "address.inc" located in the default directory.

Start of Listing 5 - Footer Include

```
1.  <HR NOSHADE SIZE="1">
2.  <TABLE BORDER="0" CELLPADDING="0"
    CELLSPACING="0">
3.   <TR>
4.   <TD WIDTH="110" ALIGN="left">
5.   <A HREF="/"><IMG SRC="/home/graphics/uwid.gif"
    BORDER="0" WIDTH="94" HEIGHT="33"
6.     ALT="[University of Washington]"
    HSPACE="5"></A></TD>
7.   <TD>
8.   Equipment Inventory Office<BR>
9.   EIO@u.washington.edu<BR>
10.  Last Modified 8/4/98
11.  </TD>
12.  </TR>
13. </TABLE>
```

End of Listing 5 - Footer Include

"Half-a" Generations

There are three distinct generations of Web and Data Server code involved in the "Half-a" concept. The need to migrate up the chain is related to the size of the application, extent of edits performed on the Web Server, the volume of transactions, the responsiveness demanded by the user community, the technical capabilities of the development staff, and the physical capabilities of the network. Each step on the ladder requires some significant level of software reengineering.

Simple and Elementary Level - rcp, rsh and cat
Moderate Difficult Level - DBConnect and Socket Extensions
Bold and Complex Level - J++ and Microsoft MTS Application

The Simple and Elementary Generation – rcp, rsh and cat

The following are samples of the code typically found in "Half-a" systems developed at the Simple and Elementary Level – rcp, rsh and cat level. Listing 6, find_asset_sql, is the code used to find an asset and all related expenditure, history and general note data. This creates the contents of the Web Server "Half-a" file. Listing 7, copy_sql_file, is the rcp function that places the Web Server "Half-a" file on the Data Server. Listing 8, run_sql, passes the SQL inquiry to the database engine by referencing the name of the file containing the inquiry as an argument passed to the Data Server "Half-a" script.

In Listing 6 there are lines of note. Line 4 calls a routine to build the particular columns being extracted. This is discussed later in this paper; see the heading titled Code and Data Base Linking Table. Line 7 is there for completeness, in the event that a specific return sequence (other than asset_id) is desired this variable will be set. Lines 27 and 28 call subroutines included as Listing 9, exp_select_sql, and Listing 10, note_select_sql, respectively.

The use of these code fragments, with multiple rcp, rsh and cat commands, drove the response time issues forcing migration to the next generation of Web and Data Server Code.

Start of Listing 6 - find_asset_sql

```
1.  sub find_asset_sql {
2.   $filename  = $user_sought . "_asset.dat";
3.   $seek_item = "'$asset_id'";
4.   &asset_sel_sql;
5.   $find_asset_where = "WHERE asset_id = $seek_item "
6.             . "AND  asset_seq = $seek_comp ";
7.   $find_asset_order = '';
```

```
$seek_stmt = "UNLOAD TO $filename "
  . "SELECT $select_str "
  . 'FROM asset_master a, '
  . 'OUTER t_names b, OUTER t_names c, OUTER class d, '
  . 'OUTER (findb:budget_no_index e, OUTER global g), '
  . 'OUTER (findb:organization_tl f, OUTER global h) '
  . "$find_asset_where"
  . "AND a.asset_type = b.table_key and b.table_name = 'A-TYPE' "
  . "AND a.building  = c.table_key and c.table_name = 'BLDG' "
  . "AND a.class_code = d.class_code "
  . "AND a.inventory_bgt[1,2] = e.budget_number[1,2] "
  . "AND a.inventory_bgt[3,6] = e.budget_number[4,7] "
  . "  AND e.biennium_year = g.global_string "
  . "   AND g.global_item = 'CURRENT-BIENNIUM' "
  . "AND a.organization = f.organization_code "
  . "  AND f.biennium_year = h.global_string "
  . "   AND h.global_item = 'CURRENT-BIENNIUM' "
  . "$find_asset_order" . ';';
if ($get_exp_note){
 &exp_select_sql;
 &note_select_sql;
}
$seek_stmt = $seek_stmt . "\n";
if ($test_sw) {
 print $chtml_file
   "<P>find_asset select workfile command : $seek_stmt";
}
$workfile = $user_file_prefix . '_asset.sql';
&copy_sql_file;
&run_sql;
}
```

End of Listing 6 - find_asset_sql

Start of Listing 7 - copy_sql_file

```
sub copy_sql_file {
 $rcp_result = `$rm $workfile`;
 $rcp_result = open(isql_dummy , "> $workfile");
 $rcp_result = print isql_dummy $seek_stmt;
```

```
 $rcp_result = close(isql_dummy);
 $rcp_result = `chmod 755 $workfile`;
}
```

End of Listing 7 - copy_sql_file

Start of Listing 8 Listing 8 - run_sql

```
sub run_sql {
 $info_time = ";
 $info_time = `$rsh_cmd $sql_user "/bin/date "`;
 if ($info_time eq ") {
 print $chtml_file
  '<P>Database Server not responding ... try again later...';
 }
 else {
  $fwd_file = `rcp $workfile $rcp_destination`;
  if ($no_unload == 1) {
   $info = `rsh $sql_user "$rsh_file $sql_db $workfile"`;
  }
  else {
   $db_exe_command = "$rsh_file $sql_db $workfile; "
      . "cat -e -v $filename ";
   $info = `rsh $sql_user "$db_exe_command"`;
  }
 }
}
```

End of Listing 8 - run_sql

Start of Listing 9 - exp_select_sql

```
sub exp_select_sql {
 $select_exp_str = $add_comma = ";
 for ($i=0; $i < $last_exp_idx + 1; $i++) {
  $select_exp_str = $select_exp_str . $add_comma
         . "$exp_field_cntl[$i][1]";
  $add_comma = ', ';
  }
 $exp_filename = $user_sought . '_asset_exp.dat';
 $seek_stmt = $seek_stmt
     . "UNLOAD TO $exp_filename "
     . "SELECT $select_exp_str "
```

```
    . 'FROM expenditure '
    . "WHERE asset_id  = '$asset_id' "
    . "AND  asset_seq = '$asset_seq' "
    . "$where_type_exp_id"
    . "ORDER BY asset_type, expenditure_id; ";
}
```

End of Listing 9 - exp_select_sql

Start of Listing 10 - note_select_sql

```
sub note_select_sql {
 $select_note_str = $add_comma = '';
 for ($i=2; $i < $last_note_idx + 1; $i++) {
  $select_note_str = $select_note_str . $add_comma
           . "$note_field_cntl[$i][1]";
  $add_comma = ', ';
 }
 $note_filename = $user_sought . '_asset_note.dat';
 $seek_stmt = $seek_stmt
    . "UNLOAD TO $note_filename "
    . "SELECT $select_note_str "
    . 'FROM note '
    . "WHERE asset_id  = '$asset_id' "
    . "AND  asset_seq = '$asset_seq' "
    . "$where_other_fields"
    . "ORDER BY asset_type, note_type, note_sequence;";
}
```

End of Listing 10 - note_select_sql

The Moderately Difficult Generation - DBConnect and Socket Extensions

This midpoint is where the beta version of OASIS now resides. The Achilles heel of the rcp, rsh and cat generation of code is the time it takes to complete all these transactions. In a large installation with a busy network and complex SQL inquiries to process it is not unusual for response times to reach 20 seconds. Changing to a persistent database process with socket level connection reduces that time in half, at least. Such interconnection software should be written in an executable language. At this time, we have settled upon a "C" Web-Server Client and a "C" Data-Server Server. Since this language is platform specific, migration to this generation requires you to give up flexibility.

The two parts of this C&C Service, both header and "C" source, are included below in Listing 11, Web-Server Client, and Listing 12, Data-Server Server. Note that these are no line numbers because line wrap was used to produce this paper. "C" and long lines do not always work together. This code is for the RS-6000/AIX platform and will require changes to work in a DEC ALPHA or other environment.

Start of Listing 11 - Web-Server Client

```
/*------------------------------------------------------------------
  oasisdevapi.h -- Oasisdev application interface definitions
 ------------------------------------------------------------------*/

#ifndef _OASISDEVAPI_H
#define _OASISDEVAPI_H

#define PROC

typedef struct Logon_
{
 struct Logon_ *next;
 char id[17];
 char account[9];
 int uid;
 char type[7];
 char owner[9];
 char hosts[512];
 char forward[128];
} Logon;

typedef struct Owner_
{
 struct Owner_ *next;
 char owner[9];
 char account[9];
 char id[17];
 char ssn[10];
```

```
 char lname[61];
 char fname[61];
 char pac[7];
 char birthdate[11];
 char avn[8];
 char college[3];
 char department[7];
 char unit[4];
 char hepps_type[2];
 char budget[7];
 char faccode[3];
 char mailstop[8];
 char class[3];
 int branch;
 char sdb_status[2];
 int category;
 char data_source[2];
 char data_status[3];
 char expires[11];
 char comment[81];
 int acctype;
} Owner;

extern char OASISDEVhost[];
extern char *OASISDEVpwdf;
extern char *OASISDEVserver;
extern char *OASISDEVsocket;
extern int  OASISDEVdacl;
extern int  OASISDEVport;

int PROC OASISDEVconnect (char *, char *);
int PROC OASISDEVdelavf (char *, char *);
int PROC OASISDEVdelowner (char *, char *);
void PROC OASISDEVdisconnect (void);
void PROC OASISDEVfreelogon (Logon **);
void PROC OASISDEVfreeowner (Owner **);
int PROC OASISDEVgetavf (Owner **, char *, char *, char *);
int PROC OASISDEVgetlogon (Logon **, char *, char *);
int PROC OASISDEVgetowner (Owner **, char *, char *, char
*);
int PROC OASISDEVmatch (char *, char *, int);
char PROC *OASISDEVparse (char *, int *);
```

```
int PROC OASISDEVputavf (Owner *);
int PROC OASISDEVputowner (Owner *);
int PROC OASISDEVread (char *, int);
int PROC OASISDEVvalidate (char *, char *);
int PROC OASISDEVvalue (char *, char *, int);
int PROC OASISDEVwrite (char *);

#endif /* _OASISDEVAPI_H */


/*----------------------------------------------------------------
  oasisdevapi.c -- Oasisdev application interface routines
 ----------------------------------------------------------------*/

/* The following routines are defined:
 *
 * int PROC OASISDEVconnect (char *, char *);
 * void PROC OASISDEVdisconnect (void);
 * char PROC *OASISDEVparse (char *, int *);
 * int PROC OASISDEVread (char *, int);
 * int PROC OASISDEVwrite (char *);
 */

#include <stdio.h>
#include <ctype.h>
#include <errno.h>
#include <netdb.h>
#include <pwd.h>
#include <signal.h>
#include <string.h>
#include <time.h>
#include <unistd.h>
#include <arpa/inet.h>
#include <netinet/in.h>
#include <sys/file.h>
#include <sys/time.h>
#include <sys/types.h>
#include <sys/socket.h>
#include <sys/un.h>

#include "oasisdevapi.h"
```

```
#ifdef _XOPEN_SOURCE_EXTENDED
typedef size_t fromlen_t;
#else
typedef int  fromlen_t;
#endif

char OASISDEVhost[64];
char *OASISDEVserver = "vitcos.u.washington.edu";
char *OASISDEVsocket =
"/home/informix/oasisdev/dat/oasisdevsock";
int  OASISDEVdacl  = 2;
int  OASISDEVport  = xxxx;  /* hidden here */

static char buff[8192], cid[12], cpw[16], tmp1[32], tmp2[32];
static int ifd = -1, seq = 0, set = 0;
static struct sockaddr_in sin;
static struct sockaddr_un sun;

/*------------------------------------------------------------------
  xalloc -- Allocate and zero out memory
 ------------------------------------------------------------------*/

static void PROC *xalloc (int size)
{
  void *new;

  new = (void *) malloc (size);
  if (new != NULL) bzero (new, size);

  return (new);
}

/*------------------------------------------------------------------
  xfree -- Free allocated memory
 ------------------------------------------------------------------*/

static void PROC xfree (void *mem)
{
  if (mem) free (mem);
  return;
}
```

```
/*-----------------------------------------------------------------
  OASISDEVconnect --
 -----------------------------------------------------------------*/

int PROC OASISDEVconnect (char *id, char *pw)
{
  struct hostent *hp;
  struct servent *sp;
  struct timeval tmo;
  char  **adr, *tok;
  int  pos;
  fd_set fds;
  fromlen_t slen;

  if (ifd != -1) OASISDEVdisconnect ();

  if (id && *id) {strcpy (cid, id); ++set;}
  if (pw && *pw) {strcpy (cpw, pw); ++set;}
  if (!set) return (0);

  if (OASISDEVport == -1) {
   if ((sp = getservbyname ("oasisdev", "tcp")) == NULL) {
    OASISDEVdisconnect ();
    return (-1);
   }
   OASISDEVport = ntohs (sp->s_port);
  }

/* Establish communications with oasisdev server */

  sun.sun_family = AF_UNIX;
  strcpy (sun.sun_path, OASISDEVsocket);

  if ((ifd = socket (AF_UNIX, SOCK_STREAM, 0)) > 0 &&
    connect (ifd, (struct sockaddr *) &sun, strlen (sun.sun_path) +
2) == 0) {
    gethostname (OASISDEVhost, sizeof (OASISDEVhost));
    goto try;
  }

  sin.sin_family = AF_INET;
  sin.sin_addr.s_addr = INADDR_ANY;
```

```
  sin.sin_port = htons (OASISDEVport);

  if ((ifd = socket (AF_INET, SOCK_DGRAM, 0)) < 0) {
    OASISDEVdisconnect ();
    return (-1);
  }

  strcpy (buff, OASISDEVserver); *OASISDEVhost = '\0'; pos
= 0;

  while ((tok = OASISDEVparse (buff, &pos)) != NULL) {
    if (*tok != '\0' && (hp = gethostbyname (tok)) != NULL) {
      for (adr = hp->h_addr_list; *adr; adr++) {
        sin.sin_family = hp->h_addrtype;
        bcopy (*adr, &sin.sin_addr, hp->h_length);
        if (sendto (ifd, "p\n", 2, 0, (struct sockaddr *) &sin, sizeof
(sin)) < 1) {
          OASISDEVdisconnect ();
          return (-1);
        }
      }
    }
  }

  FD_ZERO (&fds); FD_SET (ifd, &fds);
  tmo.tv_sec = 10;
  tmo.tv_usec = 0;

  if (select (ifd + 1, &fds, NULL, NULL, &tmo) > 0) {
    slen = sizeof (sin);
    if (recvfrom (ifd, buff, sizeof (buff), 0, (struct sockaddr *) &sin,
&slen) > 0 && *buff == 'u') {
      OASISDEVdisconnect ();
      if ((hp = gethostbyaddr ((char *) &sin.sin_addr, sizeof
(sin.sin_addr), AF_INET)) != NULL) {
        strcpy (OASISDEVhost, hp->h_name);
      } else {
        strcpy (OASISDEVhost, inet_ntoa (sin.sin_addr));
      }
      if ((ifd = socket (AF_INET, SOCK_STREAM, 0)) < 0) {
        OASISDEVdisconnect ();
        return (-1);
```

```
    }
    if (connect (ifd, (struct sockaddr *) &sin, sizeof (sin)) < 0) {
      OASISDEVdisconnect ();
      return (-1);
    }
   }
  }

try: if (*OASISDEVhost) {
    sprintf (buff, "access id=(%s) pw=(%s) op=%d\n", cid,
"xxxxxx", 2);
    if (OASISDEVwrite (buff) < 1 || OASISDEVread (buff,
sizeof (buff)) < 1 || strncmp (buff, "ack", 3)) {
      OASISDEVdisconnect ();
      return (-1);
    }
  } else {
    OASISDEVdisconnect ();
    return (-1);
  }

  return (ifd);
}

/*---------------------------------------------------------------
  OASISDEVdisconnect --
---------------------------------------------------------------*/

void PROC OASISDEVdisconnect (void)
{
  if (ifd == -1) return;

  close (ifd);
  ifd = -1; *OASISDEVhost = '\0';

  return;
}

/*---------------------------------------------------------------
  OASISDEVparse -- Parse string for token
---------------------------------------------------------------*/
```

```
char PROC *OASISDEVparse (char *str, int *pos)
{
  char *s, *t;
  int quo;

  for (s = str + *pos; *s && strchr (" \f\r\t\v", *s); s++);

  for (t = s, quo = 0; *s; s++) {
   if (*s == '(') ++quo;
   if (*s == ')') --quo;
   if (strchr (" \f\r\t\v", *s) && !quo) break;
  }

  *pos = s - str + (*s ? 1 : 0); *s = '\0';
  return (*t ? t : NULL);
}

/*-------------------------------------------------------------------
  OASISDEVread --
-------------------------------------------------------------------*/

int PROC OASISDEVread (char *str, int nch)
{
  char *s = str;
  int ret;

  while (1) {
   if ((ret = read (ifd, s, 1)) < 1) {
    OASISDEVdisconnect ();
    return (ret);
   }
   if (*s == '\n') break;
   if (*s != '\r' && s < str + nch) ++s;
  }

  *s = '\0';
  return (s - str);
}

/*-------------------------------------------------------------------
  OASISDEVwrite --
-------------------------------------------------------------------*/
```

```
int PROC OASISDEVwrite (char *str)
{
  int ret;

  if ((ret = write (ifd, str, strlen (str))) < 1) OASISDEVdisconnect
();
  return (ret);
}
```

End of Listing 11 - Web-Server Client

This listing is not available for release at the time this is being written. Contact Patrick Benson through his home page, http://weber.u.washington.edu/ ~pbenson or directly to his email at pbenson@cac.washington.edu or at 206-685-2938. Efforts are underway to have a version ready for publication at the CAUSE98 Meeting in Seattle during December.

(2020 Note – These addresses and phone numbers are no longer accurate. Please see the introduction and 'About the Author' sections for current information.)

(2020 Note – For security purposes this code is not available.)

Listing 12 - Data-Server Server

The Bold and Complex Generation - J++ and Microsoft MTS Application

This is where we are going next. You'll have to tune in for more details as they become available.

The author is not, generally, a fan of large integrated packages from one vendor. Based upon experience, such packages tend to be strong in 25 % of their functions, middle of the road in another 25%, mediocre in another 25%, and best left unspoken about for the remaining 25%. However, the Microsoft Visual Studio ™ is proving itself to be an exception. Although complex in operation, and not as intuitive as possible, all the pieces for the C++, J++ and Internet Explorer ™ fit together into a package that works.

As noted in comments about the DBConnect and Socket Level, moving up a generation of Web to Data Server interconnection imposes a cost of decreased flexibility. This will be true with migration to this generation, too. Implementation of J++ and the MTS ™ will limit you to the Microsoft NT Server environment. Such implementation is a decision to make after careful consideration.

SQL Results and Data Parsing Code Samples

Regardless of the "Half-a" generation in place, the parsing of the returned data is an area where Perl really shines. The returned data is pipe delimited, so splitting a single row into fields and counting the number you received is completed by the instructions:

```
@perm_data = split('\|,$info);
$col_count = $#perm_data;
```

If multiple rows are returned, the commands are just as simple:

```
@perm_data = split('\|\$',$info);
$row_count = $#perm_data;
@row_data = split('\|',$perm_data[0]);
$col_count = $#row_data + 1;
```

Code and Data Base Linking Table

To facilitate rapid and comparatively easy attachment of the data to its attributes, OASIS uses a Linking Table. Based upon the major strengths of the Perl language is the ability to manipulate strings and tables. In this system all fields in all data tables have a parallel entry in a memory resident control table. This table allows direct conversion of a data item's real name (in a data table), the name it is called on screens and printed on reports, it's maximum length, edit characteristics, and an indication if it is a required field.

For the asset master table, a portion of this linking table is as follows in Listing 11, asset_master linking table, below. From this table we can easily find out that the asset_type is called the Status and that it is a required one-position character entry. We also can find that the inventory_bgt is called the Budget and that it is an optional six-position character entry translated from an external table called "budget".

```
@a_field_cntl = (
 ['Status','asset_type',1,'C','R'],
 ['Description Line 1','description_1',30,'C','R'],
 ['Description Line 2','description_2',30,'C','N'],
 ['Class','class_code',06,'C','R'],
 ['Organization','organization',10,'IPorg','N'],
 ['Budget','inventory_bgt',06, 'IPbudget','R'],
 ['Serial Nbr','serial_number',20,'C','R'],
 ['Building','building',05, 'C', 'N'],
 ['Wing','location_wing', 02,'C','N'],
 ['Room','location_room',05,'C','N'],
.
.
.
['Dept. Data 2','dept_data_2',60,'C','N']
);
```

Listing 11 - asset_master linking table

The logical extension is to tie the SQL Inquiry, the returned data stream, and the data attributes together. For example, Listing 6, find_asset_sql shows the relationships among the various tables but it does not show the exact selection clause. Elsewhere in the software there is a table indicating what elements of the linking table are used for which type of inquiry. Below, in Listing 12, Selection Statement Driven By Link Table, the method of allowing the link table to drive select statement construction, freeing the programmer from maintaining the SQL when columns are added or subtracted from the data base.

Here Line 4 sets the maximum number of iterations for the builder. Line 5 does the initial setup while lines 8-11 get the first nine data elements from the table. As noted in the comments, the selects get the translations of some fields, rather than just the fields themselves; see Lines 12-16.

Start of Listing 12 – Selection Statement Driven By Link Table

```
sub asset_sel_sql {
 $before_loc= 9;  #The first 9 items.. from asset_seq to building
 $loc_start = 14;  #next part asset data starts from 14
 $row_count = $misc_end = $#a_field_cntl;
 $select_str = 'a.asset_seq';

# Get the first 9 items, up to building, then put in the translations for
# building id, organization description and class code description
 for ($i=1; $i < $before_loc; $i++) {
  $select_str = $select_str . ', a.'
        . "$a_field_cntl[$i][1]";
}
$select_str = $select_str . ', '
        . 'e.budget_name, f.org_description, '
        . 'b.table_value as name_a_type, '
        . 'c.table_value as name_building, '
        . 'd.class_name';
# Get the rest of them, no more fields need translation
 for (; $i < $row_count + 1; $i++) {
   $select_str = $select_str . ', a.'
        . "$a_field_cntl[$i][1]";
}
}
```

End of Listing 12 – Selection Statement Driven By Link Table

A full extraction statement build this way looks like the following, where the asset id being extracted is 1013579, my old computer. See Figure 5, Full Link Table Controlled SQL Select Statement.

Start of Figure 5 – Full Link Table Controlled SQL Select Statement

UNLOAD TO pbenson_asset.dat SELECT a.asset_seq, a.asset_type, a.description_1, a.description_2, a.class_code, a.organization, a.inventory_bgt, a.serial_number, a.building, e.budget_name, f.org_description, b.table_value as name_a_type, c.table_value as name_building, d.class_name, a.other_location, a.location_wing, a.location_room, a.grant_contract_id, a.inventory_req_nbr, a.total_cost, a.acq_method, a.date_received, a.ownership_title, a.capitalization, a.date_in_service, a.date_last_invntry, a.quantity, a.quantity_uom, a.manufacturer_name, a.mfr_model_number, a.replacement_cost, a.inflation_code, a.trade_in_allow, a.inventory_fund, a.useful_life, a.remaining_life, a.salvage_value, a.basis_amount, a.basis_years, a.depr_manual_amt, a.depr_unrecorded, a.depr_method, a.depr_first_year, a.depr_last_year, a.depr_accum_ytd, a.depr_yrsthis_calc, a.depr_1yrthis_calc, a.depr_priorlast_yr, a.depr_years, a.disposal_reference, a.disposal_ref_date, a.disposal_method, a.disposal_date, a.disposal_amt, a.first_year_rule, a.last_trans_date, a.last_trans_type, a.date_created, a.create_reference, a.how_tagged, a.condition_code, a.custodian_name, a.availability, a.aims_tag_number, a.dept_act_date, a.dept_act_type, a.dept_act_oper, a.eio_act_date, a.eio_act_type, a.eio_act_oper, a.gov_tag_nbr, a.dept_code, a.dept_data_1, a.dept_data_2 FROM asset_master a, OUTER t_names b, OUTER t_names c, OUTER class d, OUTER (findb:budget_no_index e, OUTER global g), OUTER (findb:organization_tl f, OUTER global h) WHERE asset_id = '1013579' AND asset_seq >= '1' AND a.asset_type = b.table_key and b.table_name = 'A-TYPE' AND a.building = c.table_key and c.table_name = 'BLDG' AND a.class_code = d.class_code AND a.inventory_bgt[1,2] = e.budget_number[1,2] AND a.inventory_bgt[3,6] = e.budget_number[4,7] AND e.biennium_year = g.global_string AND g.global_item = 'CURRENT-BIENNIUM' AND a.organization = f.organization_code AND f.biennium_year = h.global_string AND h.global_item = 'CURRENT-BIENNIUM' ORDER BY asset_seq

End of Figure 5 – Full Link Table Controlled SQL Select Statement

A variation of this scheme is used to create views and reports. To do this a list of items to be extracted is built and passed through a subroutine similar to that in Listing 12, Selection Statement Driven By Link Table. One of these, and the resulting select statement follows in Figure 6, Link Table Controlled SQL.

The "Snapshot View 1" has ten columns, they are disjoint and out of sequence. This is the declaration for the view.

@snap_fields_1 = (2, 3, 22, 23, 6, 55, 7, 9, 10, 8);

The SQL generated from this is as follows.

Start of Figure 6, Link Table Controlled SQL

UNLOAD TO pbenson_asset.dat SELECT a.asset_seq, a.asset_type, a.quantity, a.quantity_uom, a.budget, a.custodian_name, a.building, a.other_location, a.location_wing, a.location_room WHERE asset_id = '1013579' AND asset_seq >= '1'

End of Figure 6, Link Table Controlled SQL

"My Application"

Much has been written about the concept of allowing the user to take ownership of their use of an application. The Link Table provides an easy method of accomplishing this and it will be integrated into the deployed system.

Users will be allowed to tailor a number of inquiry and update screens to their own needs through their Profile. Columns will be added to the oasis_user table, see Figure 5 that will allow the user to pick and order the fields for display. Their selection(s) will be loaded into variables similar to @snap_fields_1 in Figure 6, Link Table Controlled SQL, above. A common code block will interpret and construct the appropriate SQL, and another block will parse the returned data.

A similar, but more extensive, process is being considered. This would allow the user to use web buttons and pull down lists to construct SQL that will be submitted. By restricting the user this way, as opposed to providing a direct SQL interface, the novice user has access generally unheard of while the chance for "inappropriate" activity is reduced, both without burdening the Data Base Server with views and time consuming security settings.

Data Tables and Entity Relationship Diagram

Data Tables

The current data base tables are constructed to work with the Informix engine. The limited use of any functions aside from elementary dbaccess routines means these tables should conform to any SQL engine.

Start of Figure 7 – Data Tables

```
CREATE TABLE asset_master
(
 asset_id     Char  (10) NOT NULL,
 asset_seq    Smallint,
 asset_type    Char  (01) NOT NULL,
 description_1  Char  (30) NOT NULL,
 organization  Char  (10) NOT NULL,
 inventory_bgt  Char  (6) NOT NULL,
 class_code   Char  (6) NOT NULL,
 serial_number  Char  (20) NOT NULL,
 description_2  Char  (30),
 last_trans_date  Date,
 last_trans_type  Char  (18),
 date_created   Date,
 create_reference  Char  (18),
 capitalization  Char  (1),
 date_in_service  Date,
 ownership_title  Char  (1),
 date_last_invntry Date,
 how_tagged    Char  (2),
 condition_code  Char  (2),
 custodian_name  Char  (20),
 availabilty   Char  (2),
 inventory_fund  Char  (6),
 inventory_req_nbr Char  (7),
 quantity     Integer,
 quantity_uom   Char  (3),
 date_received  Date,
 acq_method    Char  (2),
 total_cost    Money  (11,2),
 disposal_reference Char  (7),
```

```
disposal_ref_date Date,
disposal_method  Char  (2),
disposal_date  Date,
disposal_amt  Money (11,2),
manufacturer_name Char  (30),
mfr_model_number  Char  (20),
replacement_cost  Money  (11,2),
inflation_code  Char  (2),
building  Char  (5),
other_location  Varchar (30,0),
useful_life  Smallint,
remianing_life  Smallint,
salvage_value  Money  (11,2),
first_year_rule  Char  (1),
depr_manual_amt  Money  (11,2),
depr_method  Char  (2),
depr_first_year  Money  (11,2),
depr_last_year  Money  (11,2),
depr_unrecorded  Money  (11,2),
depr_accum_ytd  Money  (11,2),
depr_yrsthis_calc Smallint,
depr_1yrthis_calc Money  (11,2),
depr_priorlast_yr Money  (11,2),
depr_years  Smallint,
basis_years  Smallint,
basis_amount  Money  (11,2),
grant_contract_id Varchar (30,0),
location_wing  Char  (2),
location_room  Char  (5),
trade_in_allow  Money  (11,2),
aims_tag_number  Char  (14),
dept_act_date  Date,
dept_act_type  Char  (18),
dept_act_oper  Char  (12),
eio_act_date  Date,
eio_act_type  Char  (18),
eio_act_oper  Char  (12),
gov_tag_nbr  Varchar (20,0),
dept_code  Char  (08),
dept_data_1  Varchar (60,0),
dept_data_2  Varchar (60,0)
);
```

```
CREATE UNIQUE INDEX asset ON asset_master (asset_id,
asset_seq,
                asset_type);
CREATE INDEX asset_class ON asset_master (class_code,
asset_id,
                asset_seq);
CREATE INDEX asset_org  ON asset_master (organization,
                asset_id, asset_seq);
CREATE INDEX asset_bgt  ON asset_master (inventory_bgt,
                asset_id, asset_seq);
CREATE INDEX serial_nbr  ON asset_master (serial_number);
CREATE INDEX description1 ON asset_master (description_1);
CREATE INDEX description2 ON asset_master (description_2);
CREATE INDEX custodian  ON asset_master
(custodian_name);
CREATE INDEX bldg_loc   ON asset_master (building,
                location_wing,
                location_room);
```

Note - The following Budget Index used is from the centrally maintained index.

```
INFO - "informix".budget_no_index:

---------------------- findb@findev ----------------

Column name     Type              Nulls

biennium_year   char(4)            yes
budget_number   char(7)            yes
budget_status   char(1)            yes
organ_code      char(10)           yes
budget_name     char(30)           yes
box_number      integer            yes
on_off_campus   char(1)            yes
curr_per_bgn_dt date               yes
curr_per_end_dt date               yes


CREATE TABLE class
(
```

```
class_code       CHAR(06) NOT NULL,
class_name       CHAR(30),
expected_life    SMALLINT,
depr_method      CHAR(03),
first_yr_rule    CHAR(01),
capitalization   CHAR(01),
inflation_code   CHAR(02),
class_account    CHAR(06)
);
CREATE UNIQUE INDEX c_code ON class (class_code);


CREATE TABLE expenditure
(
asset_id       CHAR(10) NOT NULL,
asset_seq      SMALLINT,
asset_type     CHAR(01),
expenditure_id   SERIAL(00000001),
expense_budget   CHAR(06),
revenue_class    CHAR(04),
revenue_src_code   CHAR(02),
fund_code      CHAR(06),
expense_amount   MONEY(11,2),
doc_seq_nbr     CHAR(11),
doc_ref_date    DATE,
activity_date   DATE,
accounting_month   CHAR(3),
req_number      CHAR(7),
expenditure_obj   CHAR(2),
expenditure_sub   CHAR(2)
);
CREATE UNIQUE INDEX expenditures ON expenditure
(asset_id,
              asset_seq asset_type,
              expenditure_id)
CREATE INDEX req_asset ON expenditure (req_number,
asset_id,
              asset_seq, asset_type)


CREATE TABLE global
(
```

```
global_item      CHAR(18) NOT NULL,
global_date      DATE,
global_money_amt   MONEY(11,2),
global_integer   INTEGER,
global_float    FLOAT,
global_string     VARCHAR(30,0)
);
CREATE UNIQUE INDEX global_data ON global
(global_item);


CREATE TABLE history
(
asset_id       CHAR(10) NOT NULL,
asset_type      CHAR(01) NOT NULL,
history_type     CHAR(06) NOT NULL,
timestamp       DATETIME YEAR TO FRACTION,
batch_date      DATE,
batch_id       CHAR(06),
batch_user      CHAR(12),
before_value     VARCHAR(30,6),
after_value      VARCHAR(30,6),
transaction_desc   VARCHAR(30,0),
auth_code       CHAR(01),
auth_date       DATE
);
CREATE UNIQUE INDEX hist ON history (asset_id,
asset_type,
              history_type, timestamp);
CREATE INDEX hist_user  ON history (batch_user,
timestamp);
CREATE INDEX hist_type  ON history (history_type,
timestamp);


CREATE TABLE note
(
asset_id       CHAR(10) NOT NULL,
asset_seq       SMALLINT,
asset_type      CHAR(01) NOT NULL,
note_type       CHAR(06) NOT NULL,
note_sequence     SMALLINT,
```

```
activity_date     DATE,
note_text       VARCHAR (240,1)
);
CREATE UNIQUE INDEX notes ON note (asset_id, asset_seq,
            asset_type, note_type,
            note_sequence);


CREATE TABLE oasis_user
(
user_id       CHAR(12),
user_name       VARCHAR (50,20),
user_email_addr    VARCHAR (50,20),
user_pref_printer   VARCHAR (30,12),
last_access      DATE,
access_counter    SMALLINT,
security_level    CHAR(01)
);


CREATE INDEX oasis_users ON oasis_user(user_id);
```

Note - The Organization Description Table used is from a centrally maintained table.

```
INFO - "informix".organization_tl:
----------------------- findb@findev ----------------

Column name      Type     Nulls
biennium_year    char(4)    yes
organization_code  char(10)   yes
org_description   char(30)   yes

CREATE TABLE permission
(
user_id        CHAR(12),
perm_seq_nbr      SERIAL(00000001),
perm_range_type     CHAR(01),
perm_i_e_flag     CHAR(01),
perm_from_range     CHAR(12),
perm_to_range      CHAR(12)
);
```

```
CREATE INDEX permissions ON permission (user_id,
perm_seq_nbr);


CREATE TABLE rpt_scheduler
(
complete_flag     CHAR(1) NOT NULL,
submit_dtime      DATETIME year TO minute NOT NULL,
user_id        CHAR(12) NOT NULL,
rpt_key        CHAR(20) NOT NULL,
process_id      INTEGER NOT NULL,
email_addr      VARCHAR(50,20),
pref_printer     VARCHAR(30,12)
);

CREATE UNIQUE INDEX rpt_index ON rpt_scheduler
(complete_flag,
               submit_dtime, user_id,
               rpt_key, process_id)


CREATE TABLE t_names
(
table_name      CHAR(06) NOT NULL,
table_key      CHAR(06) NOT NULL,
table_value     VARCHAR(30,15)
);

CREATE UNIQUE INDEX name ON t_names
(table_name,table_key);
```

End of Figure 7 – Data Tables

Figure 8 - OASIS Entity Relationship Diagram (ERD)

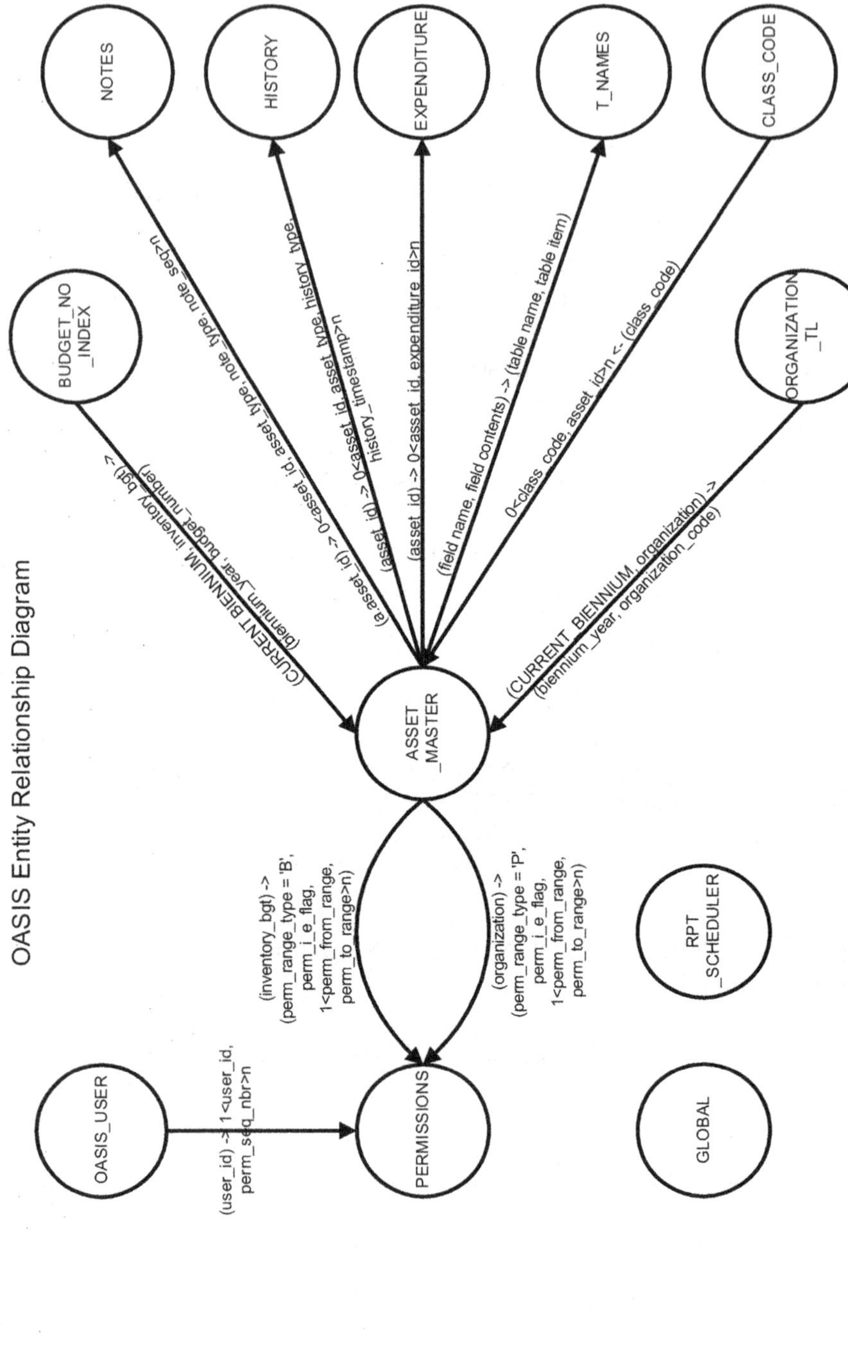

Conclusions on Web Development

Role and Problem of the Steering Committee

During development of this software and other web projects at the University of Washington it became apparent that there are distinctly different web designs needed to support record management systems, such as this fixed assets package, and data entry systems, such as a payroll time reporting package. This emergent realization reopened an area of system and user interaction design and analysis not used since the early days of on-line programming. What is a logical unit of work? Who sets it and how can a user tell when they've finished one? Is it fixed, dynamic, or both? How can it be mapped into a usable sized physical workspace when that workspace is under the control of the end user, not the developer?

A paradigm is shifting. Can you feel it? Are you as tired of that phrase as I?

As Universities, we are bureaucracies subject to movement at glacial speed. Software development today is a flood of changes. Those groups we call "steering committees", in my experience, sooner rather than later and always quickly, want to micro-manage software development. Rather than looking at the big picture and setting direction, the members quibble over minutia. How many of us have sat in "high powered" meetings and listened to a half dozen folks making $50,000 and more a year spend 30 minutes haggling over the text of a prompt? And those arguments were held when the visible world was 24 by 80 characters. A steering committee moving at glacial speed in a 24 by 80 world makes no progress and is swept away in a flood of web development. In the six weeks it takes to get on the calendars of a dozen "high powered" people for a project kick-off meeting, a prototype can be developed, deployed and two rounds of user feedback put into place. The traditional steering committee has earned a vacation, and, if it will not go, then send it packing. Who among us can take the time to wait?

Role and Need for an "Intelligence Agent"

The best reviewer of software is not the developer, their manager, the manager of the end users, but the end user themselves. It is suggested that long training sessions with management are not the most fruitful use of your time. This will not go down well but given the choice of two hours with a manager who is an infrequent user of the application and four hours with a group of three of the staff who will use the system often you will do far better with the group. This poses a challenge for Information Systems management since many, probably a majority, of the programmers entering the field today do not have the people skills necessary to complete this task. Schools are turning out many technophiles who tend to intimidate users into not cooperating or frustrate them into giving up and accepting a system that is less than it could be. Some of these newer programmers have not learned that the software is not for them, it is for the user; and beauty is in the eye of the beholder not the artist.

It may seem a trite suggestion, but experience shows that identification of a web-savvy end user that can translate the operation of user-esse into words of specification-esse is worth their weight in gold. I've called the person who can fill this role the "Intelligence Agent" not because the other users are not intelligent, but this person can be your eyes and more importantly, your ears, into the real user world.

Best Practices

During development of this project a series of working papers were created. These form the basis for a "Best Practices" model that is available. This model, as used by the OASIS team, is aimed at the Unix environment, however there is a great deal of applicability into the Microsoft NT and MTS world. The following components make up the model:

1. Design Document Summary

This serves as a document management and summary tool. The author of each document and date completed are noted.

2. Statement of Purpose

Here the purpose and level of commitment, both human and physical resource commitments, are detailed. The system owner, customer liaison and IS point of contract are identified.

3. Architecture

The development approach and rational behind that approach, the challenges anticipated from the environment or goals, and an identification of feasibility or concept testing needed before the project can go forth are outlined here.

4. Security Requirements

On this document, the various login groups are identified. This includes identification of users with special or extraordinary permissions. Access restrictions to databases or database elements (tables, rows or columns) are identified. Menus or pages with limited or controlled access are listed.

5. Entity Relationship Diagram Summary

Self-explanatory, this is a table of ERDs and the diagrams themselves.

6. Data Objects, Directories, Tables and File Descriptions

Self-explanatory. Every file, table and element, including global working storage items, must be described. The deployed directory structure is identified.

7. Object - Event - Action Matrix

This matrix lists every object (elements noted in the Data Tables and File Descriptions, all buttons that may be clicked, all anchors that may be selected) and all events. At the intersection of each object and event is the action to be taken for that instance. Construction of this matrix is a time consuming task, but when done a cut and paste of all the sheets will allow a full picture of the data inquiry, edit and update functions of the system.

8. GUI Presentation Model

This document has three sections. The first lists all the graphics used, their source and geometry for every instance, and a sample of the image. A second section describes the layout of Public Pages;

those anyone may access from the web. The third section describes the layout of Private pages; those only authorized users may access.

9. Object Navigation Model Documents

The general function and links that every page may follow are graphically shown in these documents.

10. Page Object Property Matrix Documents

This set of pages notes, for every page, every object and its use. Objects are identified by the names used in the Data Tables and File Descriptions document. The use, default value, all allowable values and comments about each object are found.

11. Interface Requirements Documents

Each interface is described in detail in these documents. It is intended that each instance of an interface will be listed in detail. For example, if there is one call to the Accounting Data Server for a Budget Number, another for an Organization Description, and a third for a Budget Status, there are three interfaces to define. For each the location, engine, performance criteria, elements, and ERD, a typical extraction request and any design implications resulting from using the interface, are listed.

12. Functional Requirement Documents

Every requirement of the system, from limiting access to producing a report or sending an email, will have its own Requirement Document. This document will identify the business goal, software need, specific data problem to solve to meet the goal, an explanation of how success in meeting the requirement is determined, and any constraints upon the system imposed by the requirement.

13. Development Environment

This section contains descriptions of the physical environment necessary for initial development of the software. It links references in Sections 3, 4, 5, 6 and 11.

14. Deployment Instructions

Plans for installation of production software may be found here. The names and functions of support software, repository used (if applicable), naming conventions and information linking references in Sections 3, 4, 5, 6 and 11 for the production environment.

15. Supporting Documentation Location

Here plans for post-implementation and change control are addressed. Included are locations of documentation necessary to support the user and system.

A blank copy of the model in Microsoft Word ™ documents is available from my homepage http://weber.u.washington.edu/~pbenson. The completed model for this project should be available before the CAUSE98 meeting to be held in Seattle during December 1998.

(2012 Note - that web site was dropped after I left the UW in 2005)

Summary

The web development environment shares only one thing in common with the 24 by 80 COBOL world, and that is hardware. During the course of this project, it became apparent to the author that two classes of changes to the software development environment have occurred; human side and business side.

Human Side Changes

The level of effort needed to support the non-technical side of the human-machine interaction was a surprise. In fact, the technical side (the actual software) turned out to be a disposable commodity, with code modules being written, then discarded and rewritten. The specification of what was to be seen and how it was to be accessed, and who actually drove deliverables changed from Information Systems and the manager of Equipment Inventory, to the actual end user. Implementation and training in the web environment requires an extremely high level of human relation skill.

The politics of "who are the important people" changed dramatically when the workspace expanded to fill all needs. When the view shifted from 24 by 80 and became unrestricted. What comes to mind is that needs expand to fill the known universe, regardless of how large or complex is that universe.

Business Side Changes

This fixed assets package was developed as a record management system. Here, breadth of view of the unit of work takes precedence over its responsiveness. Meaning it is more important to see every piece of information about an asset in a single workspace than it is to get the information quickly. To display the information so the viewer can see everything at once. The response time takes a back seat to the display. Other applications in development are data entry oriented where the responsiveness takes precedence and the end user's capabilities and choices control the unit of work. The media has become the message.

What takes eight hours in a 24 by 80 world can generally be done in one hour in a Perl CGI web environment. A list of changes that would take a week can be done before lunch.

The best technical programmers in the field today tend to have insufficient human relation skills to pull of implementation of web software. The environment is too complex and too unfamiliar. The ability to communicate person to person (faceware if you will) has been depreciated in favor of technical skill.

ACKNOWLEDGEMENTS

The following staff of the University of Washington, Computing and Communications, Information Systems deserve special credit for helping me get this paper together.

- Rick Anglin for his help with SQL and the Informix ™ database engine.
- Dan Groves for his help with Perl and Unix.
- (2012 Note - Tragically, Dan was fatally injured in an accident. The IT world was diminished by his passing.)

- Rita Johnson for her work as the Equipment Inventory Office "Intelligence Agent".
- Ed Lightfoot for permission to publish.
- Ping Lo for the DBConnect and Socket Extensions process.
- Jerry Luiten and Mike Pingree for encouragement and four NT boxes in six weeks.
- Denny Sullivan for editorial mastery.

- **Edith Shen** ... A very special thanks goes to Edith for help with programming, design, development, implementation, training, troubleshooting, documentation, DBConnect, UNIX, Perl, and helping me keep my sanity.

OASIS, THE WEB BASED CLIENT-SERVER FIXED ASSETS SYSTEM – THE PRESENTATION

This presentation was a long one. The original 90-minute block ended at the start of a two-hour box lunch and I was still answering questions when the afternoon session speakers interrupted.

What follows are the slides and my notes from the presentation. I've transferred my notes from the questions and answer session that ran through the lunchtime. In my opinion, this is my most significant presentation about application sockets and database sockets because it includes the C-code necessary to implement them.

Slide 1

Good Morning

Thank Host - _________John_________

Pat Benson, Senior Computing Specialist, U of W in Seattle. *** Seattle, where it doesn't rain a lot, it just drizzles constantly from October to June.

Feel free to contact me by email. My address is on the slide, or you can use the email window on my homepage.

We've got a lot of information to cover so hold your comments and questions until the end.

Remember John Walsh's opening comment, "That you show what you are doing."

What I intend to do is give you an overview of the underpinnings of a Fixed Assets system that runs over the web with CGI controlled dynamic HTML and an INFORMIX database on three-tier architecture. Most of what I'll present today are practical examples that apply to many projects. This presentation parallels a 40-page paper in the conference materials. Both the paper and these presentation slides will be posted on my web site when I get back to Seattle. A presentation, where the basic web to database concepts used were first discussed, was made last year at the First Perl Conference. That paper is attached to my web page now.

Some of the material here is not there, some that is there is more robust, and I'll tell you about those areas.

Will cover - Concept of Web 'SPACE' - 3-Tier database access from the web - Authentication and Access - Gentle Standardization - Some specific advice on use of Perl Tables - Some General advice for Web development.

Slide 2

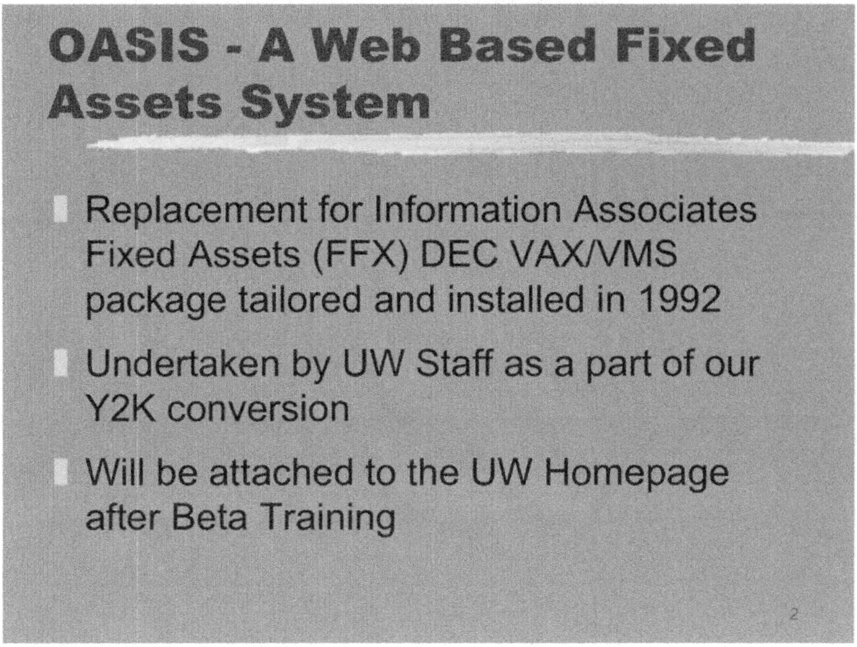

We only purchased the Fixed Assets portion of the whole IA Package. OASIS is a stand-alone system, not linked to the financial or purchasing software. Both an advantage and disadvantage.

Full featured with report writer that allows for file creation for download, email, batch and ad-hoc report writers, on request standardized and routinely scheduled reports. It has the features of Depreciation, Budget Replacement Cost, Annual Inventory.

Y2K because the package, as installed at the U of W, is not compliant in Depreciation or reporting.

Because it will be attached to the UW Homepage, the application must conform to the common look-and-feel of the other pages there. A method to centrally control this has been developed (CHTML), and I will discuss it later.

Fixed Assets is a "tail of the dog" application. It is not absolutely necessary to have a real-time system. The institution could exist for some time (in fact it did on the older system) without a computerized AP. This is so unlike, say, payroll, where blowing a run is a short path to the front pages.

Slide 3

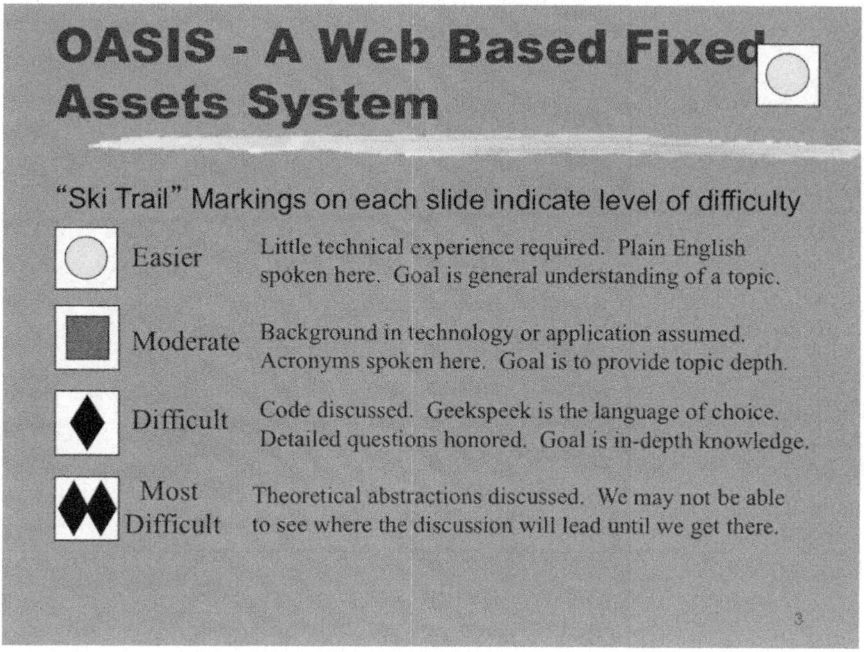

The notification that my paper was accepted the committee wanted to know how technical and difficult it would be. They introduced, as a guide, the idea of ski trail markings. I thought that was a was a grand idea and have included one of the markings on each slide.

Most of the slides are rated Moderate and Difficult.

Slide 4

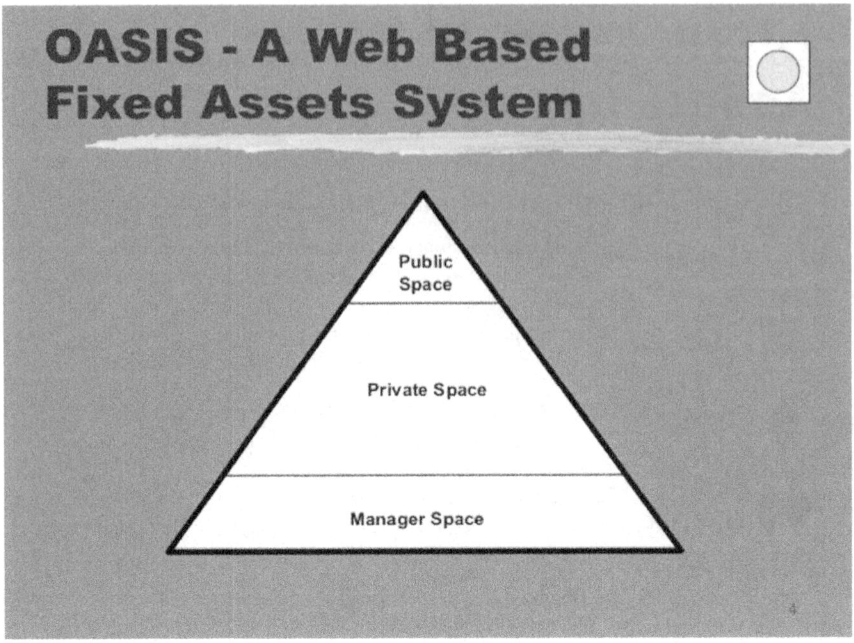

The Concept of Space - A general introduction to Institution and Enterprise wide web applications.

Every application you deploy should have a consistent look and feel that exudes the very character and essence of the institution's goals and its opinion of itself. The more the general public uses the page the more important is the consistent look-and-feel. You want the public to KNOW this is your page without having to read it carefully. BUT - Avoid the "Ransom Note" effect – David Frazier of Moorehead State's line.

However, constructing an application so every employee sees the institution's mascot the same way, page after page after page, is counterproductive and frustrating.

Typically, the material making up the consistent look and feel will initially use up the top 20% of the page. This is the highly visible and expensive real estate. After folks look at it day after day, week after week, it will it be scaled to something more realistic.

Slide 5

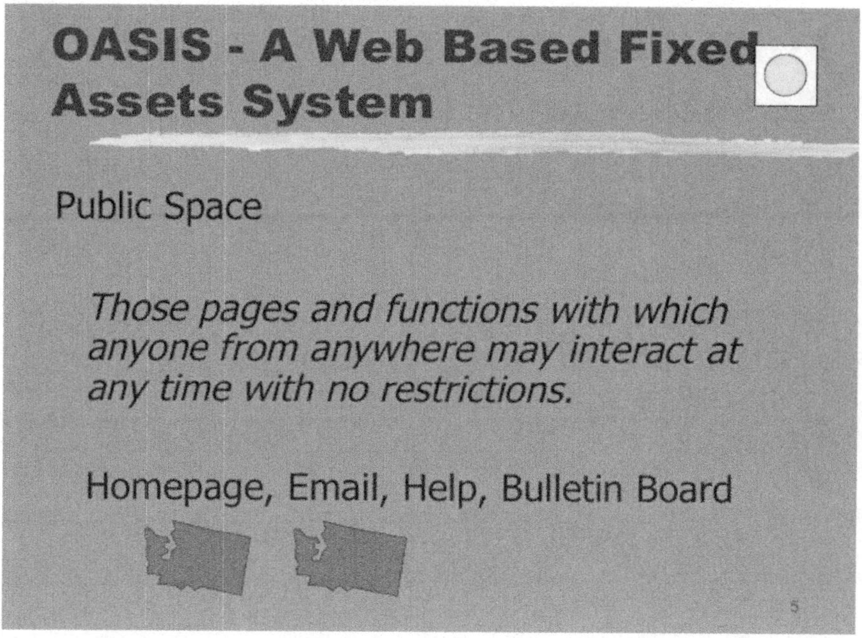

Public space, the top of the pyramid, is how you want the world to see your institution.

School colors, something to attract new students, something to show the taxpayer/parent where their money is going. Many good and bad examples out there.

I'm going to bring up two homepages, U of W and WWU, to show different approaches. This is not to compare the two ... BUT ... I want you to think for a second about them. What do you think the school is like? Are you drawn to it?
These two schools compete for the same geographic and demographic population covering the NW 1/4 of the US, Alaska, Canada, Hawaii, and the Far East. UW (37,000) is arguably the finest graduate school west of Minneapolis, north of San Francisco and east of Tokyo. WWU (11,000) is one of the most respected undergraduate liberal arts schools in the country, public or private.

Menu "stuff" is Javascript replacement of an IMG SRC with OnMouseIn and OnMouseOut events.

Slide 6

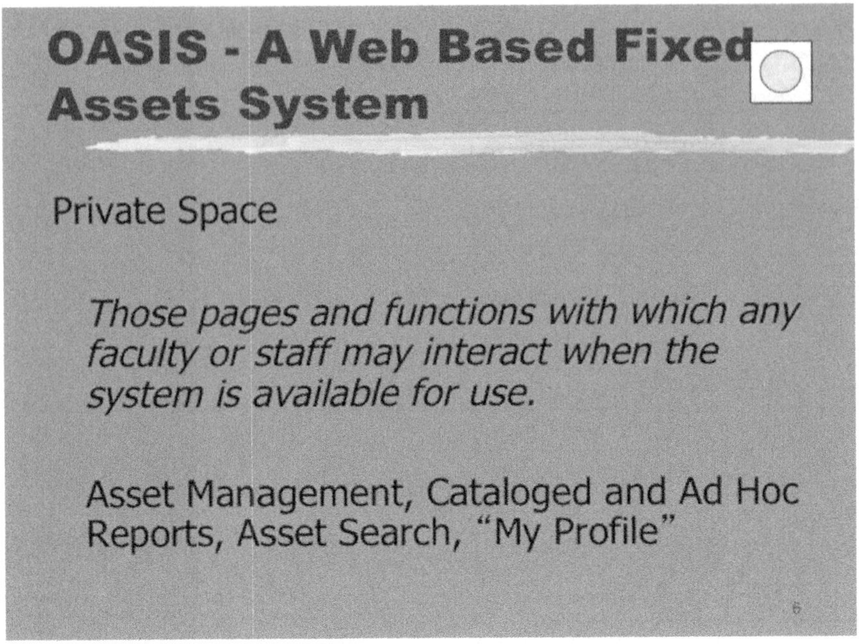

Private space, the pyramid's body, is how the members of the institution want to see their work.

This is where the user community lives and breathes. Most will bookmark pages past your public space menu so be ready for that.

THE FOLOWING TEXT SKIPPED DUIRNG THE PRESENTATION

Defining this is as close to the old-fashioned world of COBOL programming and those wonderful old 24x80 screen layouts as we get anymore. One of the challenges faced is, in fact, breaking the link to those old methodologies. Once had a user design a screen that was 36x92. It was a thing of beauty and it broke my heart to tell him I couldn't do it for him on a B-6800. Today … well if he brought it to me today, I'd ask "Why so small?"

Slide 7

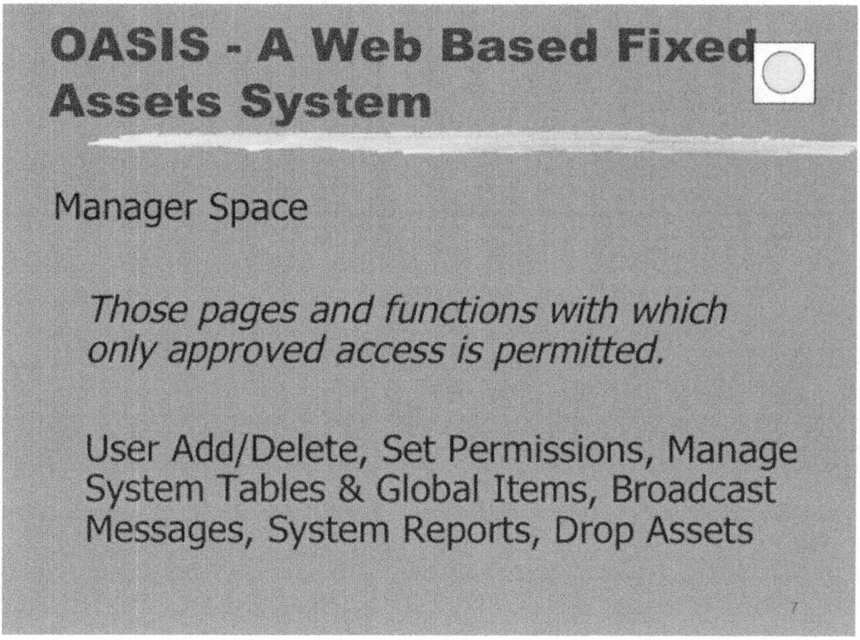

Manager space, the foundation, is where management controls what it wants the members to be able to see and do.

There are places you do not want the average user to go. This is the place.

Access is restricted in a manner that allows system managers to change in real-time the permissions and access authority of a user. They may turn the system on or off, to start and stop the report writer, and to post broadcast messages.

Slide 8

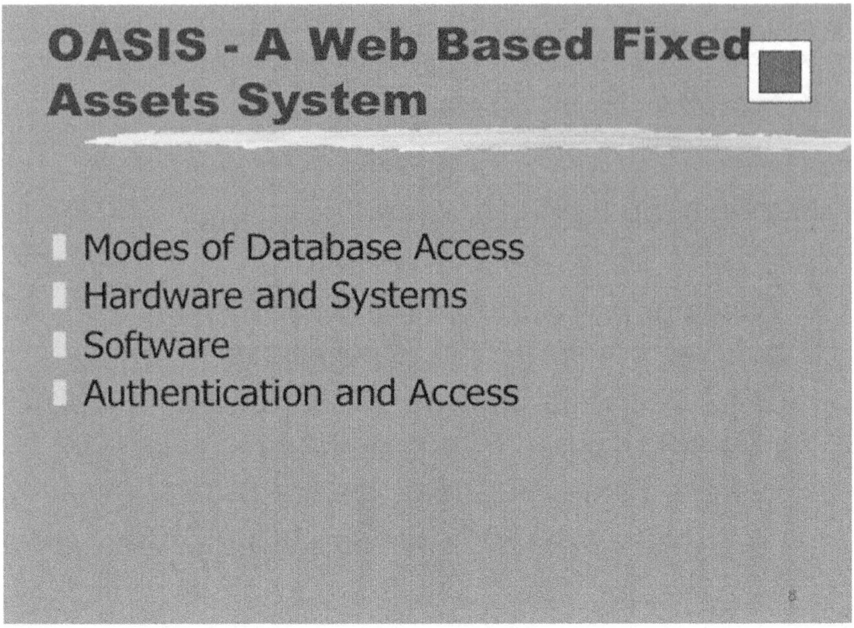

New Topic - First Blue Square Slide

This, and the next four slides, are included to introduce general topics we'll be covering during the next few minutes.

The paper Includes data tables and an ERD, see pages 29-35. (2020 Note – These page numbers will get you close but, due to reformatting, probably are not exact.)

Slide 9

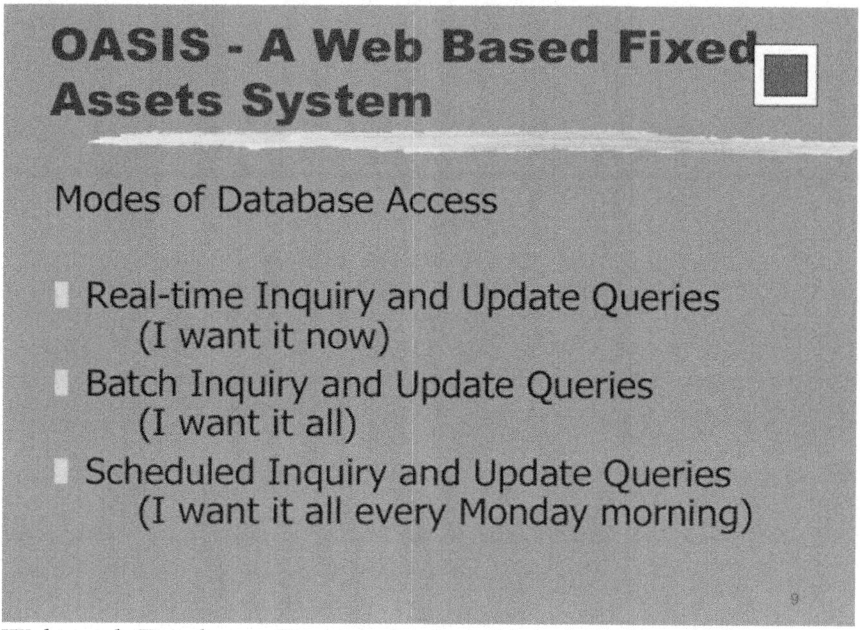

Web and Database Communication Link has 3 generations ... specifics will be discussed later. I just want you to be ready for it.

Types of Inquiry drives the type of access. There is no one-size-fits-all in this environment.

1. Real time inquiries are those with strictly web output. Submitted directly to the Database Engine. "Tell me everything about asset 884991." You'll hear about the ship again.

2. Batch Inquiries generate a working file the viewer may send to the web, printer, email or download. Passed through a FIFO queue process (later). "Get me a listing of all the PC's, XT's, NT's and related desktop equipment." [NOTE - Class Code 7012*, 16-18,000 items.]

3. Scheduled Inquiry and Update Queries are generally meet systems management needs. Daily Activity, Depreciation Calculation and Posting, End of Year/Biennium Reports. Managed by Third Party Scheduler product (later). "Run depreciation on the 5th of January, March, May and November; on the 7th of April,

June, December; and on the 4th the rest of the year except July. Run it on the 15th then."

Slide 10

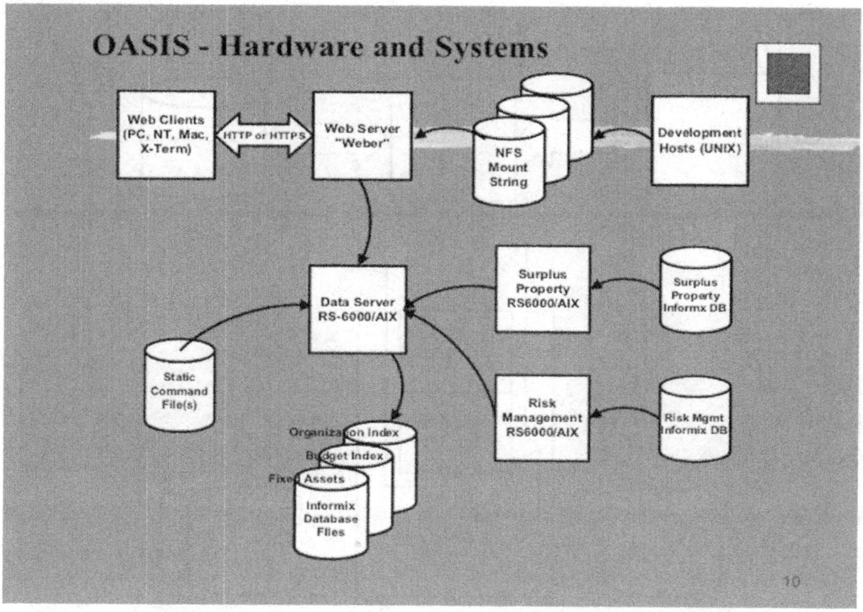

As of August 7, and subject to change hourly. This is fairly representative of an "average" Three-tier web deployment.

1. Web Clients - Intel, Mac or Term, HTTP/HTTPS - Modem, thin and thick net, home-grown, UW fiber optic, Weber - 7 DEC 3000/700 Boxes

2. NFS Mount String - 30 Gigabytes. Development hosts - Just about anything that runs a flavor of UNIX.

3. Data Server- RS6000/AIX with 7 Gigabytes of storage

4. Informix database
5. Static Command Files to tweak the environment.

6. External links to Surplus Property and Risk Management - Both are RS6000/AIX with 1-2 Gigabytes of storage, and the Informix database.

Slide 11

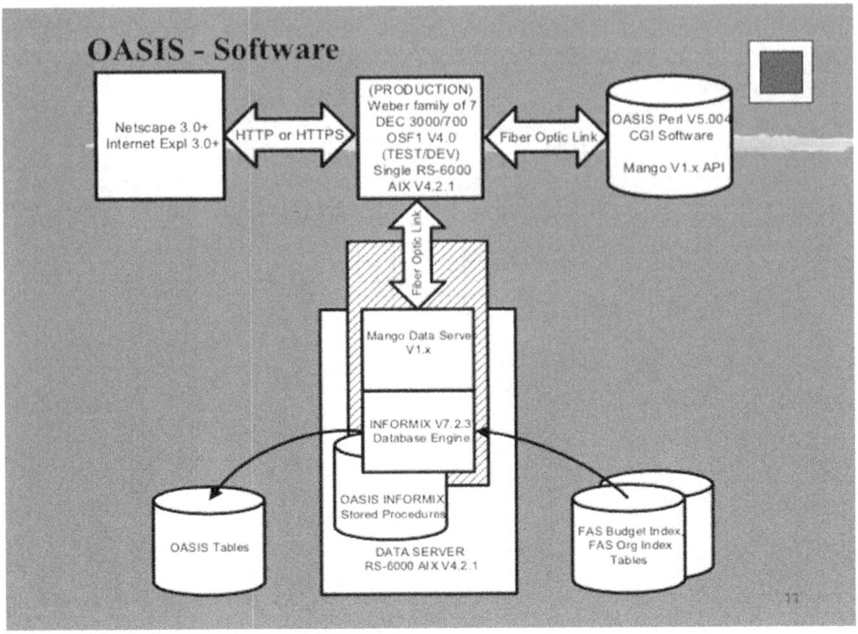

As of September 4, and subject to change hourly.

1. Web Clients - Netscape 3.0+, IE 3.0+ on Intel, Mac or Xterm

2. Weber -PRODUCTION 7 DEC 3000/700 Boxes running OSF1 Version 4.0
- TEST/DEV 1 RS-6000 running AIX Version 4.2.1

3. Development software - Perl 5.004, Assorted text editors (PICO) for the CGIs. The Mango API is in development to support this project.

4. Data Server is RS-6000 AIX Version 4.2.1. Here too is the Mango System, data server WILL BE COVERED IN JUST A BIT. The database engine is Informix Version 7.2.3.

NOTICE THE "I" STRUCTURE - Much done on the top, by and for Microsoft, Netscape, Apache ... and much done on the bottom by and for Microsoft, Informix, Ingres, Oracle ... BUT LITTLE DONE IN THE MIDDLE. Will be address downstream.

Slide 12

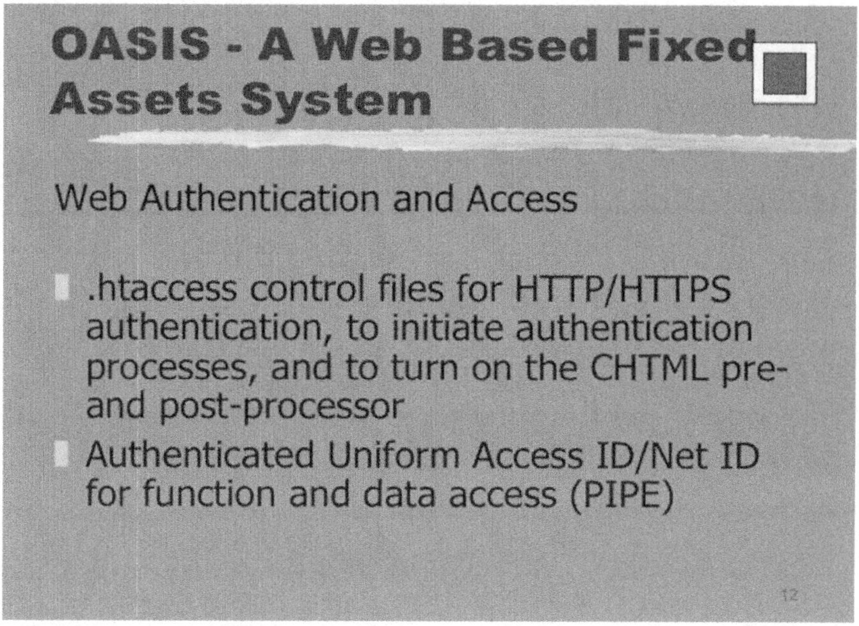

CHTML Here means "Conditional" not "Compiled" which is a Microsoft word. Although our acronym has been around for several years, I'll bet we end up changing it. Our use will be discussed later.

The paper has examples of .htaccess files for both authentication and for the CHTML processors on Page 11.

Will discuss PIPE next.

Slide 13

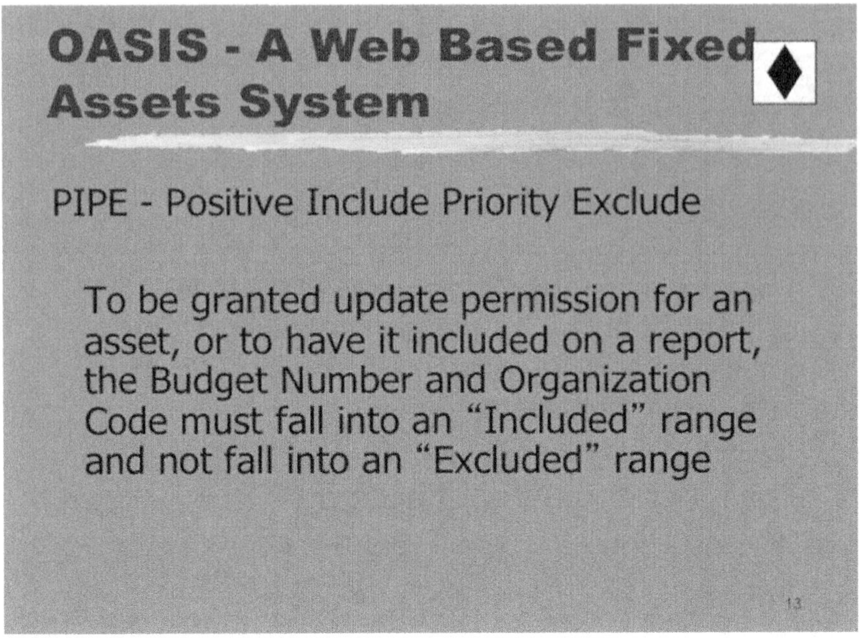

UW has used a six numeric position budget number chart of accounts for 25 years.

To identify administrative departments as separate entities from budget units, a ten position Organization Code was developed. The goal was to allow accounting roll-ups to administrative units by attaching users to organization codes and placing budgets under this organization structure.

This was to simultaneously give an organization's staff access to all appropriate budgets and restrict access to information outside their organizational span of control. It should have provided a data summary structure resembling tree roots. This concept of budgets and organizations still works in a computerized batch mode.

Unfortunately, after binding this concept to the University, the organizational structure changed. Budgetary restrictions, departmental expansion and unit realignments caused organizational trauma.

Moving the School of Biotechnology from the College of Arts and Sciences to the College of Engineering while reducing staff, forced the reporting tree roots to be cut from one place and grafted onto another. Now, to provide proper access, we must include all the organization codes that used to be under A&S EXCEPT the few that now belong to Engineering.

Both staff and budgets will cross rigid organizational boundaries; so, must software and data access controls.

Slide 14

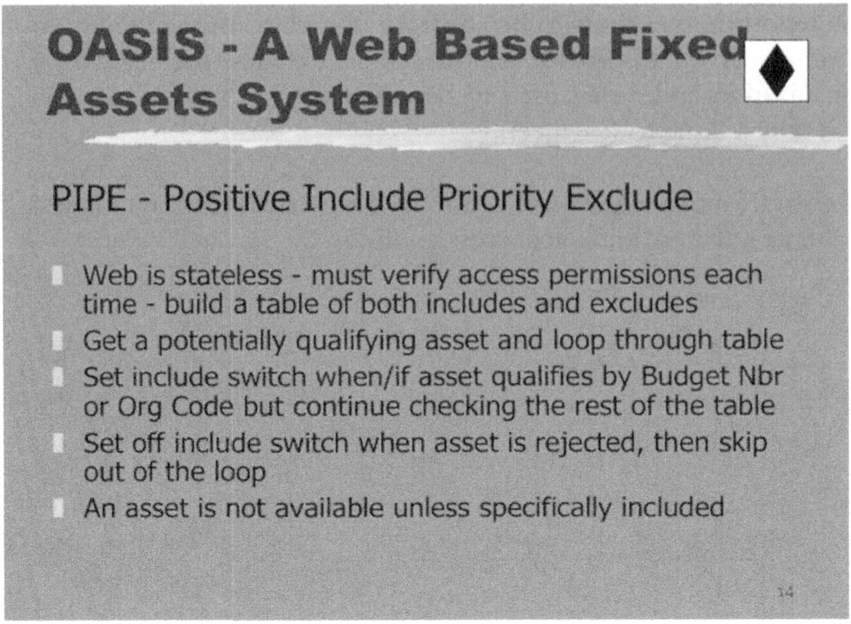

Constraint - MUST Always look up the user to verify they have access. Web is stateless … like the original implementation of CICS when there was nothing like a terminal scratch pad area. That may be where web programming is today ... and will be until the technology expands.

Must build a table of permissions each time a transaction comes down the line.

Both COBOL and Perl examples follow.

Practical Example at conference:

- Your child asks both you and your spouse to borrow the car.

- You go over all the things you need to do and then say, "It's OK with me if it's OK with Mom."

Slide 15

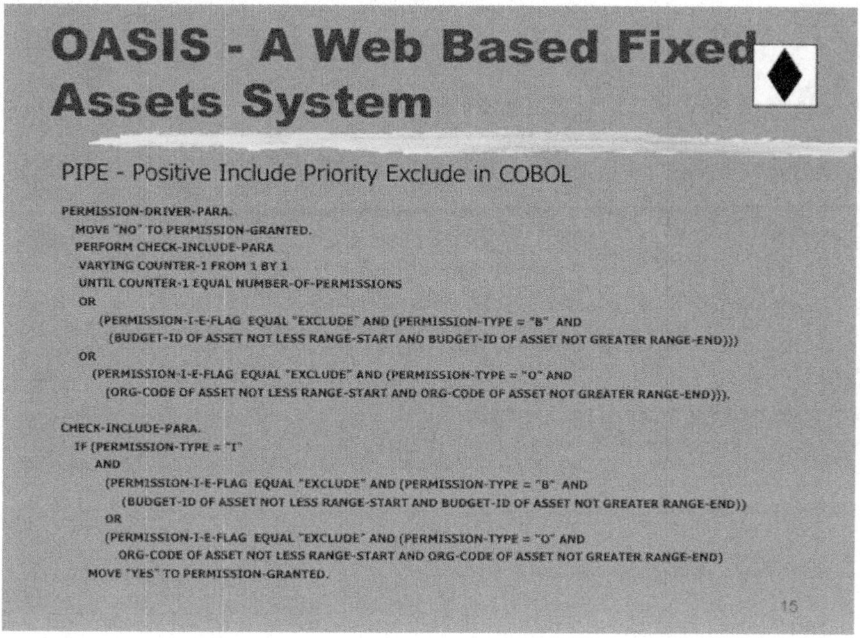

COBOL Code Example.

Dense code, may want to check out your handout or wait until I get this on the web.

Bet you never thought you'd see COBOL in a web presentation!

Slide 16

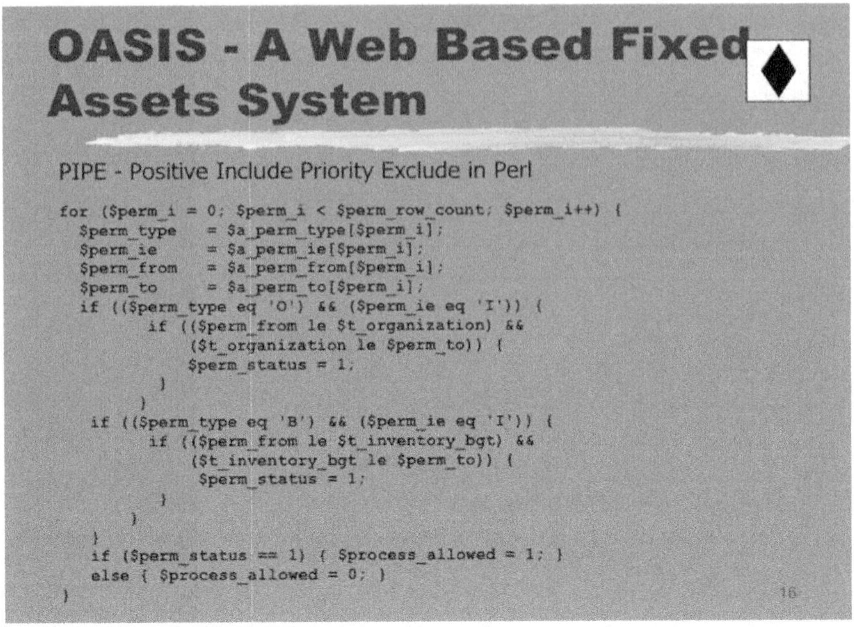

Perl Code Example.

Much shorter than COBOL.

Slide 17

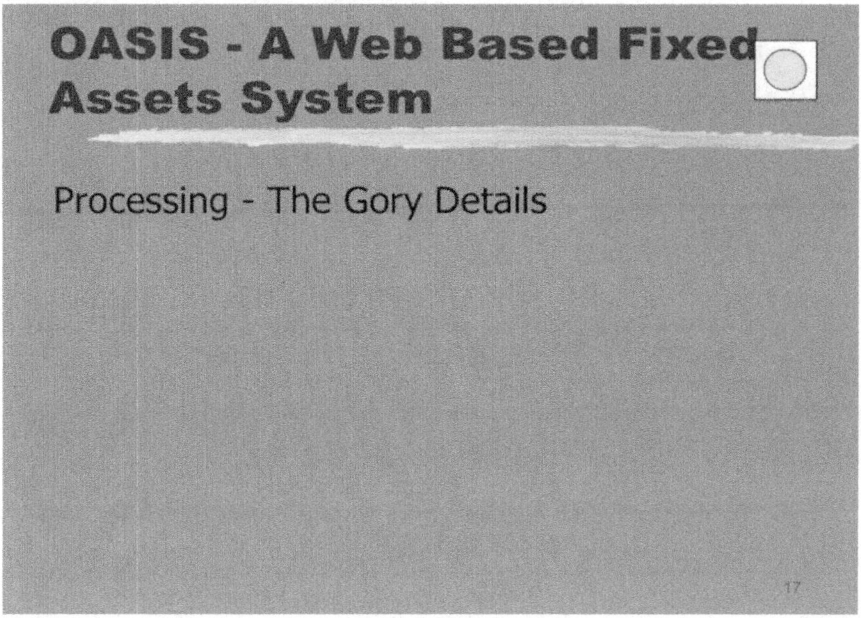

Think of this as the flat spot on the ski run. A chance to stop, take a deep breath, clear off the inside of the goggles. Let your heart stop racing and your legs stop shaking.

Slide 18

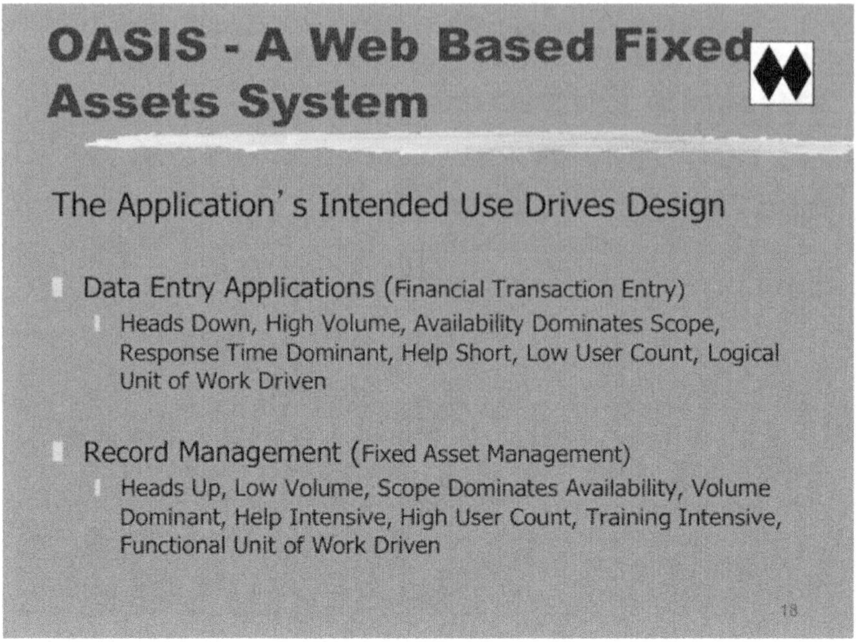

Watch Out, Double Black Diamond here. Theoretical question here.
Looks simple ... but this is the proverbial paradigm shift.

ARE YOU AS TIRED OF THAT PHASE AS I?

Points at conference

- You do not want any data entry query transactions to hit the database because the volume and speed are access killers
- You are OK with record management transactions hitting the database because they are relatedly few (compared to data entry apps).

Before, available hardware and software drove what IS did ("Software First then Hardware" adage).

Now, everything from desktop platform, browser software, communication network, web server hardware and software, database engine and platform, EVERYTHING depends upon the target environment. Important questions are different. "What is a logical unit of work?", "Who sets it and how can a user tell when

they've completed one?", "Is it fixed or dynamic, or both" "How can you map a logical unit of work into a useable sized physical workspace what that workspace is under the control of the user, not the developer?"
The Public Space and Private Space environments may be vastly different in Look, Feel and Operation.

Here are two examples of vastly different applications with which I am involved at this time.

Conference – compare FASTRANS (data entry) with OASIS (records management)

Slide 19

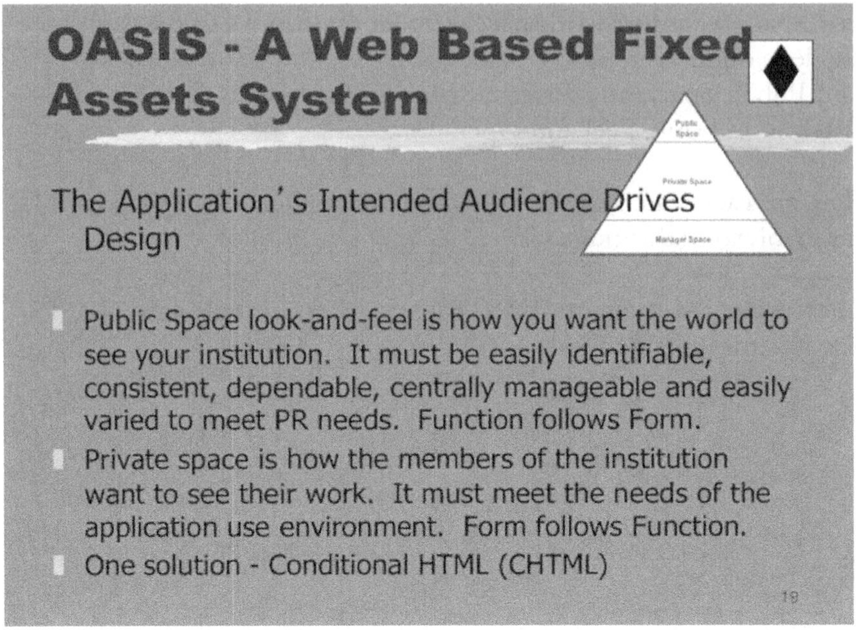

This quick review goes back to the pyramid from an earlier slide (#5).

Public or Private Audience?

Quick review of Public and Private spaces.

Remember what you thought and how you felt about the two home pages. They show very different uses of public space. You need to always ask yourself - What am I saying about us with this page - sort of like shining your shoes and combing your hair just before an interview. Do not underestimate the PR side of your public space.

As more and more students use the web to select their college – a part of many – maybe most- high school curricula will include this as a routine part of class work.

CHTML - Conditional in Unix World, Compiled in Microsoft World. We have a good idea whose acronym will survive any shakeout.

Slide 20

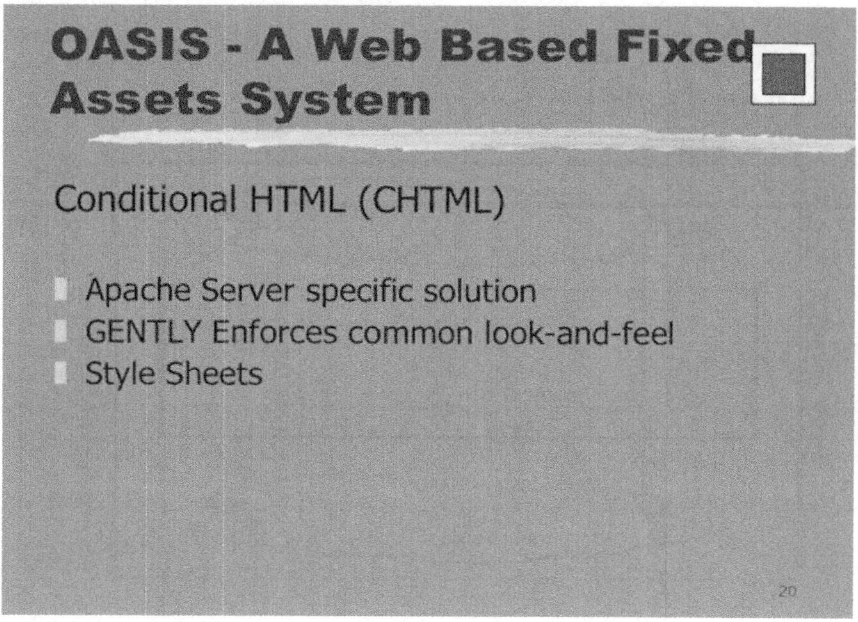

CHTML - Conditional HTML

Implemented via modification to the Apache Server.

Goal is to provide mechanism for GENTLY enforcing a common look and feel across the institution's public space; and, if desired, across the application private space.
Uses HTML Style Sheets. Where the application is located determines the content of the header.

The argument has been made that in an Object Oriented world common objects could be used ... and this is true ... but generally objects are compiled in not just picked up and used. This is an arena where things are changing quickly.

Slide 21

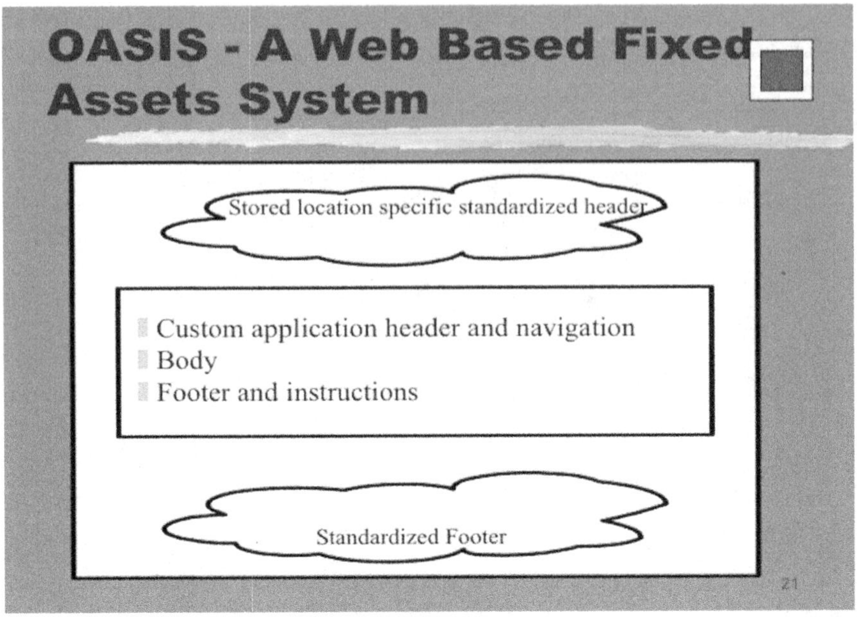

CHTML - Conditional HTML

Result is a fuzzy view of what will be in the page header and the style of your body (if style sheets are used). Font and size may be determined by a central organization, unless you hardcode fonts and that forces the web client to conform to your code's specification. Is this likely? All the time?

Your application must be able to conform. Leave lots of spaces.

Clear view of the application specific header and navigation tools, the body, and footer.
Another Fuzzy view of what will be in the footer, what it will look like, graphics and so forth.

Example follows.

Slide 22

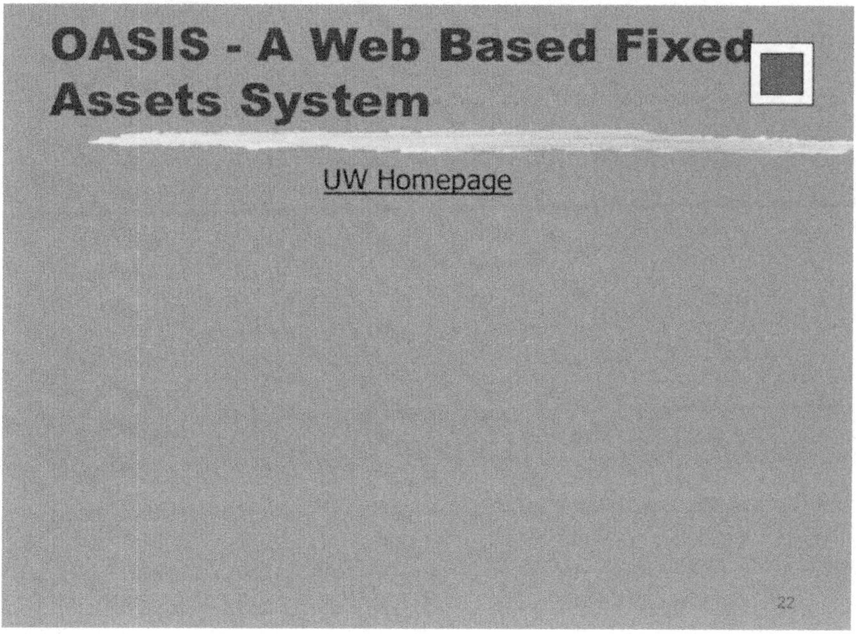

(2012 Note – In this area there has been much change. The basic thought, of using tables not frames, may no longer be an issue.)

Point out that this is done with tables ... not done with frames.

Title, purple bar with navigation links

Javascript for menu selection and expansion only applies when the browser version supports it. You can see the control logic on the next slide.

Slide 23

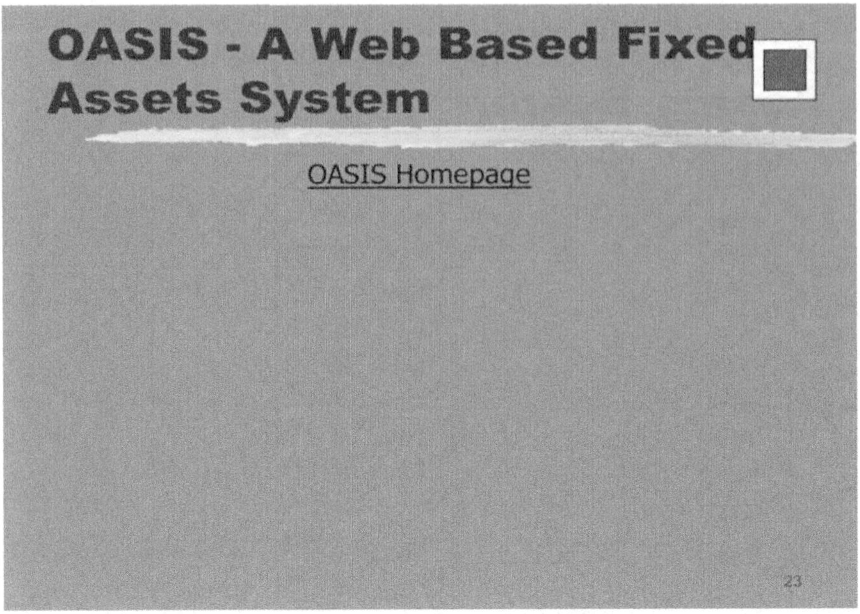

(2012 Note – In this area there has been much change. The basic though, of using tables not frames, may no longer be an issue.)

Note that CHTML pre and post processors add the title and blue bar. We'll go into that next.

Slide 24

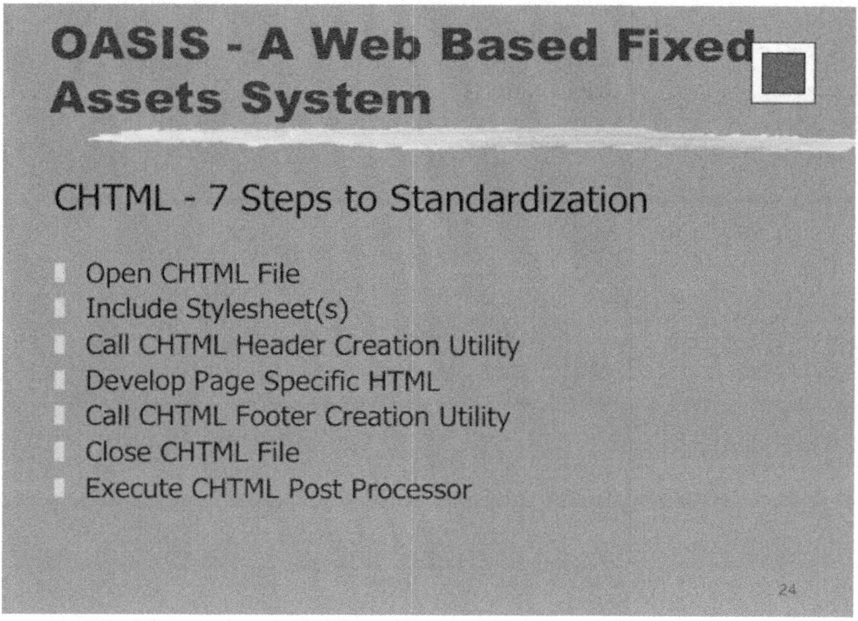

This and the next seven slides will cover CHTML - Conditional HTML

Again, implemented via modification to the Apache Server.

Remember - The goal is to provide mechanism for GENTLY enforcing a common look and feel across the institution's public space; and, if desired, across the application private space.

Uses HTML Style Sheets. Where the application is located determines the content of the header.

See pages 13-16 in the paper.

Slide 25

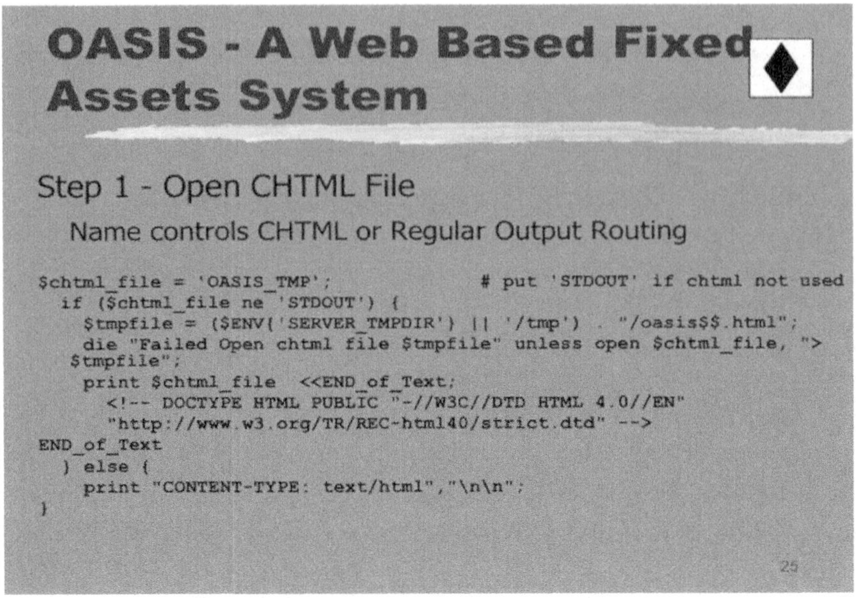

Note the name $chtml_file controls where output will be sent when the code is completed.

Either end up with the "normal" HTML content_type statement used by Perl.

(2012 Note – The POINTER notes were my way of reminding myself to point the laser pointer at a particular area of the wall/frame/screen etc. that the audience saw.)

POINTER TO "CONTENT-TYPE: text/html"
-OR-
CHTML DOCTYPE commands.
POINTER TO
"<!-- DOCTYPE HTML PUBLIC "-//W3C//DTD HTML 4.0//EN"
"http://www.w3.org/TR/REC-html40/strict.dtd" -->

Slide 26

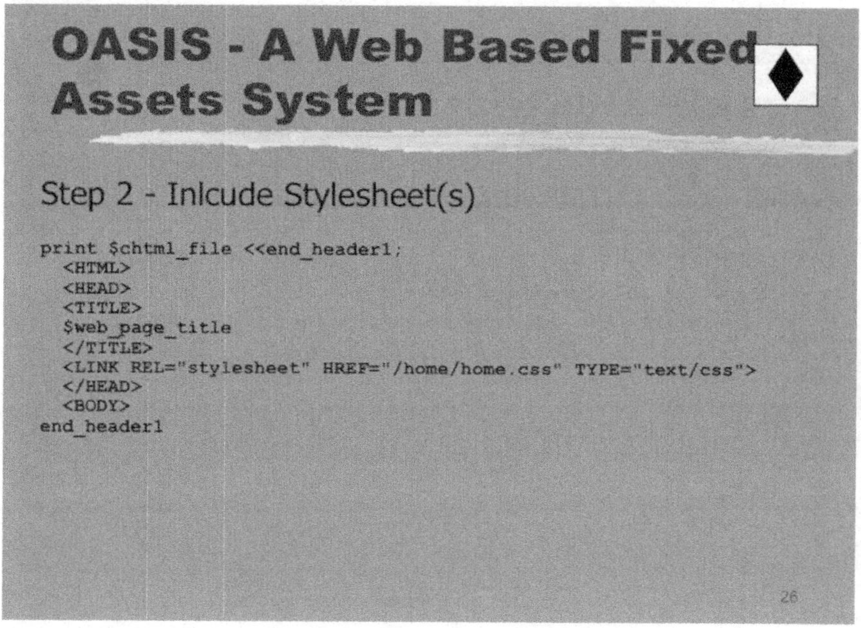

This is the normal "Print Here" Perl process. Sends a block of output to a file.

The LINK REL= brings in the style sheet. In this case it is the homepage style sheet.

Slide 27

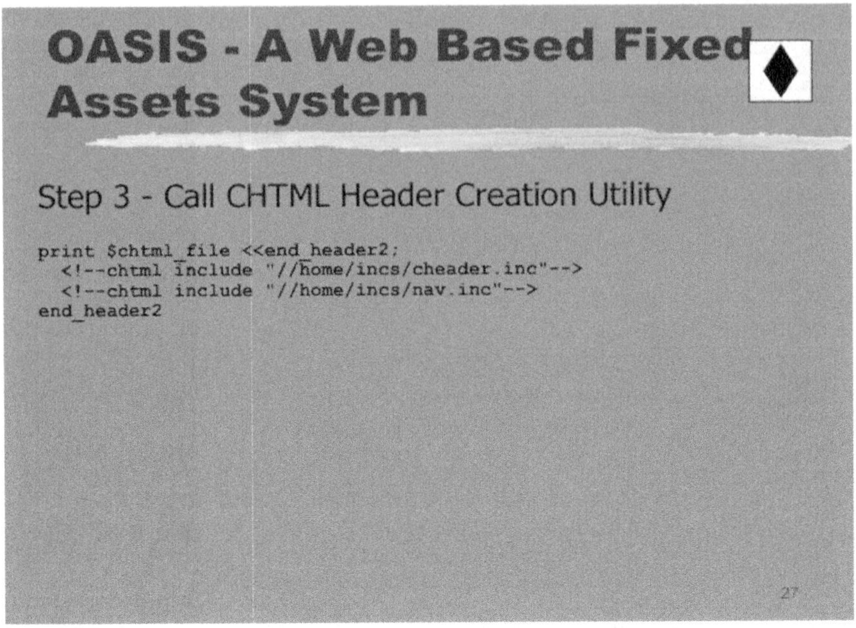

The comment special text <!--chtml is what trips the post processor to do something with the code in the otherwise ignored comment block.

Here we add the CHTML Header and bring in the standard Navigation Links (the purple bar and its format).

Slide 28

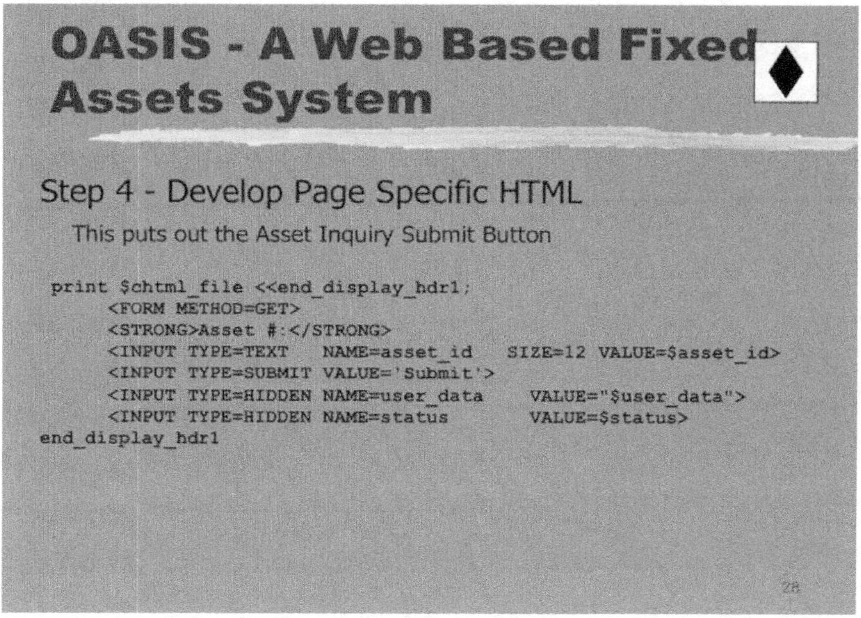

Standard Perl commands to construct a Submit button.

Slide 29

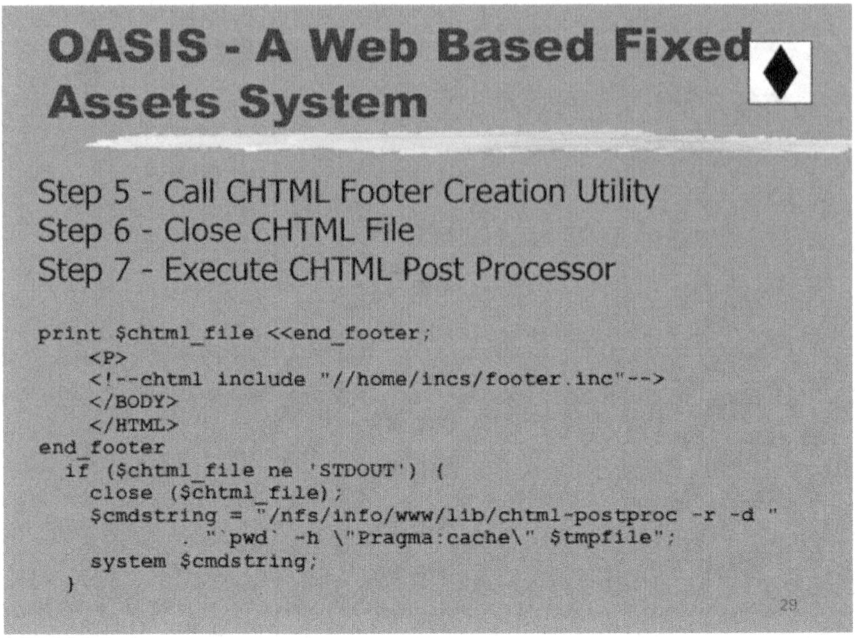

The final three steps are completed in quick succession.

Another HTML comment containing CHTML commands, here it is the standard footer include.

POINTER TO footer.inc

Brings in a file address.inc to fill in the address block, and that file contains a command to display the most recent date of any file within the directory path first accessed.

END OF CHTML!

POINTER TO conditional close statement
POINTER TO construction of cmdstring and system call

The close is conditional ... if "normal" HTML the file is not done. If CHTML then the file is closed, and the Post-Processor is called (giving it the name of the file as a parameter).

Slide 30

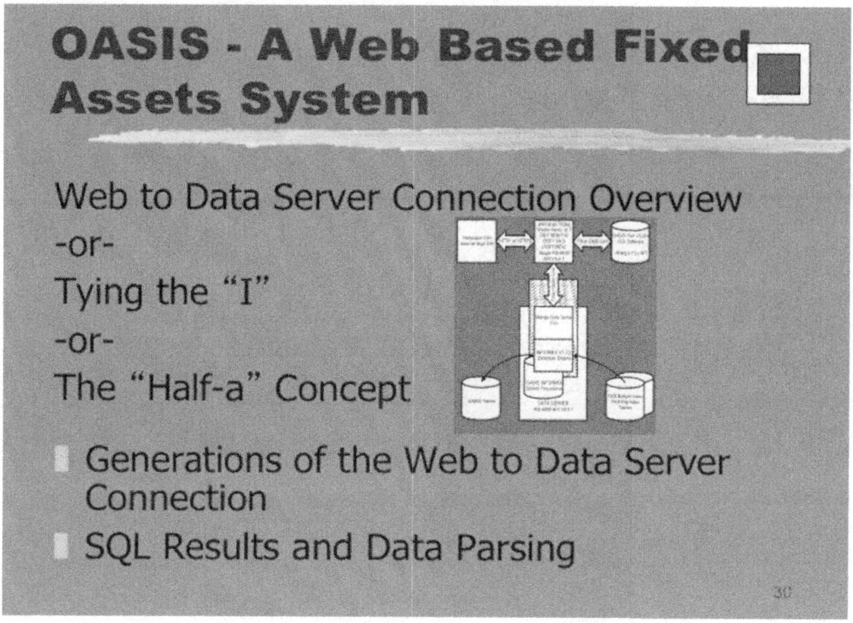

NEXT TOPIC - HOW TO TIE THE TOP AND BOTTOM OF THE "I" TOGETHER.

Remember this picture of the software architecture from earlier?

Lots of web software vendor work across the top
POINTER ACROSS TOP

Lots of database vendor software work across the bottom
POINTER ACROSS BOTTOM

Here is where the real work needs to be done. Our work shows that the majority of the time taken to meet a need is expended in here ... over 50% of the time.
POINTER ACROSS MIDDLE

Yes, I will still get to the Mango Server.

Slide 31

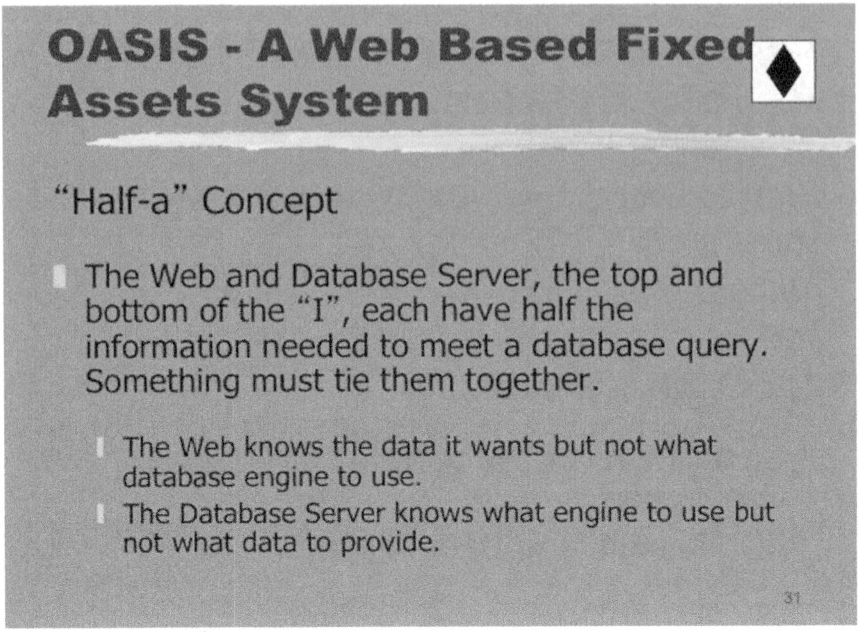

See the Slide

Slide 32

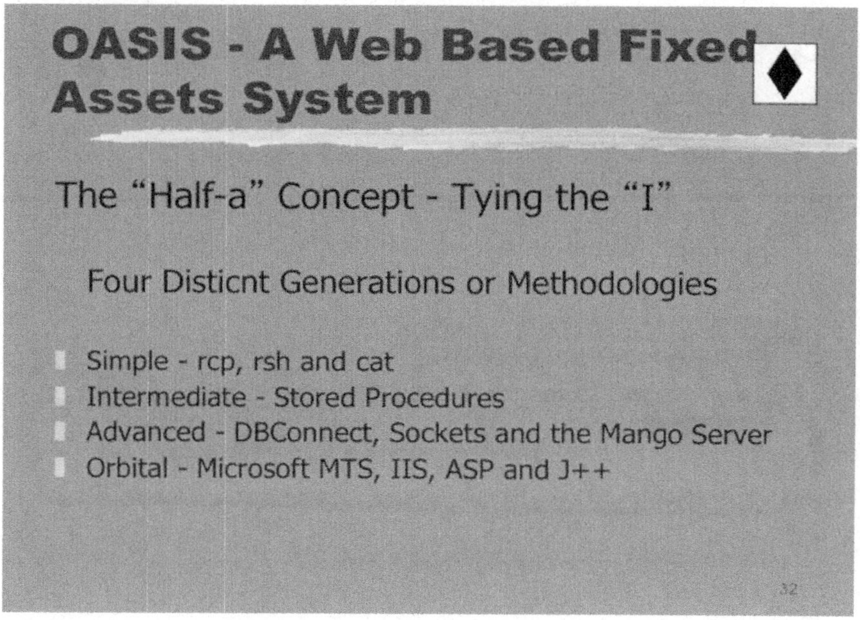

We'll go through these generations next.

OASIS today has moved from the Simple (Perl Conference paper, homepage, go to it) through the Intermediate (an "exciting" Beta session) to the Advanced.

Orbital may be just beyond our needs at this time.

Each step down, or up depending on how you look at it, makes you less database vendor and platform independent and incurs a software development and maintenance cost. This cost may be quite high, 80-120 hours for the jump from Simple to Advanced even after the Mango Server was written for us.

Slide 33

A good start, cheap and easy to build methodology. Slow but secure.

This is the method your local UNIX gurus will give you when you first tell them of your need. To them it is a no-brainer.

See the Perl Paper on my homepage, has cut and paste examples.

For out "baseline" asset, the RV Thompson (1 asset master, 100 expenditure notes, 100 general notes, 200 history notes) this required 16-24 seconds to complete.

BRING IN THE BOAT

See the paper, pages 17-19 for practical examples.

(2012 and 2020 Notes – This may be a cryptic note until you get the backstory. The US Navy provided the UW a large research vessel, the R.V. Thompson, in support of a grant to map the world's ocean bottom. Big work with big money coming to the UW. As part of this, the Office of Naval Research, ONR, was given responsibility to audit that the funds and equipment were being used appropriately. As part of the initial audit, the ONR auditor would randomly select 50 or so assets from our fixed assets database. If these could be found where the system said they were, if the UW Equipment Tag on the equipment matched the government and UW records, and if the condition, use, etc. matched what the source of funds demanded, then the auditor would assume the rest of them were, too. It was a cost-effective way to watch out for the public's money. The first audit after we installed OASIS resulted in an equipment "sled" being randomly selected. The sled was on board the R.V. Thompson somewhere out in the eastern part of the Indian Ocean. The auditor was going to pull another asset when the Asset Manager suggested we give send the ship an email and ask the crew to verify the tag. Not only did they agree, they set up the first video chat I'd seen and showed the ship's fantail, the sled with the USN tag and the UW Asset Tag clearly, albeit jumping about in the very early morning hours "way out there." The auditor was very impressed, and the UW received a very good note from the ONR.)

Very easy to migrate from one database engine to another. Only have to change the parsing code to look for a different field delimiter.

Slide 34

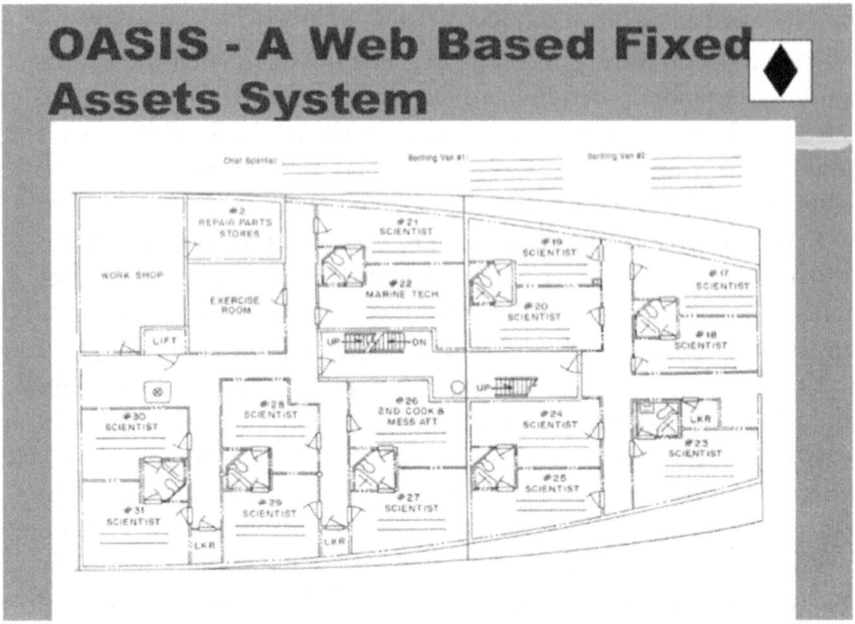

Required us to rewrite all the access logic so we stopped at this generation just long enough to test it.

The "baseline" asset, the RV Thompson (1 asset master, 1,000 expenditure notes, 100+ general notes, 2,000+ history notes) this required 14-18 seconds to complete.

BRING IN THE FLOOR PLAN

Implies that it takes 2-6 seconds for Informix to compile a moderately complex Select statement in ISQL mode and to pipe delimit the results. This time was consistent with testing in an INGRESS environment.

Further removes you from total vendor independence.

Slide 35

Where we are today.

The Mango Server was named after a bottle of Papaya-Mango juice being drunk at the time the prototype was completed.

For out "baseline" asset, the RV Thompson (1 asset master, 1,000 expenditure notes, 100+ general notes, 2,000+ history notes) this required 6-10 seconds to complete.

BRING IN THE BOAT

(2012 Note – this alluded to having the image appear to sail through the screen from lower left to upper right with a recording of a Washington State Ferry whistle en route. A pal at Microsoft loaned me a special pre-release version of a pending PowerPoint version to make this happen. It was a very effective display. For some years I was called "the boat guy" at Educause conferences.)

Slide 36

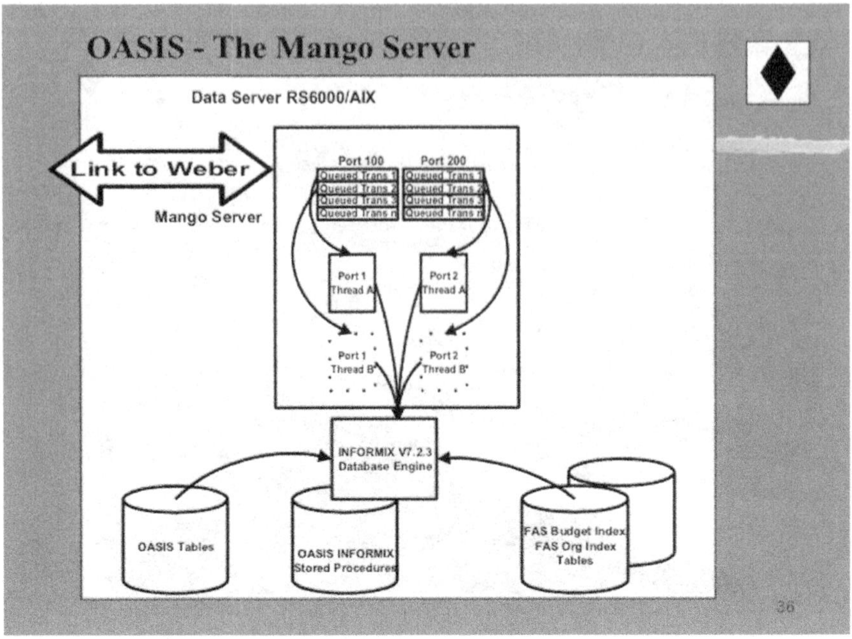

Promised I'd get here.

As of September 4, and subject to change hourly. An implementation of the INTERSOLV ODBC tool for INFORMIX databases. Constructed by U of W staff. For Object-Oriented folks this is an Active-Data-Object (ADO).

1. All transactions from Weber are through the Mango API and are directed to the Mango Server. The Mango API on Weber and the Mango Server on Vitcos keep this connection “hot”. Encryption will be available soon so this may be used with more sensitive applications. This is machine independent code ('C' program) that allows for rapid business resumption if need be.

2. Server code accepts the transactions at specified ports, queues them, and passes them to code that presents the commands to a database stored procedure. Each port supports multiple threads. Here we have a 2-by-2 Mango Server. Ports may be extended horizontally and Threads on a Port vertically. --- If two Ports are available, quick transactions and slow transactions may be sent to

different Ports. This allows the web app designer to tweak for performance on the fly.

3. The database engine accepts the commands, fills the parameters in the stored procedure, completes the query and returns data by way of a 'cat' command. --- Once opened, a connection stays open and uses one of the Informix licenses available to application software.

Benefits to the user of the Informix "the show must go on" philosophy.

Slide 37

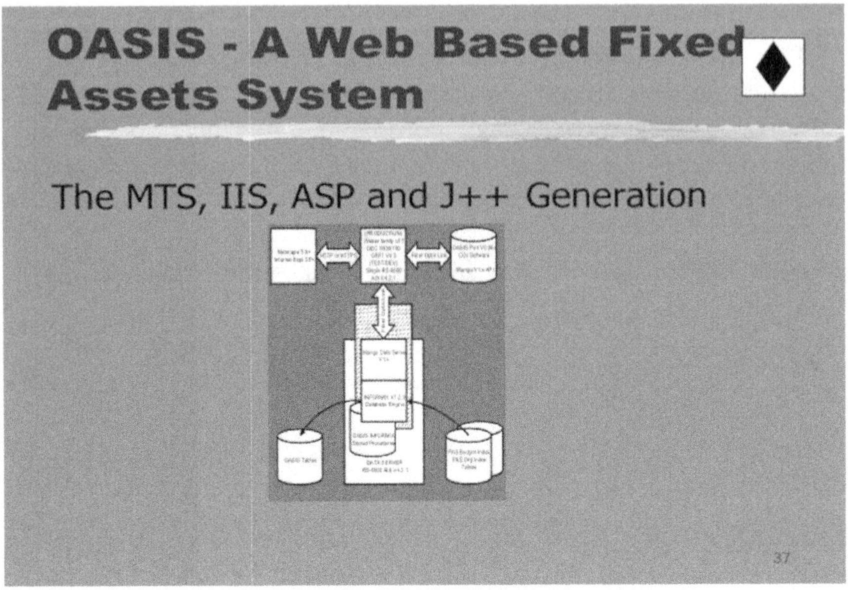

At this time the Transaction Server and IIS limit the application residence to an NT platform. ASP is reputed to improve performance; however, I have not seen an example of it improving performance in the middle of the "I". Visual Studio 6.0 begins to address this topic.

BRING IN GRAPHIC. (2012 Note – that is the picture centered here)

Much has been written about the benefit, in terms of security and business resumption, of the three-tier architecture and IIS appears best suited to a two-tier (where the web and data server reside on the same platform).

In a recent edition of the MSDN (Microsoft Developers Network) email (Mon Sept 7), in the Resources Section there is a note that the example company "Duwamish Books" system has now been constructed into a three tier architecture with Visual Studio 6.0; but my attempts to get to the page referenced showed it to be missing or moved somewhere and I couldn't find it. I assume this means MS is moving toward a three-tier IIS, a good move.

(2012 Note – This technology has changed greatly since 1998!)

If web server is compromised the data is secure. KEY POINT!

If the data server is down the web server can provide information to the user about that.

Remember, it appears the response time bottleneck is in the passing the commands to the data server and returning the response. Perl is slowest choice here … C is best.

J++ does hold promise in its speed at parsing the returned data. Loops are a strength. This may tip the scales in favor of the complete Microsoft solution. It certainly helps.

Slide 38

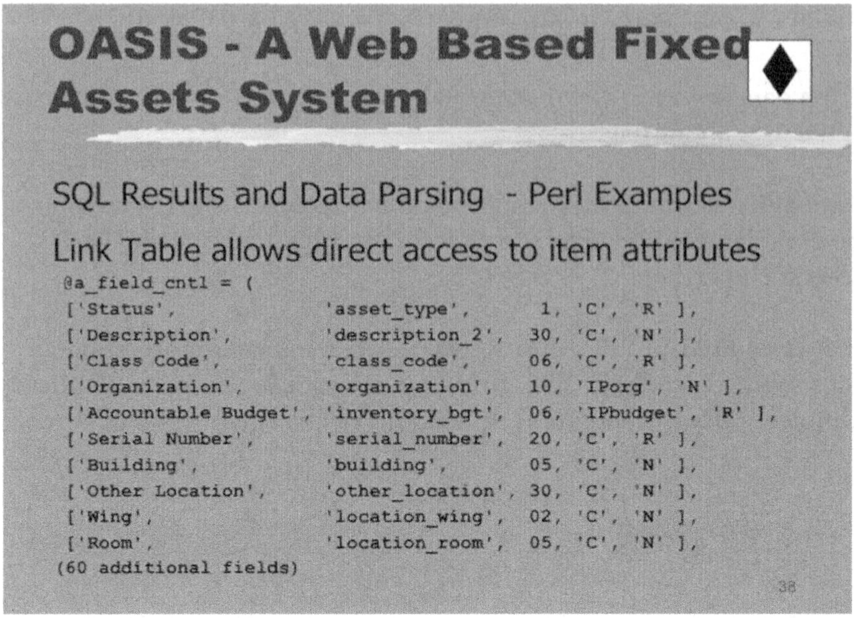

OK - New Topic

What do you do with the data you get?

How to control the display, set edit and required field flags in one easy step.

Link tables.

One of the strengths of Perl is string manipulation. This is part of a 60+ item table that is made a part of each asset management page by an "include" statement.

Slide 39

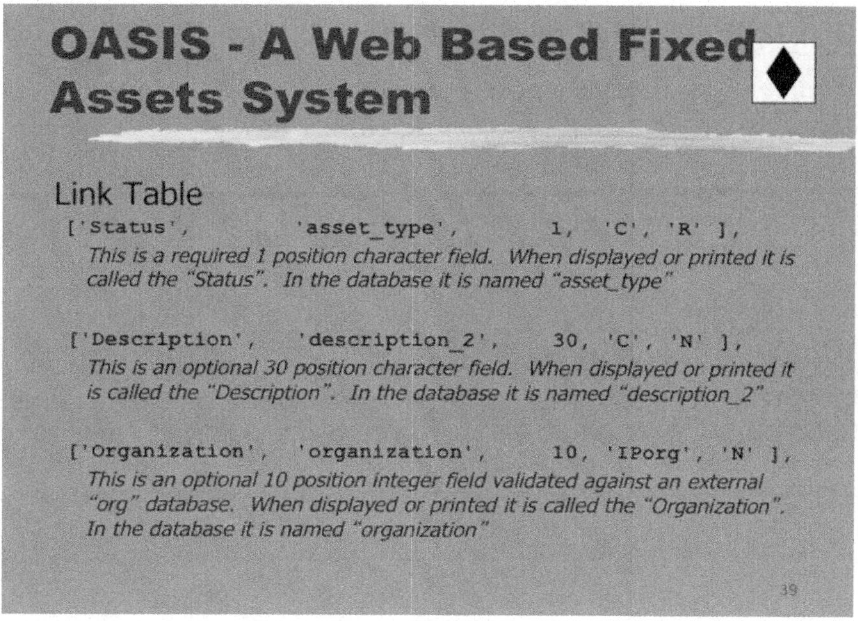

See the Slide. This is how the table describes three items

See Paper page 28 for a full selection statement including links to external databases.

Yesterday in a tech session a 40,000-line VP process was shown with about 500 data elements, this –OR– C-code could do the same with much less code and support issues.

Slide 40

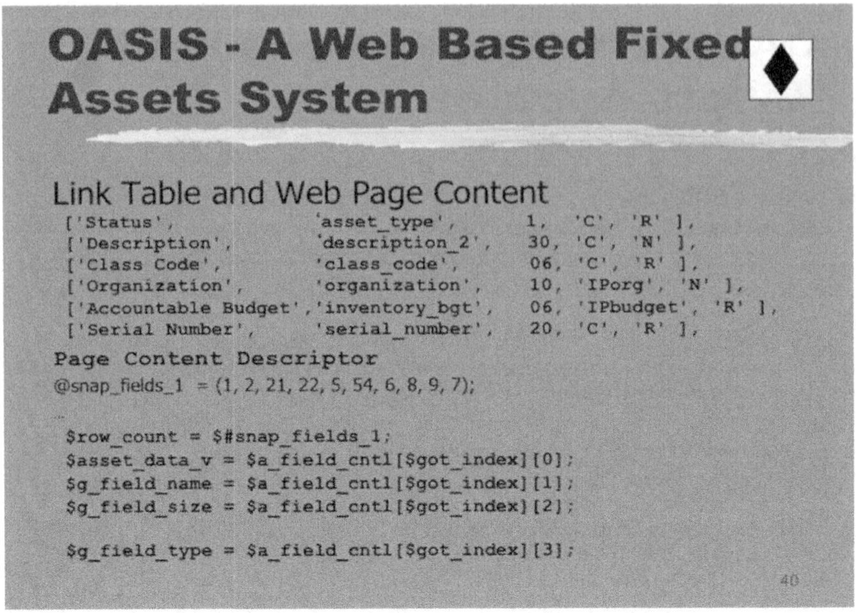

Here is an example of how the Link Table is used to generate a web page.

The "snapshot view" is a quick reference page of key pieces of asset information. It includes IN TWO COLUMNS because that's the way the user wanted to see it:

Description (1) Status (2),
Class code (21) Requisition(22)
Manufacturer(5) Budget(54)
and so forth.

POINTER BACK AND FORTH BETWEEN snap_fields_1, THE TABLE ENTRY FOR Status, AND THE BREAKOUT OF THE FIELDS, ESPECIALLY ON $got_index USE TO GET TITLES.

Next we'll see how this is rendered.

Slide 41

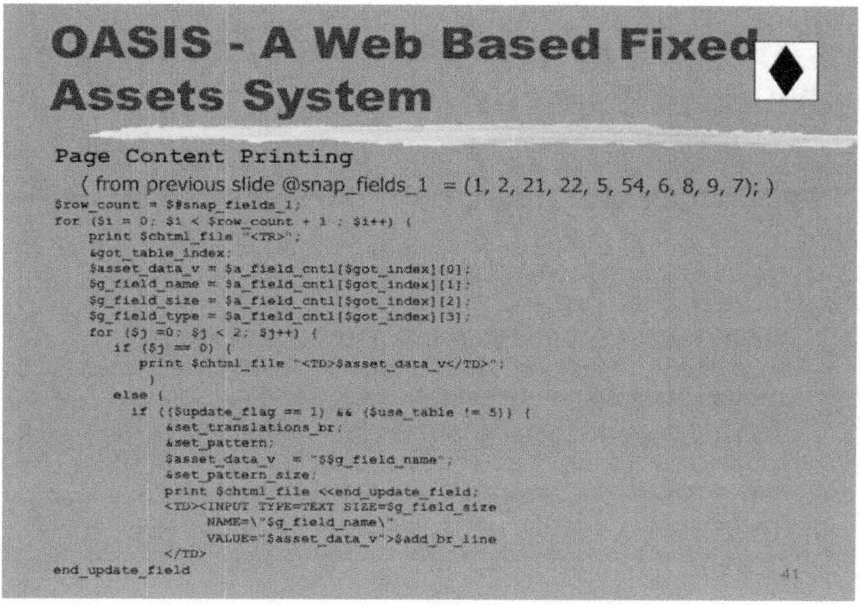

The print (and notice the CHTML file name here) is for a table item description (name from the table) and the data itself.

POINTER TO for AREA

The number of entries in the snap_field_1 controls the number of loops here ... add an item there and it automatically changes the iterations here.

POINTER TO $g_field_xxxx AREA

Here we split, in order of appearance in snap_field_1 the items.

POINTER TO LOWER for LOOP

Here we had a 1-2 table that loads the description and the data.

POINTER TO &set_pattern

These two subroutines set the patterns (character, date, dollar etc.) from the main Link Table.

Slide 42

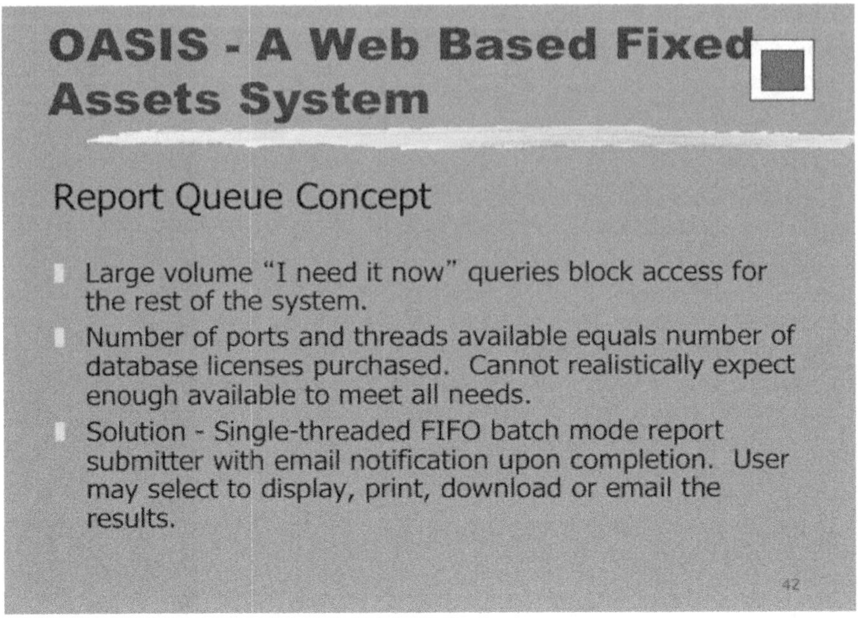

New Topic - Another Breather

These are some of the things we discovered during development.

Give user the data and let them do whatever they want/need … get out of the business of writing one-shot reports for them. It is not that difficult and empowers them.

Slide 43

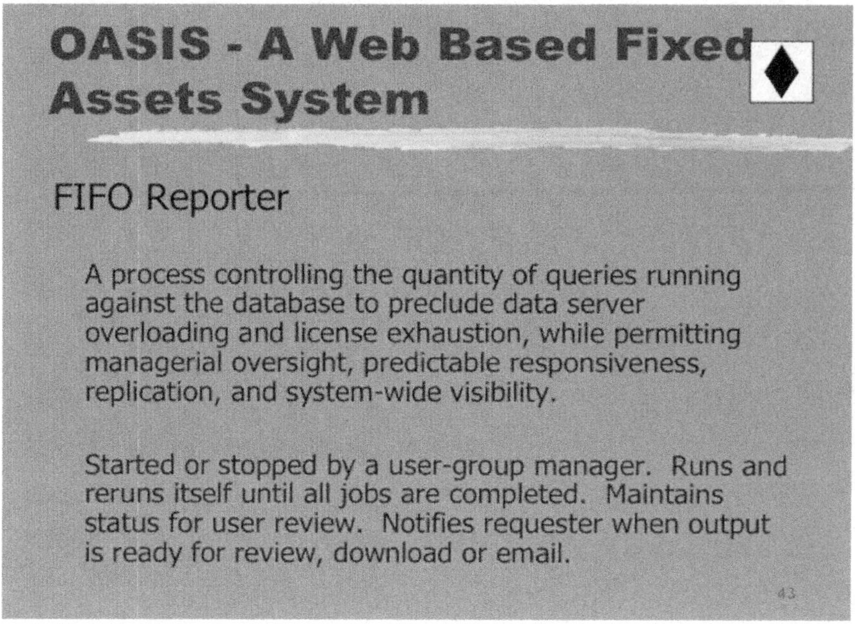

This is our solution. A First-In-First-Out reporter.

(2012 Note – Edith Shen suggested that we leverage some of the capabilities of Informix and get an estimate of the number of rows a query could be expected to return – then use that information to send "quick" queries through one FIFO queue and "slow" ones through another. This was a great idea and it became a key part of gaining user acceptance.)

Slide 44

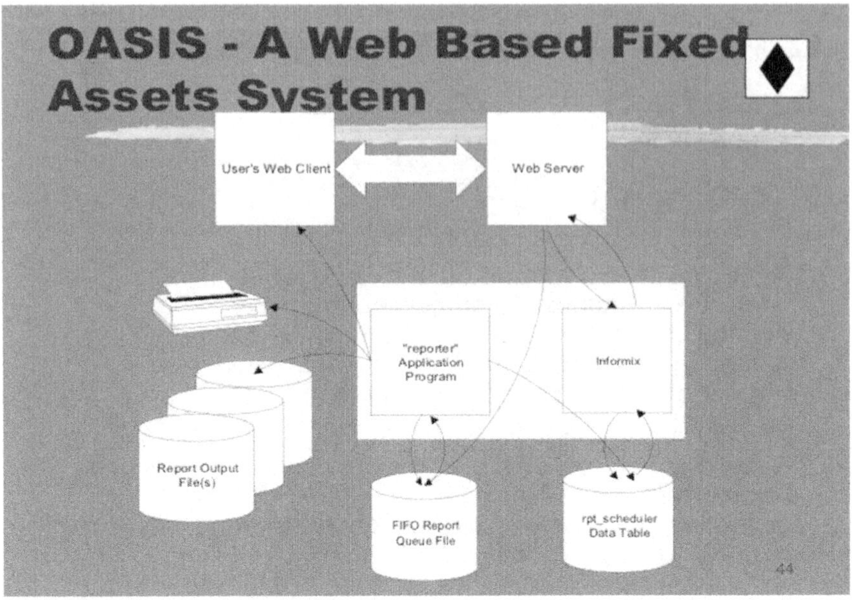

Complex Process

1. User makes a request that will force a report or inquiry identified to go into the queued process.
2. Web Server passes the request to the database engine
3. Database engine, using a stored procedure, inserts it into the rpt_schedule Data Table and passes the successful insert back to the Web Server
4. Web Server then adds (open extend) the query to the FIFO Report Queue File
5. At a quiet point, the "reporter" process (a self croning job) reads the file to see if any new entries have been added
6. Finding one it reads the SQL, issues the query and waits for it to complete
7. When the query completes the reporter sends the output where told by the user (hold on disk, print or email); then Updates the status in the rpt_scheduler and Queue File
8. When a status request is made by the user, through the web, it is passed through the Web Server to Informix
9. And Informix passes the status back to the Web Server ... the status comes from the database not from the Queue File

Slide 45

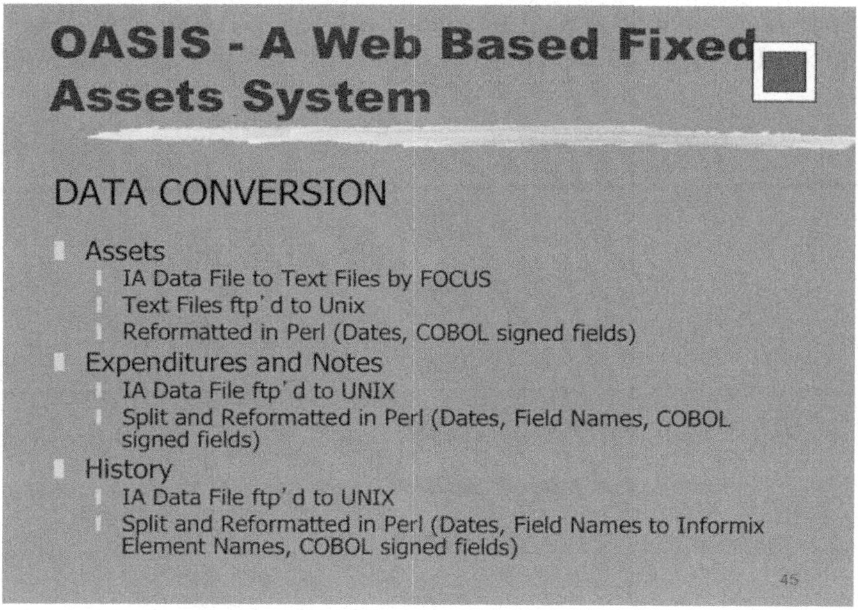

NEXT TOPIC - This applies to those folks with the Information Associates package.

Perl Code easily meets challenges here.

Assets - User identification and extraction process is cumbersome. Package allows duplicate Asset Id's if the status is different so the file has to be sorted. Unix sort not up to the volume so VMS sort used (fast and reliable). Date formats MMDDYY, YYMMDD, DDMMYY with an occasional CC thrown in.

Counts

- 127,700 asset masters
- 164,000 expenditure records
- 69,000 notes

Expenditures and Notes - The local modifications at installation time built a special type of the package Note to contain signed COBOL dollar amounts. Had to split Note-Notes from Expenditure-Notes.

History - COBOL Dollar amounts (same as Assets, Expenditures and Notes). Field ID conversion to data base name (e.g., TA205 to "Building"). NUMBER OF RECORDS (970,000 TOTAL RECORDS ACROSS ALL TYPES) WAS SURPRISING.

Slide 46

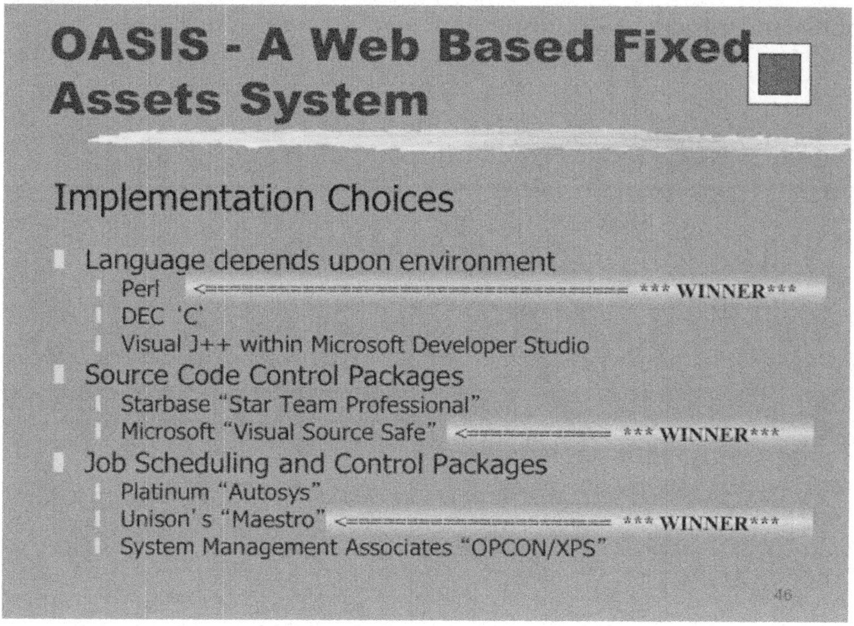

Language

Perl chosen due to skill availability, transportability (we did not know the project's host until well into design), cost (somewhere near $0 for us). The version of 'C' used differs (based on another project - FASTRANS) so badly that transportability concerns precluded its use. J++ was not, is not, stable enough and I am concerned about the ability of IIS and MS-SQL to handle the volume of records.

Source Code Control

Visual Source Safe chosen because it allows linking of NTFS, Win95 and Unix (under Samba) files. The competition was tough between these two. Star Team was, in the opinion of the evaluation team, too difficult to install and administer.

Job Scheduling

Tough competition here, too. SMA's OPCON/XPS was my personal favorite since we have a substantial and long-term investment in Unisys mainframes and that product can use the result of a Unix job to cause an event on a Unisys platform, and use that result to cause events on Unix platforms. Maestro proved more robust and easier to administer.

Slide 47

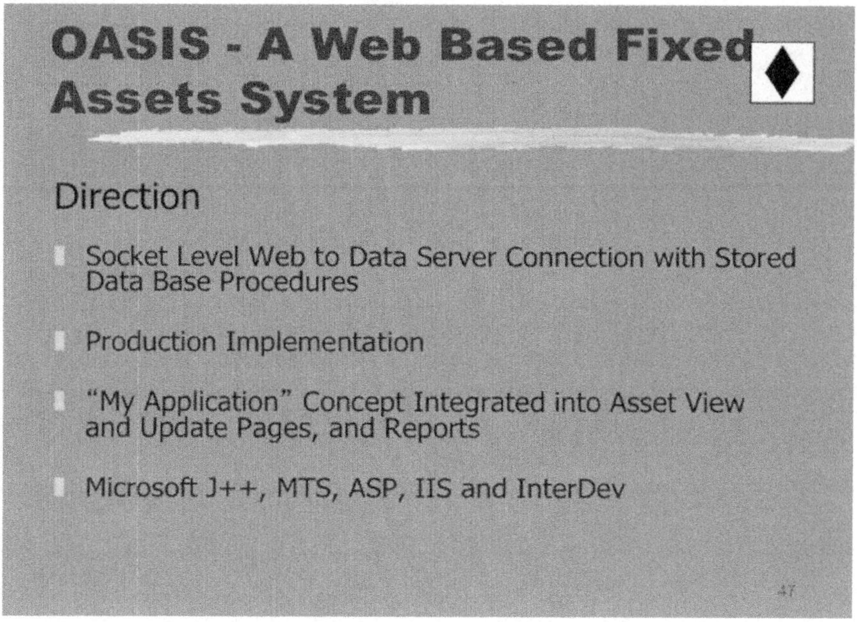

The Beta version continues to be wrung out by the user group. Three user "drag races" of 16,000 asset inquiries caused some problems we are addressing.

In the paper, Pages 19 - 25, there is a copy of the Web Mango API. This ALPHA version is for a single port with two threads. View it as a sample of how an API may be written. Later versions and a copy of the Mango Server HOPEFULLY will be available at the CAUSE98 meeting in Seattle this coming December.

(2012 Note – Those page numbers are wrong for this publication!)

Production implementation delayed by lack of training facilities. At the largest University West of St. Paul and North of San Francisco!

"My Application" extensions to the Link Table will allow users to construct their own type of input and update pages. It is unknown how many actually will do it.

Microsoft J+, MTS, ASP, IIS and InterDev. We're keeping up on this technology. The InterDev - Visual Studio product line is proving, to me, that it is well worth the investment. J++ exhibits faster looping than Perl, ASP's reputation is growing, IIS is an unknown to me at this time.

Slide 48

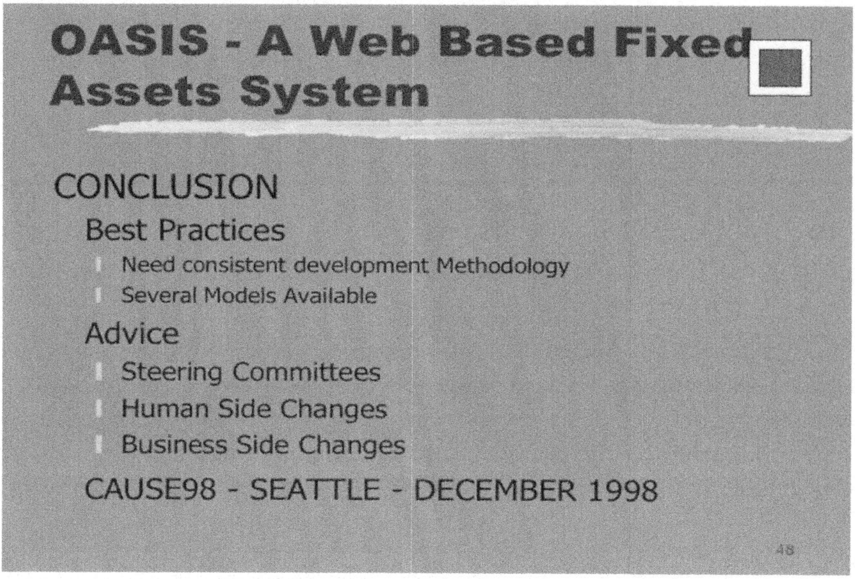

BEST PRACTICES

These are my opinions.

As this project emerged from initial thoughts to Beta implementation, I recognized the need to have some consistent way of documenting the system as it was being developed.

Working from ideas from Christine Comafort's Best Practices, I developed a series of 15 documents that apply to web development projects in a multi-platform, multi-OS environment. A listing of these forms and a short description of their function is included in the paper, Pages 37- 39.

Christine's original work may still be found at her site, www.christine.com. I will add blank versions of my work to my homepage.

ADVICE - Steering Committees

Those groups we call "steering committees", in my experience, sooner rather than later and always quickly, want to micro-manage software development.

If they won't look at the big picture or if takes six weeks it takes to get on their calendars remind them a prototype can be developed, deployed and two rounds of user feedback put into place "before we meet again".

The traditional steering committee may have earned a vacation, and, if it will not go quietly, then send it packing.

ADVICE - Human Side Changes

The process of web development is ongoing and will be chaotic to users. The technical side of a project is disposable...difficult for some managers and staff (accounting) to understand. Deliverable form and format set by end user not IS or management of end using dept ... also difficult for some.

Who are the "IMPORTANT PEOPLE" shifts when the view of data changes from 24x80 to UNLIMITED? The need expands to fill the known universe.

ADVICE - Business Side Changes

Remember there are VAST differences in data management and data entry applications ... the end use drives project design not the hardware, software or staff available. In data management breadth of scope is more important than response time. Remember the boat, 300x200 FIELD display.

Perl versus COBOL 1 to 8 hours.

The best technical programmers in the field today come from schools with names that end in "Tech". These crank out technically well qualified programmers who lack the breadth of application knowledge and people skills to work in the user community. If the user community won't use it, then it is a waste of time and money to build it.

CAUSE98 - SEATTLE - DECEMBER

A follow-up to this session, with a live demonstration, copy of the Mango Server and API, and the Best Practices Model. When you get there expect darkness falling at 4, first light at 8, and I can darn near guarantee it will be cloudy and rainy, 38-48.

Thee will, however, be coffee available on every corner

Section 3 – (1998 CAUSE) OASIS, A Web Based Fixed Assets System

The presentation at 1998 WebDevShare led to a presentation at another national conference, the 1998 CAUSE conference. This would be the final such conference because the group merged with EduComm and the two formed Educause in 1999.

The presentation focused more on systems development, management and operations costs than on technical issues. My slot was shifted to the last day because of a conflict with a keynote, and there were few attendees, maybe 25, who chose this session over the Gartner Group review of salaries and direction in higher education. There are no sour grapes here, it is tough talking against the big-guns of the industry.

To keep down the volume of pages containing only transitional slides, most of the slides with the seven topics (which were displayed with check-offs between the topics) have been deleted.

Here are the slides with the notes used then and my additions resulting from questions and comments.

Enjoy.

Slide 1

(2012 Note - that web site and email address were dropped after I left the UW in 2005)

Thanks _____KEN_______ and thank all of you for coming.

I plan to be done in time for some questions. When I get to the Best Practices part of the presentation, start getting your questions together.

What I intend to do is give you an overview of the development cycle of web applications based upon our most recent experience. Most of what I'll present today are practical examples that apply to many projects, and especially to web projects.

We installed a Fixed Assets system that runs over the web with CGI controlled dynamic HTML and an INFORMIX database on a thinnest client three-tier architecture.

I presented a very technical paper with a parallel presentation about the system code and processes at the Web Dev Share Conference held at Indiana University last October. The paper and the

PowerPoint may be found on my homepage. In addition, there is a paper and presentation from the first Perl Conference, held in Santa Clara during August 1997. That paper goes into the basics of programming secure web SQL database applications within the framework of a three-tier architecture.

Slide 2

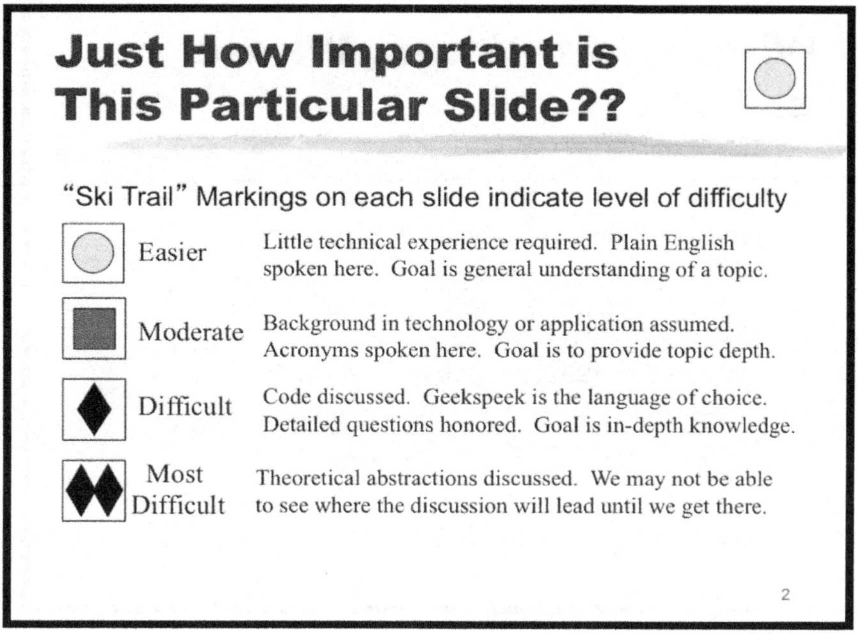

At this time of year, especially this far north (further north than the most northerly tip of Maine), many of us think about skiing.

I've marked the slides with the international ski trail level of difficulty signs so everyone knows when they should pay attention and when they can talk with their neighbors.

Most of the slides are rated Moderate and Difficult.

Slide 3

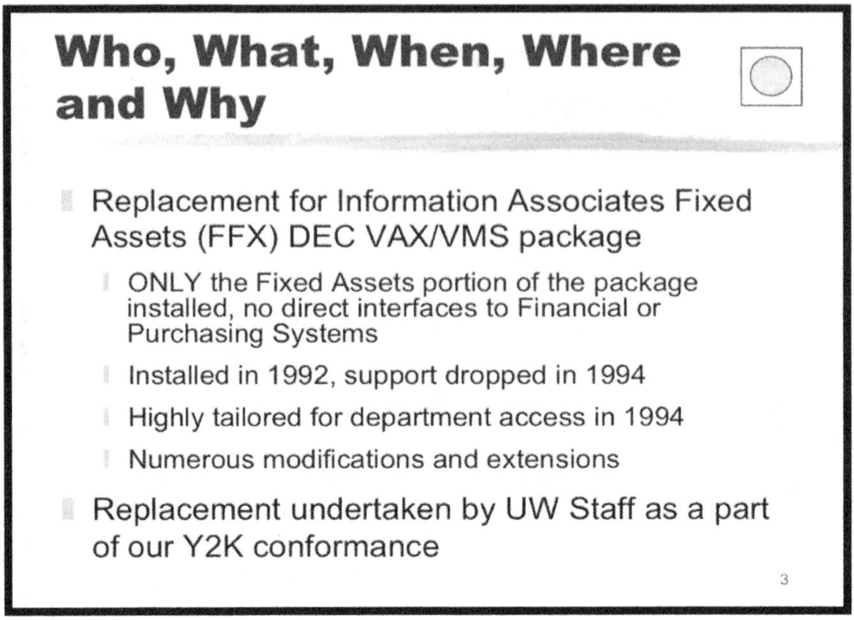

Why did we do this.

We only purchased the Fixed Assets portion of the whole IA Package. OASIS is a stand-alone system, not directly linked to the financial or purchasing software. This is both an advantage and disadvantage. It is a "tail of the dog" type of application, but it is a do-able, easy to isolate process with a small core of highly trained users.

Y2K project because the package, as purchased and installed at the U of W, is not compliant in Depreciation or reporting.

With all the talk about Business Practice Re-engineering during the conference I feel I must say that this was NOT a BPR driven project. In fact, we are replicating many of the bizarre business practices built into the great-grandfather of this system. A card-based system dating to the early 1970's.

On the technical side, however, it does conform to Steps 3, 4 and 5 of the Systems and Process Re-Engineering Model outlined yesterday by Ms. Bruno, Ms. Vrana, and Ms. Welz during their session yesterday.

Slide 4

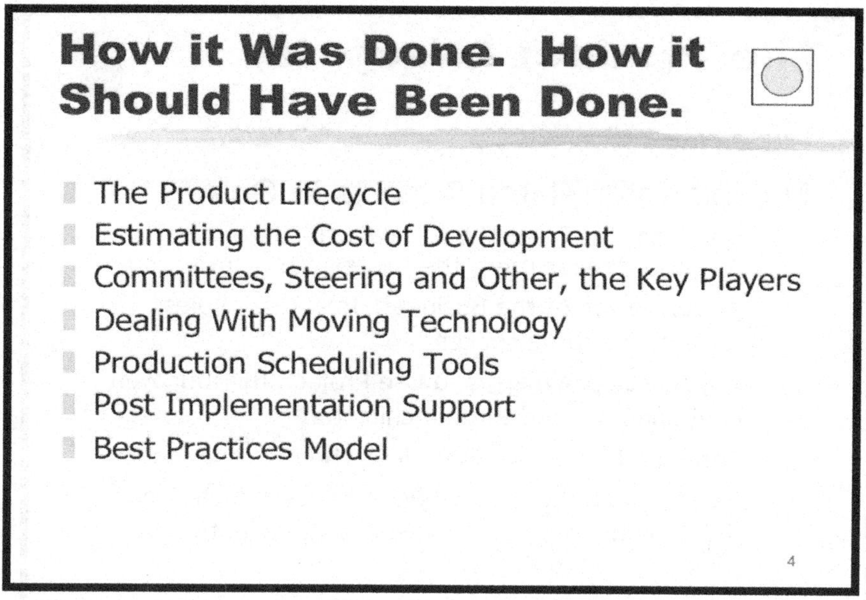

(2012 Note – This was the transitional slide used to show progress and topics that would be covered. It appeared many times but I've only put it here one time.)

Slide 5

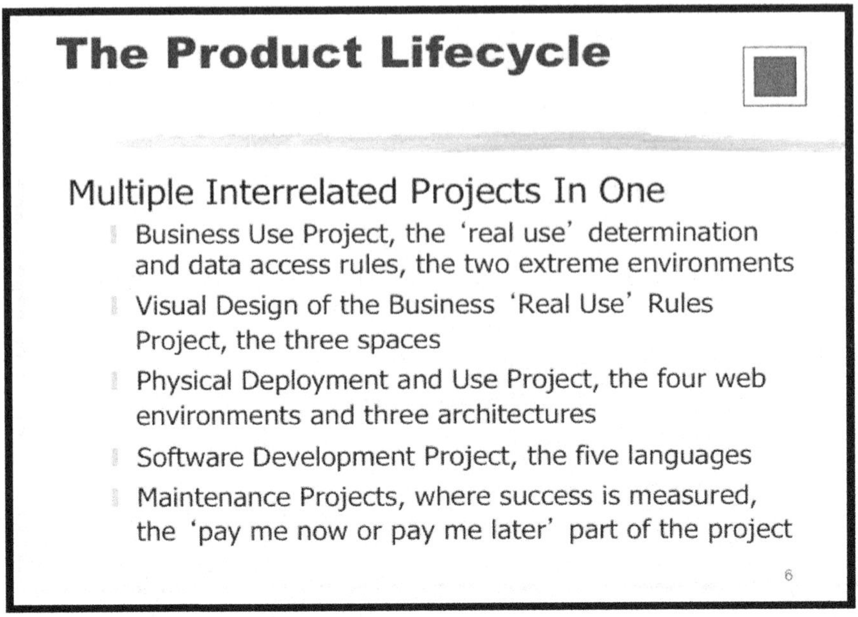

Although all Application Development projects will have these five characteristics, web development projects are more affected due to the shortness of the development cycle. I estimate that web development and deployment takes 1/8 to 1/2 the time of COBOL application, and, more importantly, with a corresponding decrease in maintenance costs.

We'll cover these items one-by-one.

Slide 6

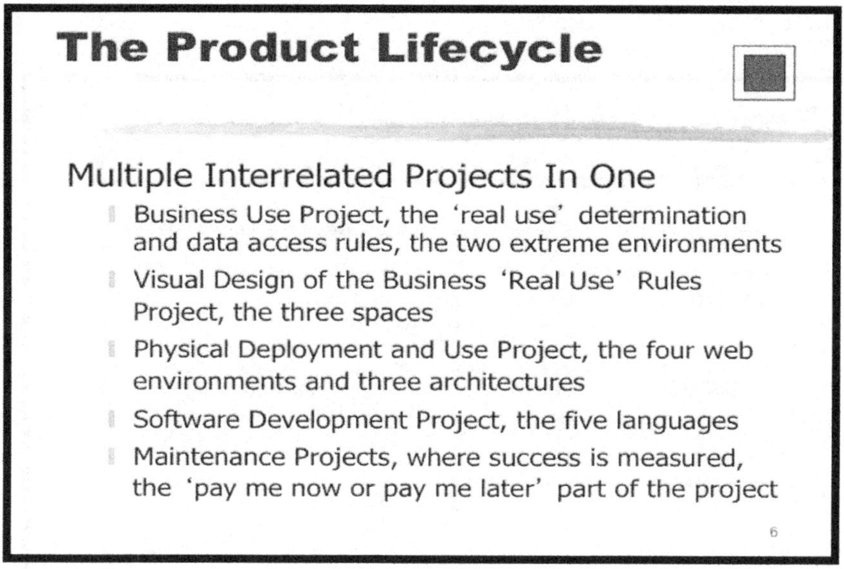

First ... What is the real user community?

Most of the development I've done in the last 25 years has reflected the needs and desires of one key user or a set of users who work in one office. In the 24x80 world, with the associated high cost of development, that was understandable, but with the ease of leveraging the power of the web to include additional functionality, this is no longer a factor.

I strongly suggest that, from now on, avoiding the single point of contact development scheme of the past.

Slide 8
(2020 Note - There were two of these in the original presentation, so there is no Slide 7 here.)

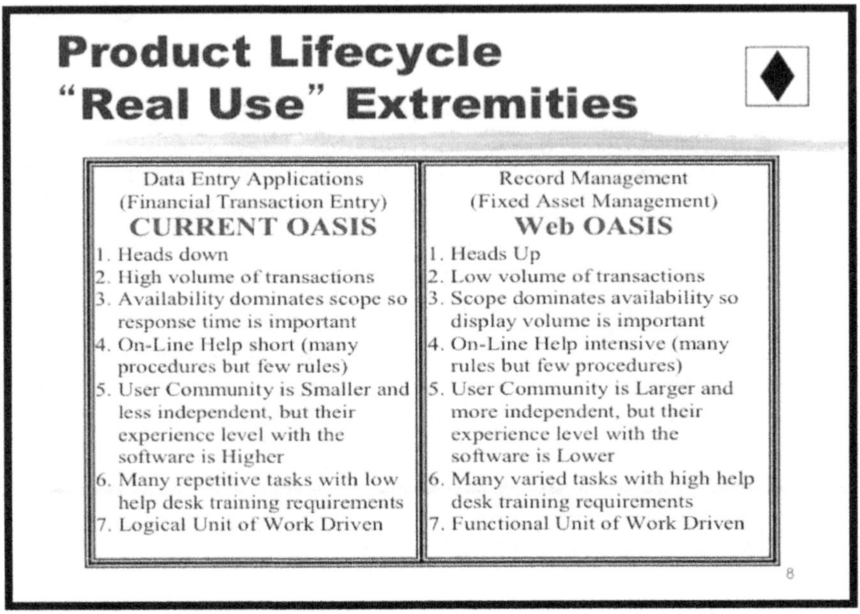

Second ...What does the real system really use?

This table shows the two distinctly different uses of current IA package (left) and the new web application (fight). The IA package was a part of a larger financial management system, the real use (fixed assets records management) is very different than the designed use (financial transaction entry).
1 - Heads Down/Up - Less thinking is required during a data entry operation than during records management activities.

2 - "Transaction Volume" High/Low - Major design issue.

3 - "Scope of a Unit of Work" High/Low - Currently, 3 to 8 screens must be used to do what can be done on 1 web page.

4 - "Help" For Financial Transaction Entry, the user instructions are pretty much "Key what you see" and since the purchased package is really just a part of a larger financial accounting package, the current OASIS inherited that philosophy. The new web application is very different.

5 - "User Community" Small-Dependent-Experiences / Large-Independent-System Naive. Very different views of the target audience.

6 - "Tasks" Repetitive /Varied - Record Entry / Record Management - The "Real Use" is Record Management.

7 -"Unit of Work" For Web OASIS, the instructions are much more complex than for payroll time entry. For example, just listing the data elements and their edits that are necessary to build an approved asset will take up several pages of help text.

Slide 9

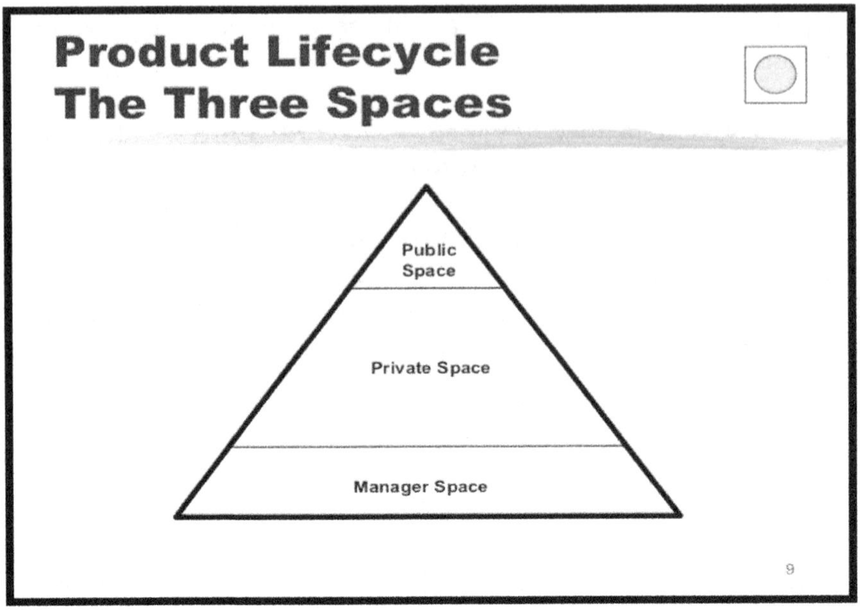

The Concept of Space - A general introduction to Institution and Enterprise wide web applications.

As we developed the package it became evident that every application you deploy should have a consistent look and feel that exudes the very character and essence of the institution's goals and its opinion of itself. The more the general public uses the page the more important is the consistent look-and-feel. You want the public to KNOW this is your page without having to read it carefully. Just looking at it should let them know just whose page it is.

However, constructing an application so every employee sees the institution's mascot the same way, page after page after page, is counterproductive and frustrating. And for gosh sake, avoid those dancing mailboxes!

When we started, the material making up the consistent look and feel used up the top and bottom 20% of every page. This is some highly visible and expensive real estate. After folks looked at it day after day, week after week, it was scaled to something more realistic. Today we use 10% of top and bottom in Public Space, and 10% of the bottom in Private and Manager Space.

Slide 10

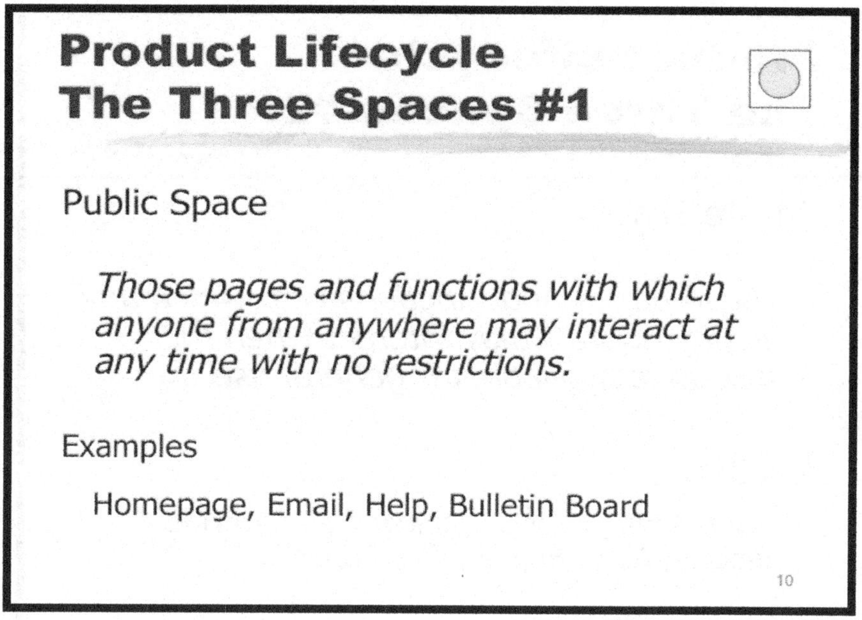

Public space, the top of the pyramid, is how you want the world to see your institution and application.

Remember, anyone, from anywhere, at any time, must be able get to your public pages.

Slide 11

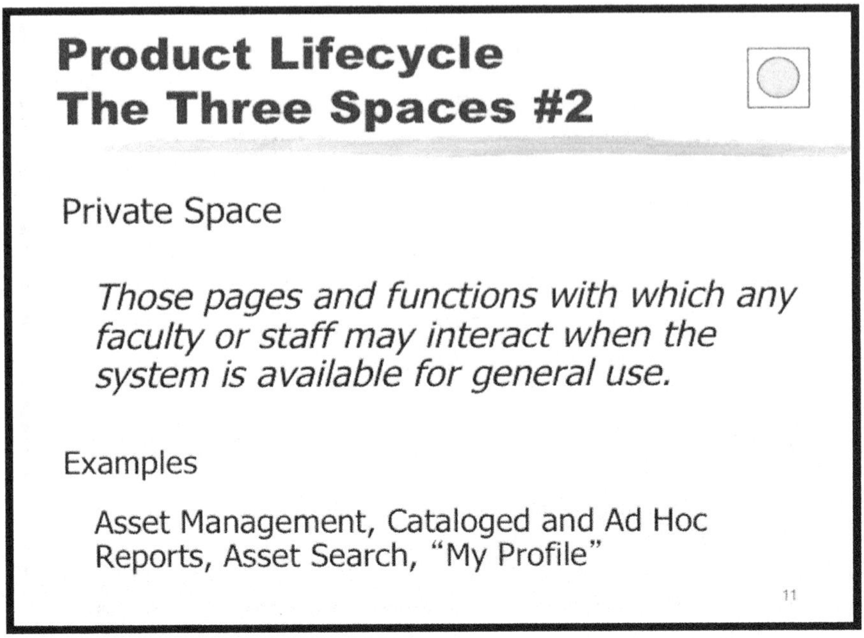

Private space, the body of the pyramid. This where the user community lives and breathes. Most will bookmark these pages, past your public space menu, so be ready for that. Users will not follow fixed access paths, which are difficult to enforce on the web anyway. This is a major difference between web and traditional 80x24 applications.

Slide 12

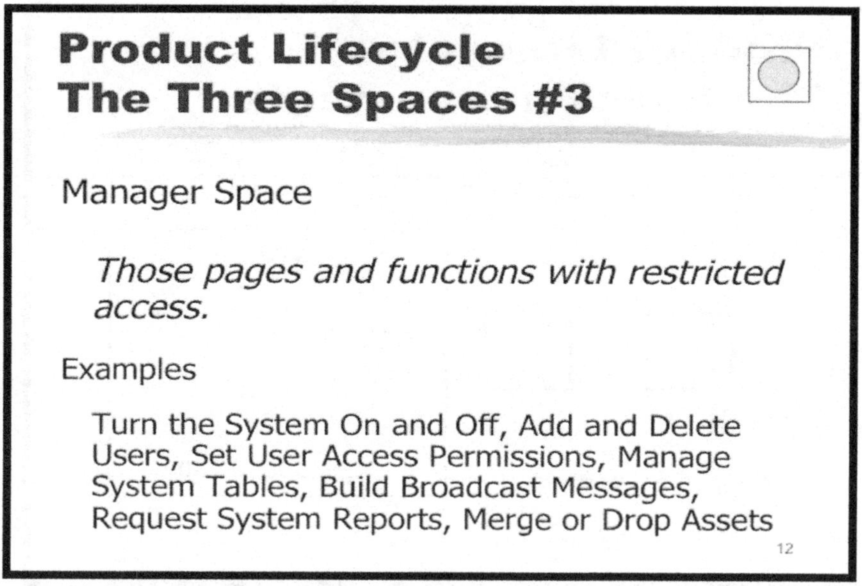

Manager space, the foundation, is where management controls what it wants the members of the user community to be able to see and do.

Simply put, there are places you do not want the average user to venture. This is that space.

Access is restricted in a manner that allows system managers to change, in real-time, the permissions and access authority of a user. They may turn system access on or off, to start and stop the report writers, and to post broadcast messages.

Slide 13

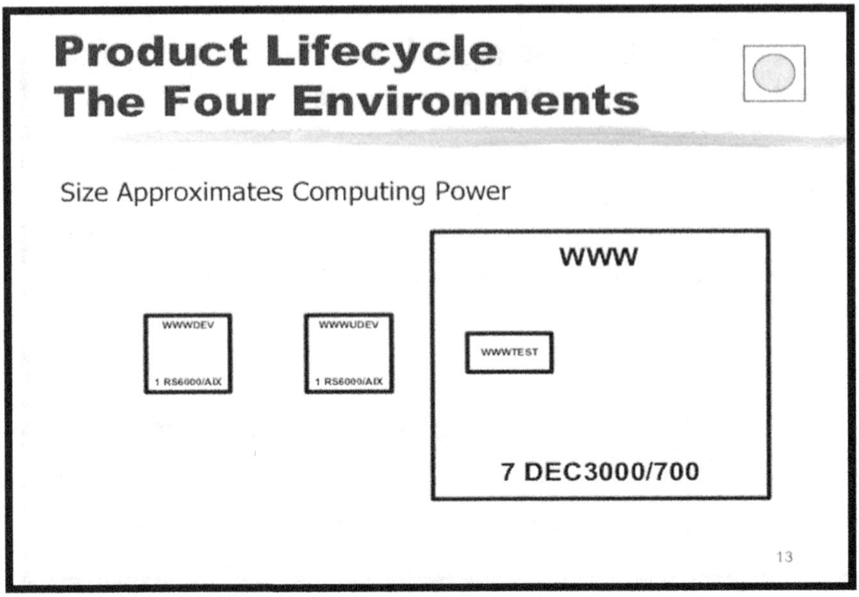

We've found a very useful Four Environment set-up.

1 - Initial development in a protected area, IS ONLY, the WWWDEV environment.

2 - To give selected enterprise users a view, we push into a controlled access area, WWWUDEV environment.

3 - When it is necessary to see the effect of the real-world web environment on the package, we push into a production look-alike, but controlled access area, IS ONLY, the WWWTEST environment.

Note that these three environments run on our INTRANET ONLY.

4 - FINALLY, when the package is ready for prime time, push it into production with world access, the INTERNET

Slide 14

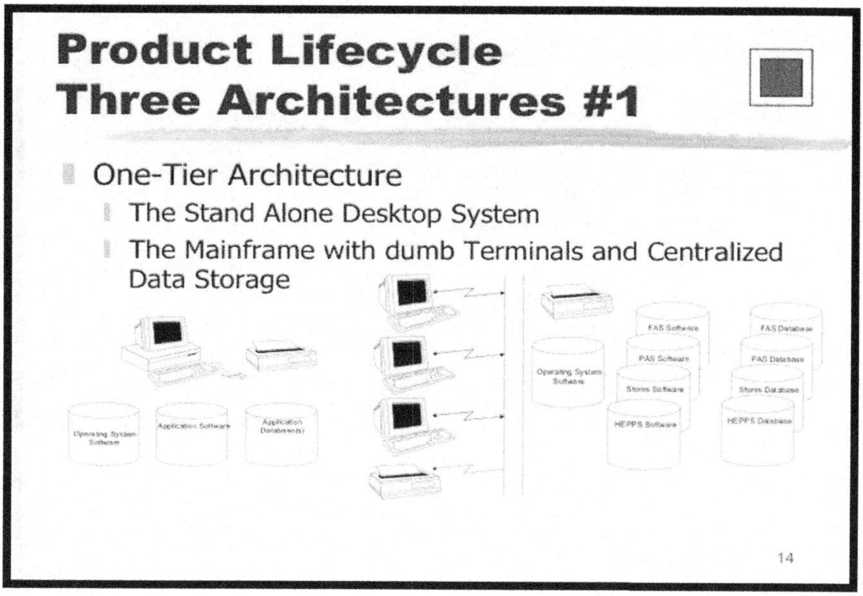

This may be old news to a lot of you, but it serves as a jumping off point to other discussions.

One-Tier
1 - Stand-alone desktop systems
2 - Mainframes with dumb terminals and central data repositories

Essentially the stand-alone system. If any part goes down, you're stuck on sitting on the chair lift, so to speak, and in keeping with the ski area slide markings.

Slide 15

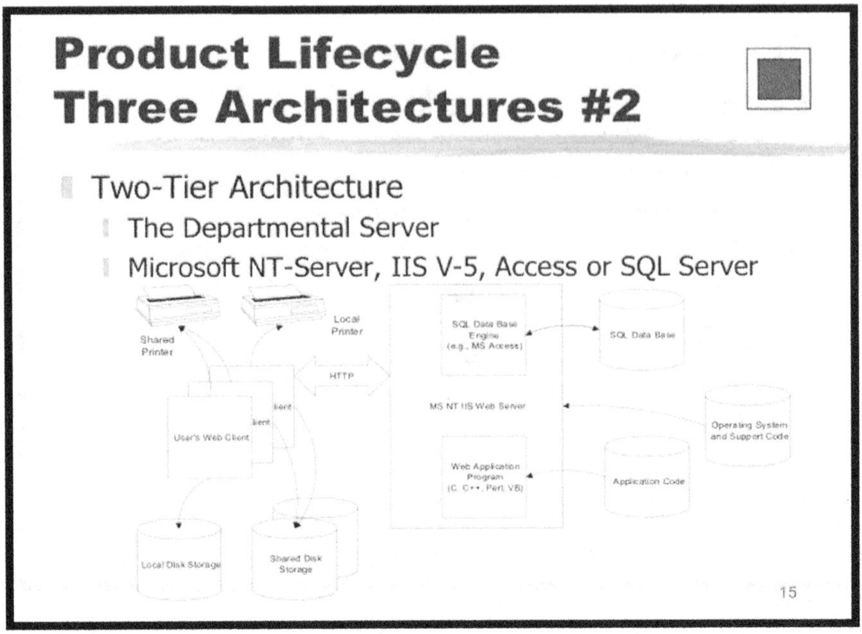

Two-Tier - The Departmental Server

The notation about MS IIS Version 5 is because they are trying to put up a three-tier on their web demo site, the Duwamish Book Club, but the last time I checked they seem to be having problems (up Sept 6, down and gone Sept 9). I have not personally had the time to check it out, but I am reliably told it works well with pooled user-ids ("nobody") but the overhead of using specific user-ids seems to be a problem. Using the specific id's incurs tons of overhead in opening, authenticating and dropping user-ids.

Generally restricted in the number of records, complexity of data structures (especially when grouping with MS ACCESS rather than SQL SERVER), number of users. Most of these I've seen tend to be for smaller and less powerful hardware. I cannot recommend Access for anything beyond the most basic prototyping or One-Tier applications. It just is not intended for that level of use, especially when constructing views and issuing "group by" commands.

The biggest problem with the Two-Tier architecture is that WEHN, not IF, your web server is compromised so is your data.

Slide 16

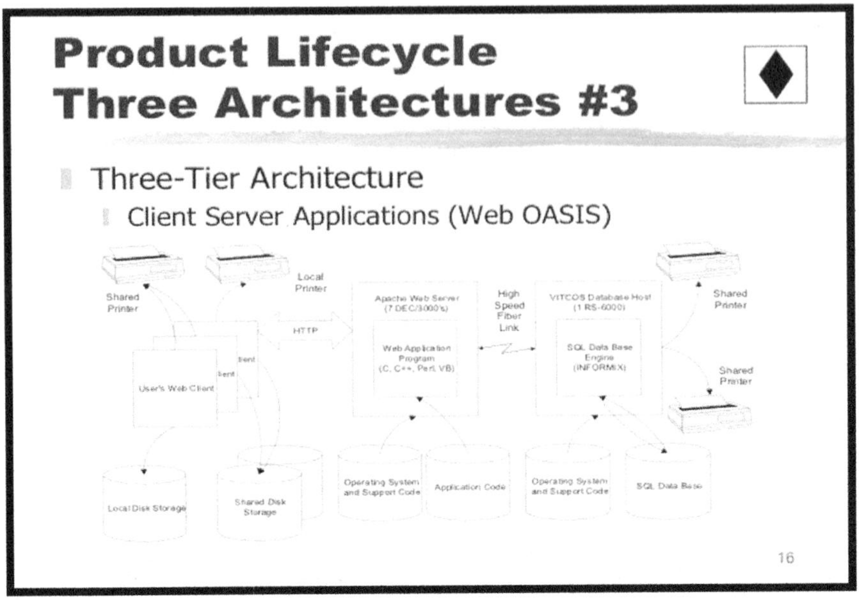

Three Tier Client Server Applications (like OASIS)

This is a thinnest possible client - server process. All that is required on the client is a browser. We use a very short Javascript that allows us to tell whether the version of IE or Netscape is 3.x or below or 4.x and above. It is, however, optional. This allows multiple, parallel and redundant web servers. If the designer and / or their management are responsible, it will have a secure socket connection (SSL) to the database server (HTTPS access)

Typically, this arrangement provides access to more services (high capacity printers, email, large scale file storage, etc.).

In addition to improved security (since your data sits behind a firewall, only your web servers are hacker sensitive) it allows tweaking each section for the primary use. The web server is tweaked for response time to and from the network, while the data server is tweaked for response times to and from the data base. Your networks are tweaked for the components. And, the user is responsible for their client tweaking.

Slide 17

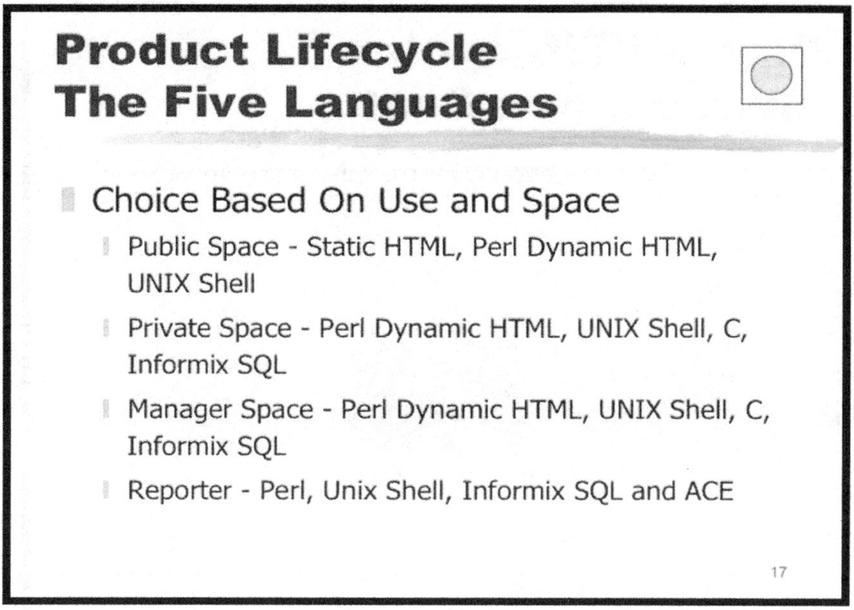

Five Languages

These are what we used. Each has a separate use in one or more spaces of the application as it runs today in a Three-Tier architecture.

The languages represent "Price and Performance" driven choices. We recognize that better response times may have been realized, but the target audience includes all windows, desktops, Macs and X-Terms. Our standard is version 3.0+ of both IE and Netscape.

Slide 18

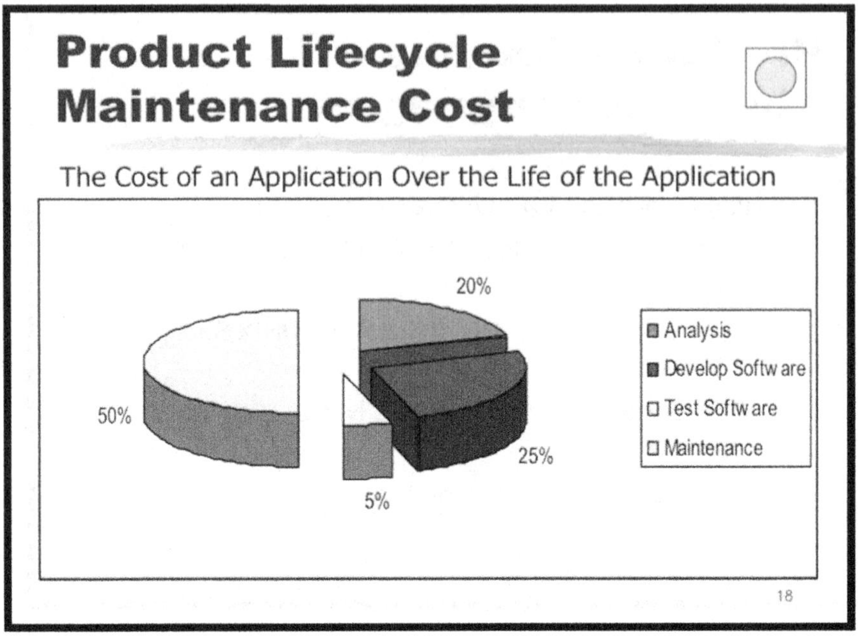

Lastly, this should be old news, too. But in a minute, I hope you will see it used in a new way.

What I tell people is to build anything as if someone else was going to maintain it BUT their name will still be on the product. Such development, where the programmer feels they own the product, facilitates both maintenance and reusability.

We'll talk about reusability again a later in the Best Practices Section.

(2012 Note – This slide appeared twice in the presentation. Once here and again three slides later with the following dialogue.)

It may be difficult to measure the cost of development, but it seems easier to measure the cost of maintenance. Given the 50/50 relationship between maintenance and development, by computing the cost to maintain you compute the cost to develop.

Sort of like figuring out the purchase price of a car or house from the monthly payments.

Slide 22
(2020 Note - Slides 19, 20 and 21 were transitional and are not included.)

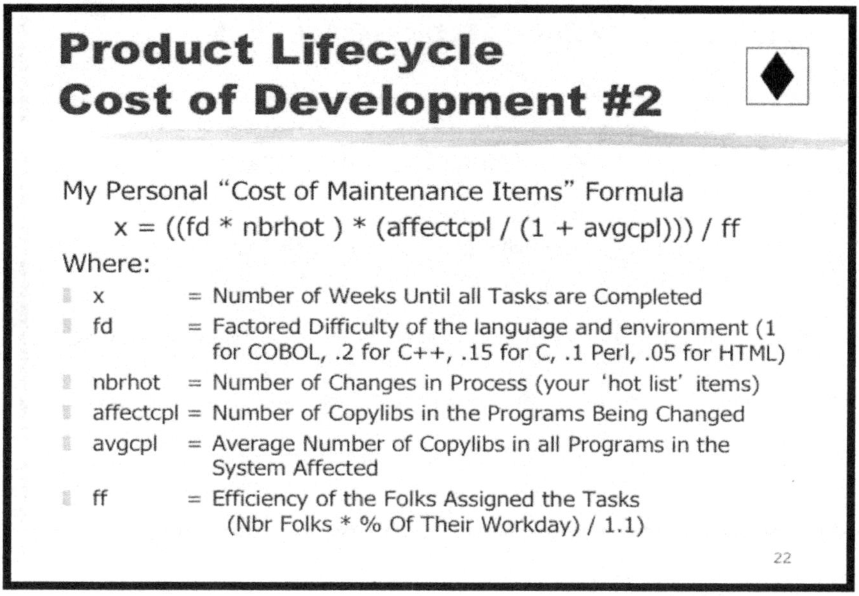

This is the method I've used. It yields a decent result. Try it out and see if it works for you. I suggest that, initially at least, you use it backwards from the completion time of a different project, one where you know "x". Use it to figure out your local "fd", which has to be tweaked as your staff and their working environment changes.

I'm open to criticism of this formula, send me an email with your observations. Maybe we can work on it and come up with a better one.

Check out Page 8 of the handout for this and the next slide. I'll go over the factors.

Slide 23

Product Lifecycle Cost of Development #3

Examples:

x = ((fd * nbrhot) * (affectcpl / (1 + avgcpl))) / ff

- fd and nbrhot represent the staff skills and workload
- affectcpl and avgcpl represent complexity of code faced
- ff represents the staffing and commitment to the project

Example	x	ff	ff1 # folks	ff2 = % hrs	fd	nbrhot	affectcpl	avgcpl
New Perl	0.07	0.682	1.00	0.75	0.10	2	4	16
C++ Chg	0.28	0.682	1.00	0.75	0.15	4	8	24
COBOL Chg	4.27	0.909	2.00	0.50	1.00	8	16	32
OASIS	30.56	1.091	2.00	0.60	0.10	125	8	2

23

Here are some examples:

"x" is in weeks because that is how I measure things. OASIS, the last line, about halfway through the project I estimated completion would take 30.56 weeks and it took just about 32 weeks to get to a final Beta Version.

"fd" is based upon the ability of you or your staff to write code in a particular language in your particular environment. I've taken a lot of flak over rating COBOL as tough (a value of 1.0). The language itself may be easy, but the mainframe environments are not. I would challenge someone who said that a mainframe IBM or Unisys environment was user friendly at all, let alone as user friendly as the worst UNIX or NT ones.

"nbrhot" reflects my experience that the more things on a programmers' hot-list, the more fragmented your business environment and, therefore, the more fragmented your computing environment. Do fewer things faster and you'll get more things done. More haste, less speed. Additionally, when you experience deliverable creep you can quickly show the effect on the final delivery date by adjusting this factor.

"affectcpl" and "avgcpl" are a way of factoring in the complexity of code written at the site. Where staff routinely use more copy libraries, I've found they are quicker at developing code that uses a few, but not too many, copy libraries. The strength of C, Perl and OO languages is in the use of library routines. On the other hand, we're rewriting a COBOL app that has programs using up to 48 copy libs when the average faced is 4. The whole application is a pain and is taking a lot of time to make Y2K compliant.

"ff" is to factor in how much time the staff can actually dedicate to working, as opposed to communicating. The formula (Nbr Folks * % Of Their Workday) / 1.1) factors for the mythical man month. After about 7.5 folks on the job, any additional staff don't add much more project team bottom line.

Slide 26

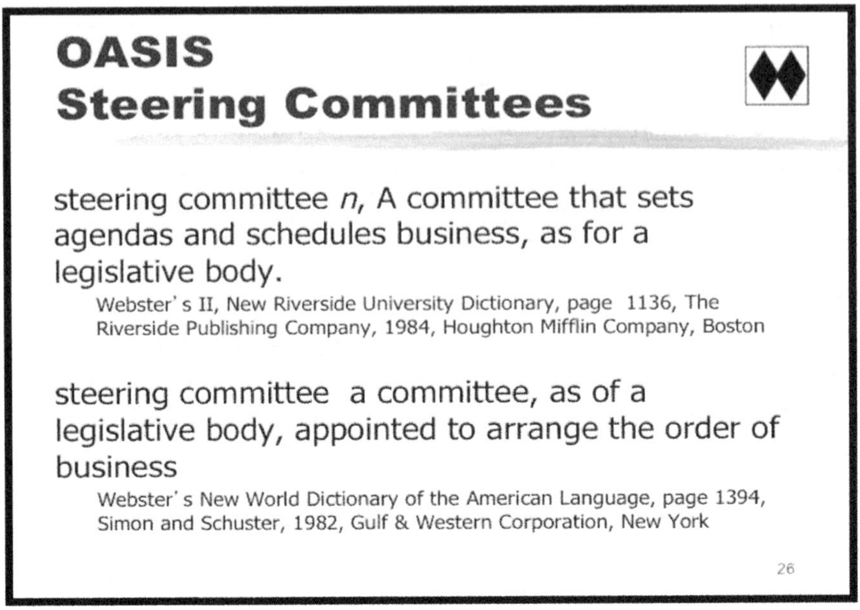

Notice the double diamond. If the person next to you has dozed off (and you know them well enough) give 'em a quick elbow to the ribs.

Here are a pair of formal definitions.

As soon as your steering committee recommends anything be put on a screen, they have ceased steering and started designing the application. Remember a giraffe is a dog designed by committee.

DO NOT LET THIS HAPPEN. THIS IS WHERE PROJECT DELIVERABLE 'CREEP' STARTS.

In my opinion, the direction received from a steering committee should be straight forward and simple. They should say "go in that direction and do this". Examples are as in Lewis and Clark's Charter from Jefferson to "Traverse the Louisiana Purchase and map a way to the Pacific Ocean" or JFK issuing the challenge that the nation "...should have as our goal to send a man to the moon and return him safely within this decade." Don't say how, just say "do it".

Slide 27

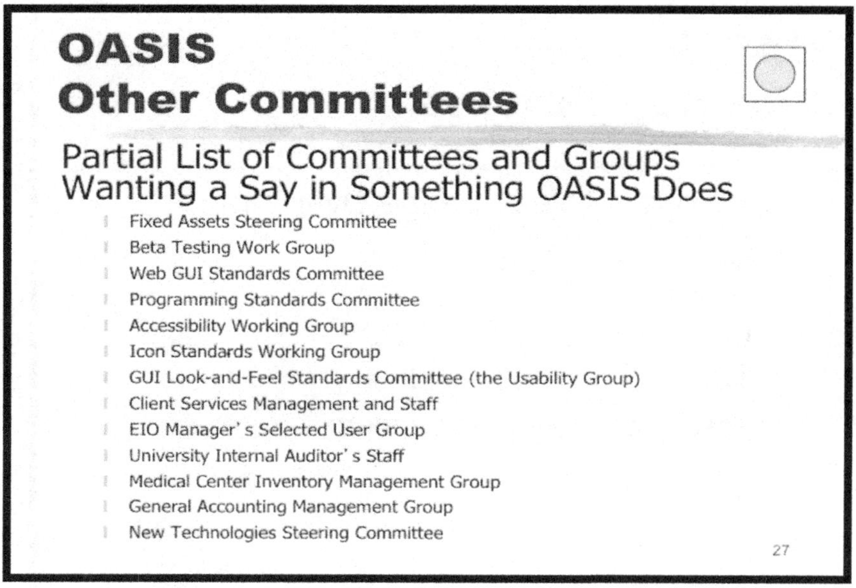

This list of 13 is not to complain about committees and meetings. It is to re-enforce to you that web applications and programming are such hot topics that everyone wants to be a part of it. Assure that you factor into your "X" part of your formulae the time and complexity the multiple overlapping and contradictory directions given by the committees you will face.

Slide 28

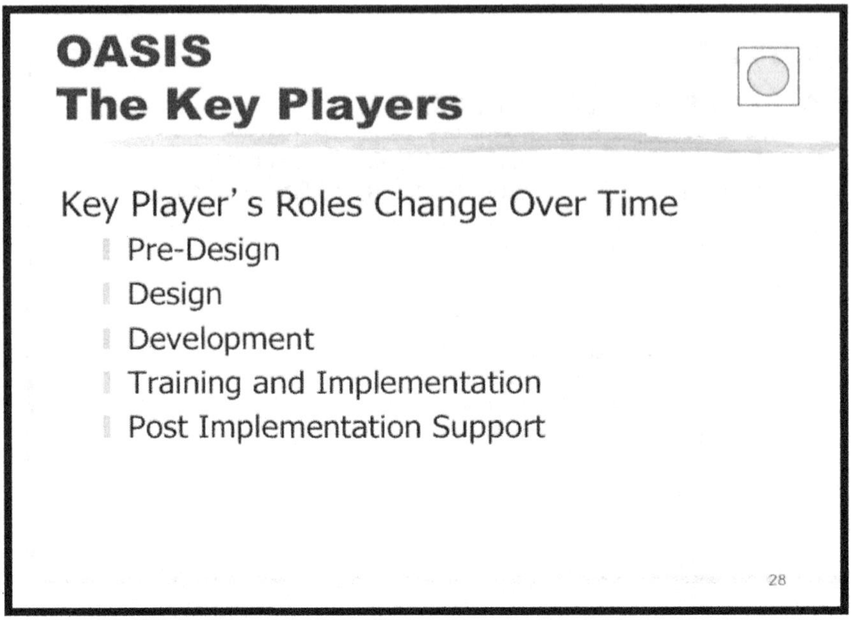

Here is an area where web development projects differs substantially from that found in the older 24x80 world.

I'd like to bounce through some of the things that took up a lot of our time. Things that, if we'd been able to do differently, would have saved us a lot of pain and suffering.

Slide 29

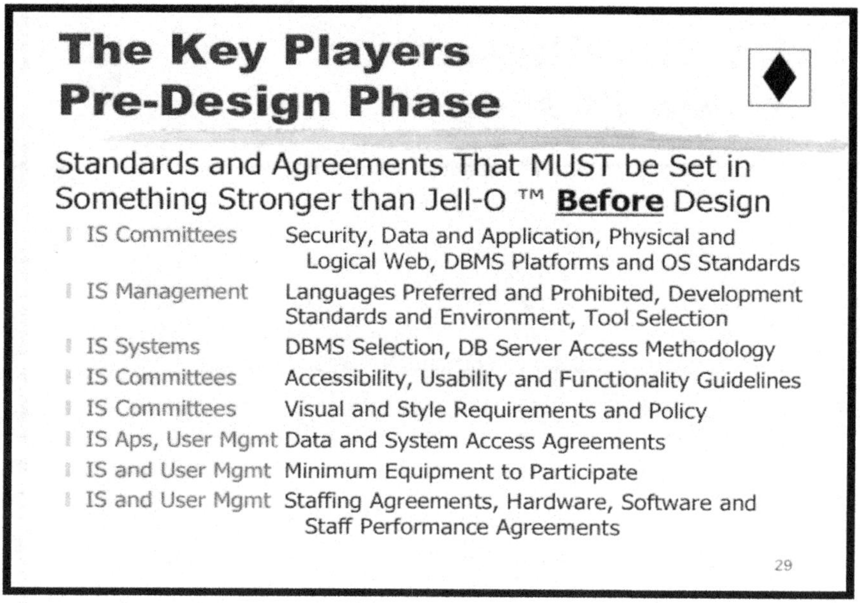

SET STANDARDS FIRST!

More or less in the order I think they should be done since there are many dependencies in here. As your site gains expertise in web projects these should become second nature.

These are issues we had to address on the fly since this was a leading-edge project. The cost of addressing these issues was 25% or so of the total price of the project.

If you're starting a web development project and are the first one in your organization out there, remember the distance between the leading edge and the bleeding edge is short, very short.

Slide 30

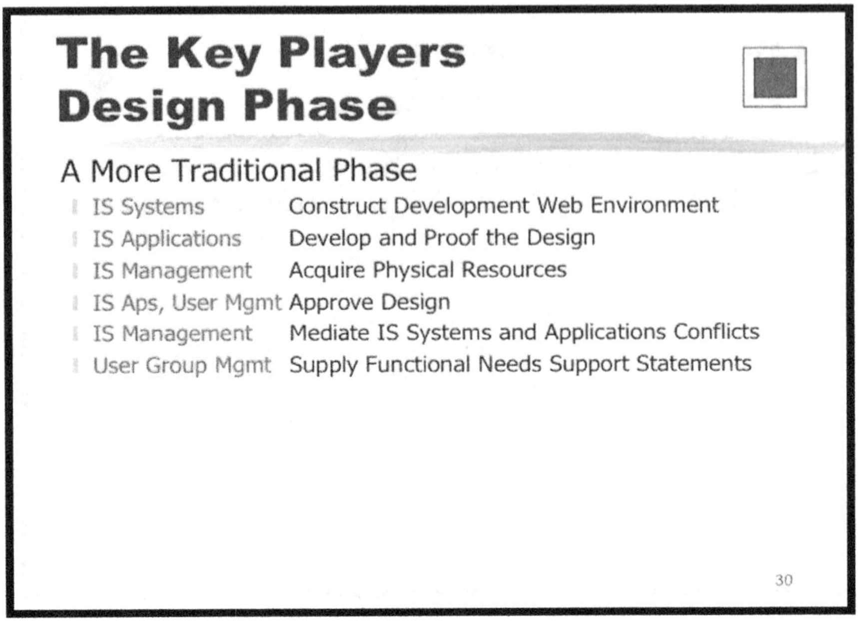

The Design Phase.

Again, these are more or less in the order I think they should be done since there are dependencies hidden here.

Design is the most technical, and also the most artistic part of the project.

The most important task on this list, in my opinion, is mediating conflict between IS Applications and Systems programmers.

Slide 31

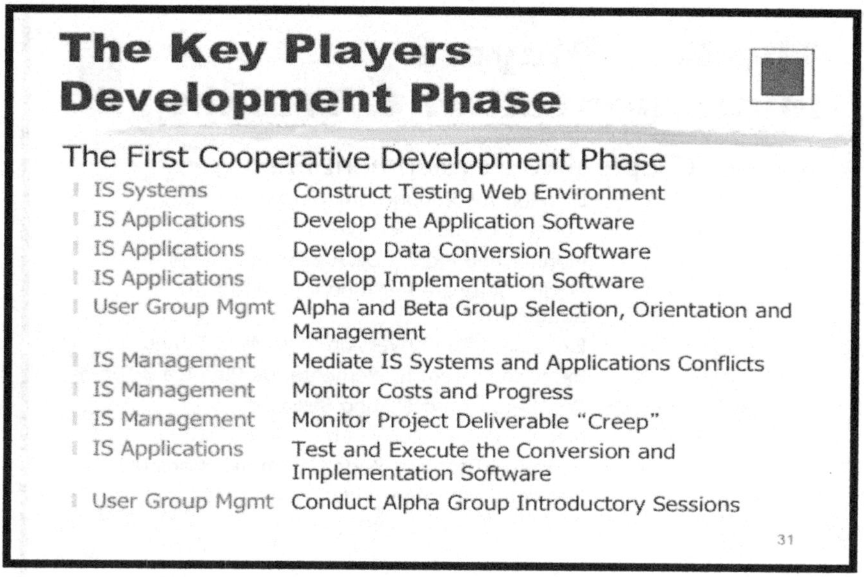

The Development Phase

Still, these are more or less in the order I think they should be done since there are many dependencies in here.

In my opinion the most important here is Monitoring Project Deliverable "Creep"

Slide 32

Implementation and Training.

Again, more or less in the order I think they should be done since there are many dependencies in here.

Given that web applications are so quick to develop and deploy, you should expect to go through these steps over and over and over.

In my opinion, Most Important is Managing the Test User Group.

Slide 33

Lastly, Post Implementation, but then is any web application ever really finished?

Again, these are more or less in the order I think they should be done since there are many dependencies in here.

Since stale web pages are death, you'll go through Final Deployment many times. For example, as you push through the four environments.

Tuning is the most important thing on this page. In a few moments we'll go over the cycle of performance tuning.

Slide 36
(2020 Note – Slides 34 and 35 were transitional and not included.)

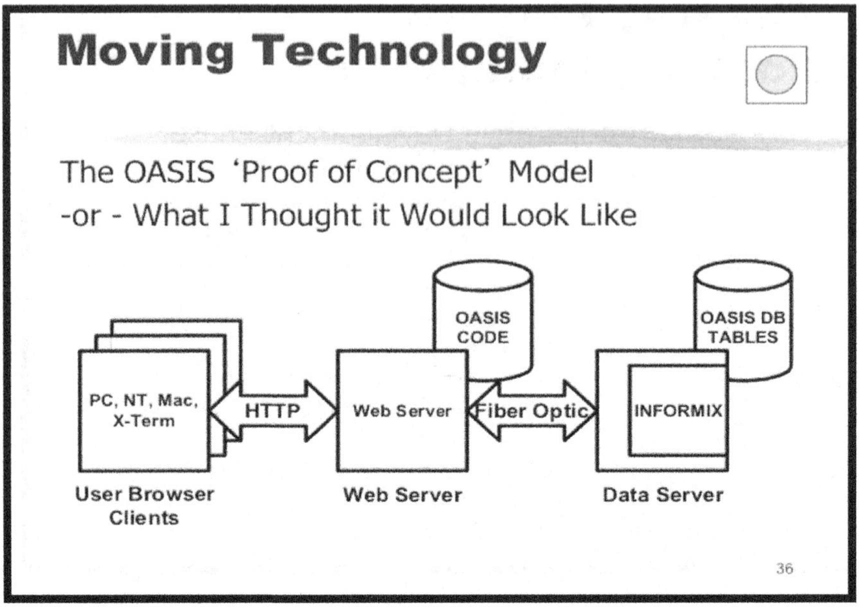

I dreamed of a simple three tier architecture written in Perl, with an rcp, rsh and cat mechanism for passing inquiries over and data back from the data server to the web server.

If you go to my homepage, you'll find a paper describing this dream world that I presented at the First Perl Conference in 1997. I think it is still useful because it provides a good introduction to how web CGI's work.

(2012 Note – That is the paper in Section 1 of this publication)

Slide 37

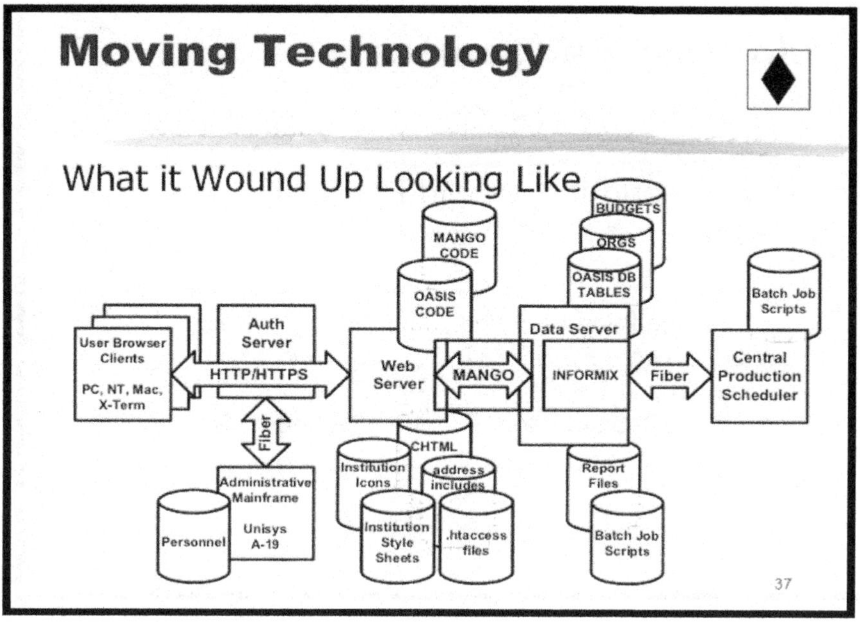

What I ended up with is a Perl application, an assortment of 'C' wrapped programs, interfaces to central financial tables, common style sheets, institutional icon files, a tailored API and data server in C, and a remote production scheduling interface.

These additions are the effects of reality checks, committees, systems security specialists, standards to reduce net traffic.

The reality hits taken added to the robustness, improved responsiveness and reduced exposure to hackers. So, it was good that the changes evolved.

Slide 38

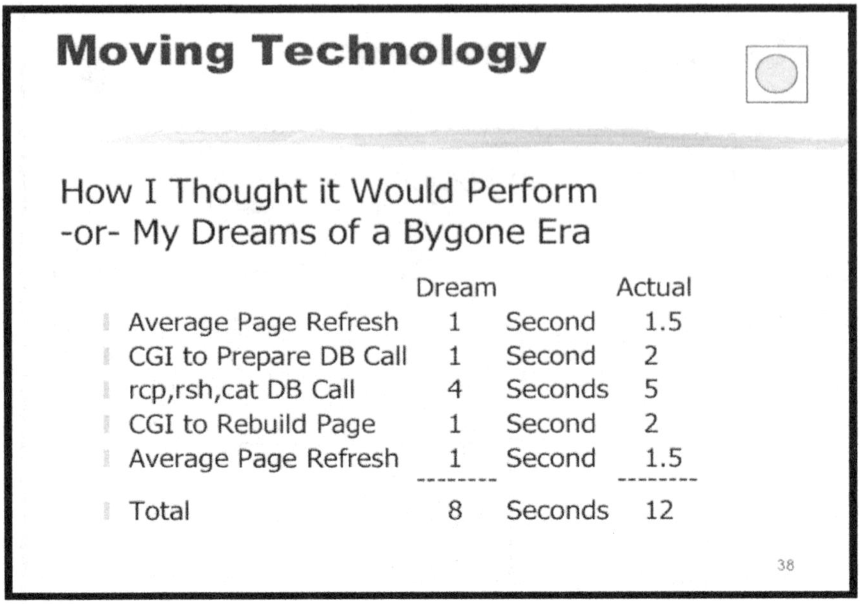

These were the best times we could muster. When this came to light the original rcp, rsh and cat concept had to be abandoned. The Database API and Server, the "Mango" arrow you'll see referenced in this presentation, were added and the Informix database engine was tweaked to fix web network problems.

Slide 39

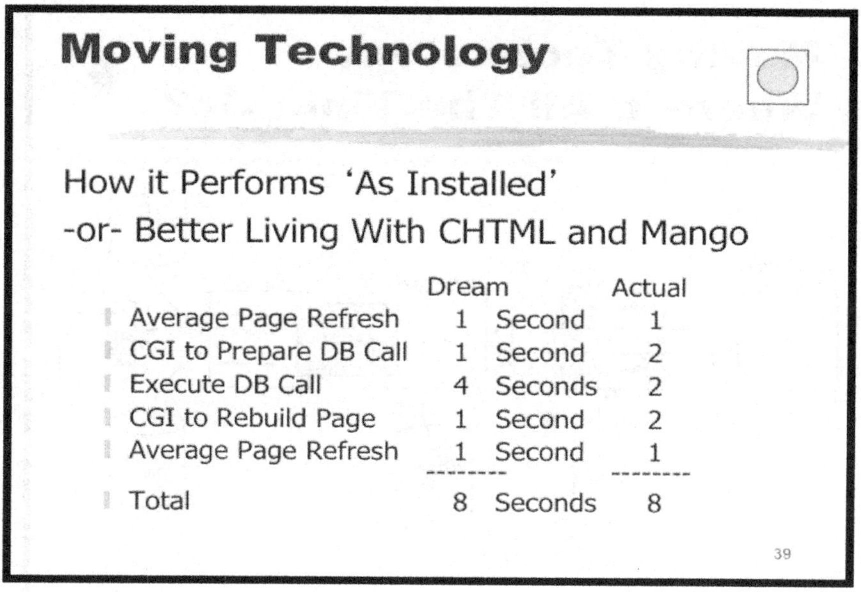

This is where we are today.

Eight seconds seems to be a baseline for SSL Dynamic HTML where caching is disabled, at release level 4.0 or better of the IE or Netscape browsers running on a Windows Platform, a Mac, or an X-Term

CHTML, a process whose name has been taken by Microsoft for a different use and will probably change, reduces network traffic by putting all HTML into a cached file on the web server then bursting it to the client. If a single app is active it reduces throughput, but when your net takes 1.3 million hits a month it works like a champ to reduce traffic and improve overall performance.

Slide 40

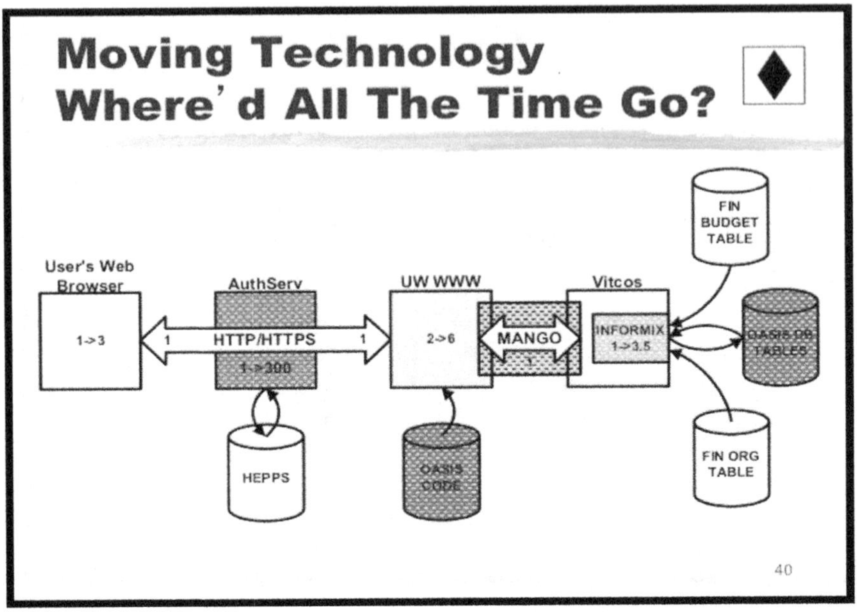

These are all "best guess" time estimates. Tools to get accurate counts are not available ... yet ... We will have to build or buy some.

The problem we face is that adding code to measure the times affects the times themselves. Heisenberg's Theory of Uncertainty comes into play. Your attempts to measure something affect that which you are measuring.

Slide 43
(2020 Note – Slides 41, 42 and 43 were transitional and not included.)

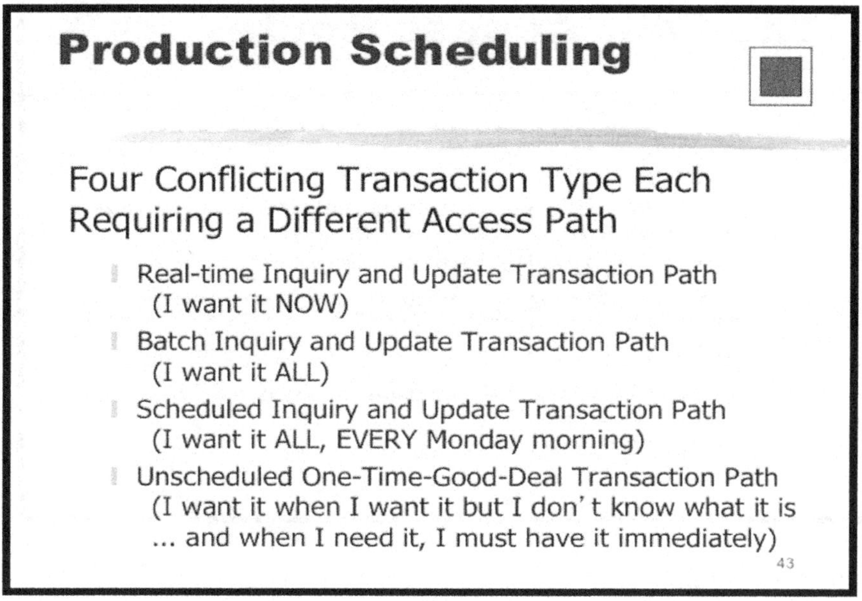

(2012 Note – From a deleted transitional slide)

One of our goals was to eliminate the work of writing a job scheduler for this application, since there are going to be many systems and therefore many schedules … and left to their own devices, none of them would be the same and all of which will have to maintained separately.

We identified four distinctly different scheduling problems.

There is a different solution for each … remember that the goal is to reduce the cost of maintenance during development to reduce the cost of the development itself.

Slide 44

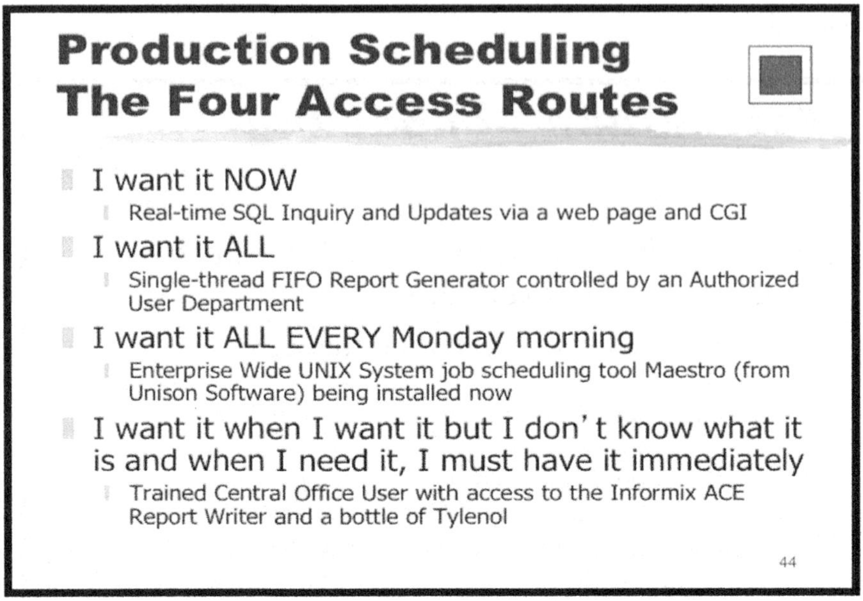

The system implications of each of these are distinct and different.

These solutions minimize development, operation and maintenance costs.

(2012 Note – Maestro is a registered trademark)

Slide 46
(2020 Note – Slide 45 was transitional and is not included.)

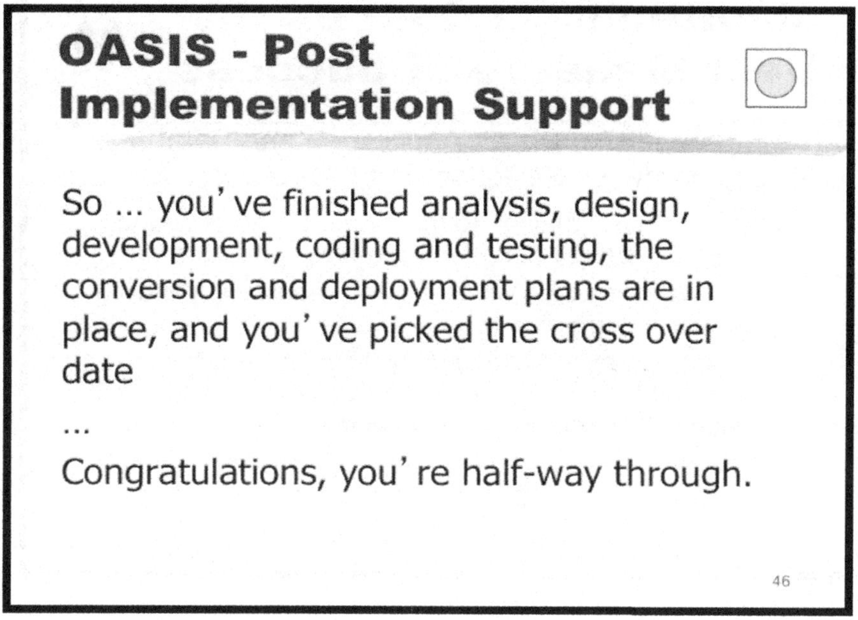

You deploy the production version, everyone pats you on the back, the boss authorizes a lunch out at a fine restaurant on the company expense account.

And then reality sets in ... you are only halfway through.

Slide 47

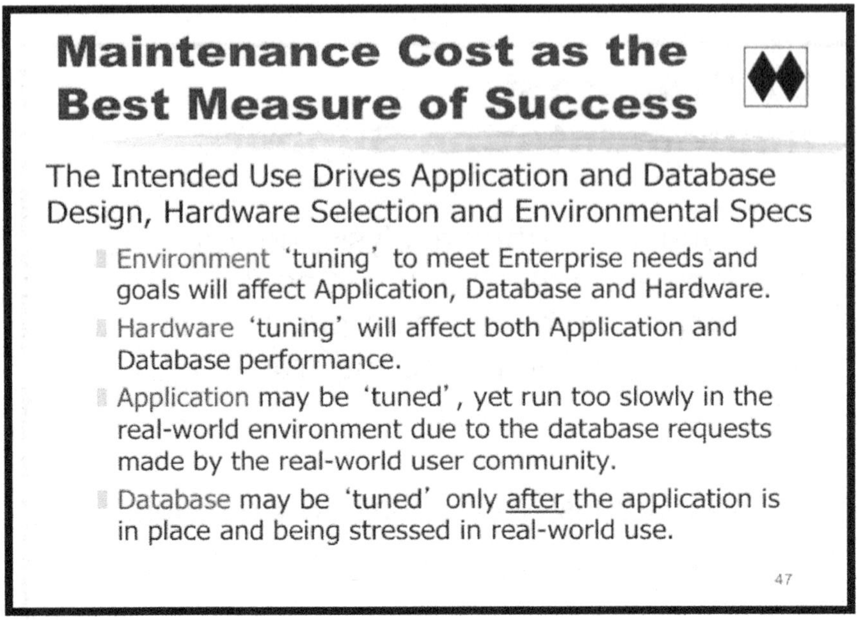

Watch Out, Double Black Diamond here. Theoretical question here.

This brings us back to one of the earlier slides. Each component of an application simultaneously enhances and limits the abilities of the other components. The key is to optimize them to support most fully the intended use.

All four components of the application must be tuned, as I mentioned earlier. And tuning of each component affects every other component.

Think of it as a pyramid

- Database
- Application
- Hardware
- Environment

YOU WILL CYCLE THROUGH THESE FOUR MANY TIMES BEFORE A FINAL ENVIRONMENT IS SET, AND ITCAN NOT BE DONE UNTIL THE SOFTWARE IS DEPLOYED AND IN PRODUCTION FOR SOME TIME, PERHAPS EVEN MONTHS!

Slide 48

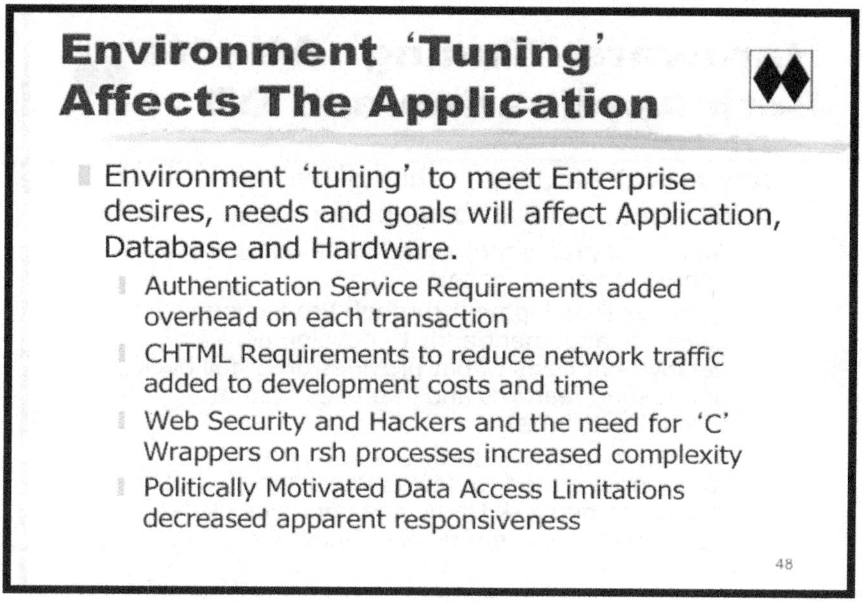

These are topics we have dealt with during the project that arose due to changes or emerging standards in the environment.

None of these topics is frivolous ... all are necessary.

Remember, especially the first time you go through this process, that the distance between the leading edge of technology and the bleeding edge of technology is quite short.

Slide 49

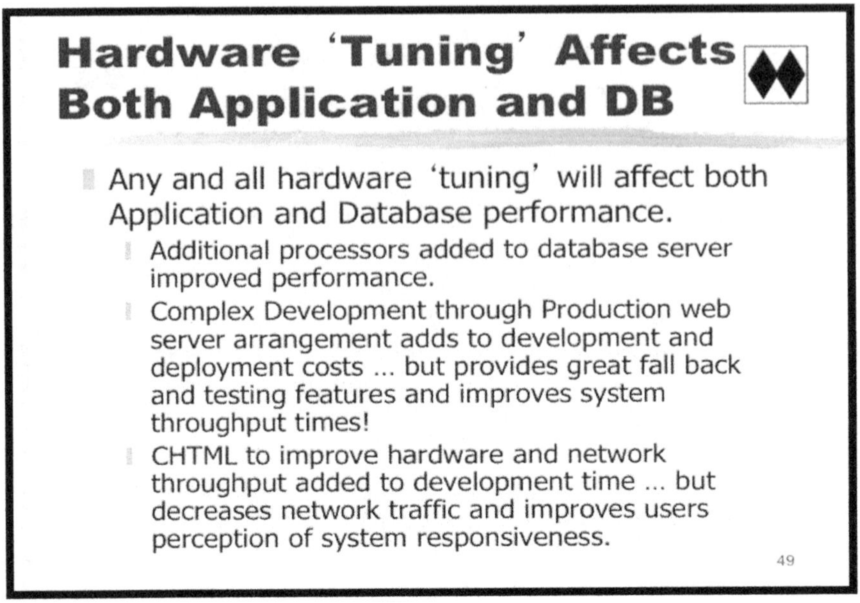

Again ... these are issues that came up as development progressed.

Slide 50

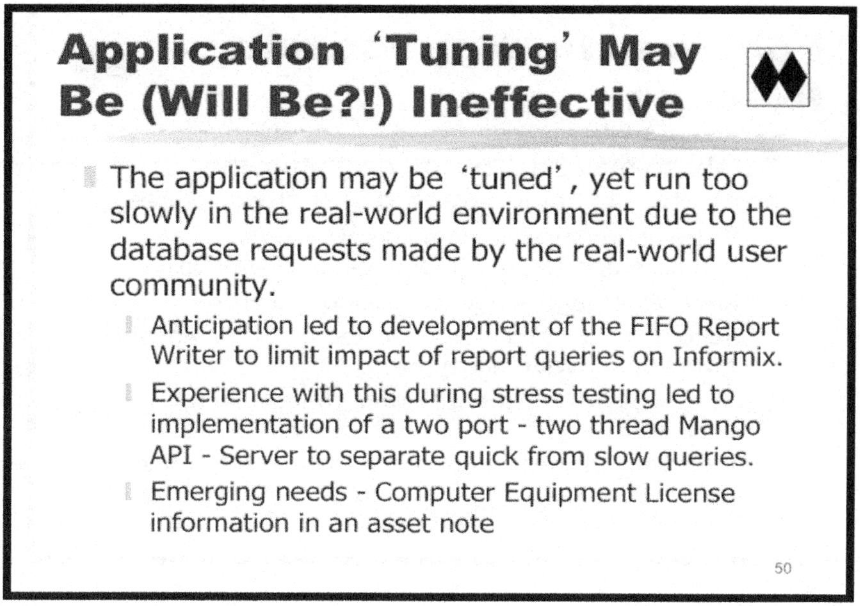

This was a tough one to learn. We took a shot based upon instinct and the action of the proof-of-concept model developed during 1997, and still had some major surprises along the way.

Some of the surprises were pleasant ... some were not.

Slide 51

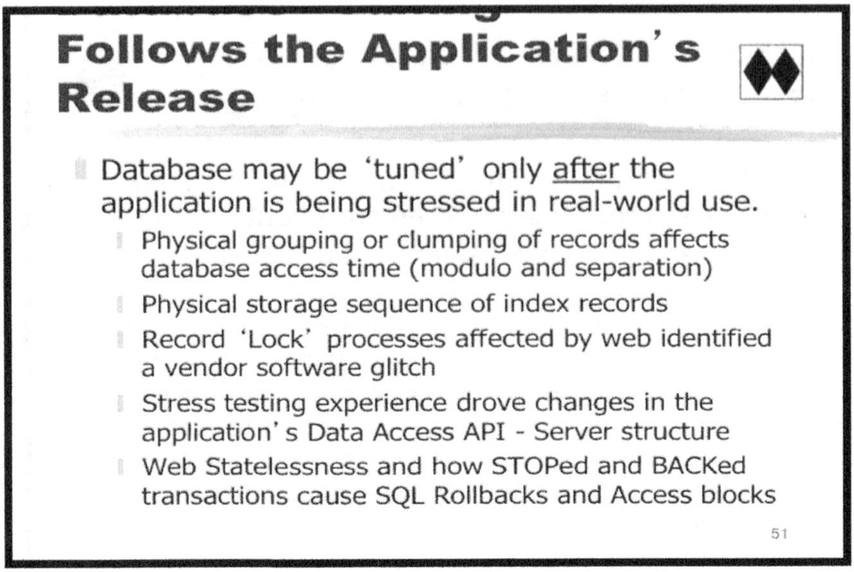

(2012 Note – The heading used to say "Database Tuning Follows the Application's Release. The first two words drifted off the top of the slide somewhere between PowerPoint in 1998 and 2012.)

Database Tuning requires that you must determine who is the "real' user, not just who is your point of contact in the user community during design.

Upon release to Beta I was worried about performance until my Director, Ed Lightfoot, reassured me, saying, "I've never seen one of these that performed worth a damn in Beta. They all need database tuning. And, this seems truer in these Client Server applications."

Note - The Vendor's glitch was not releasing Shared Locks when the client was a web application. The file containing all the locks filled up and the system hung.

Slide 53
(2020 Note – Slide 52 was transitional and is not included.)

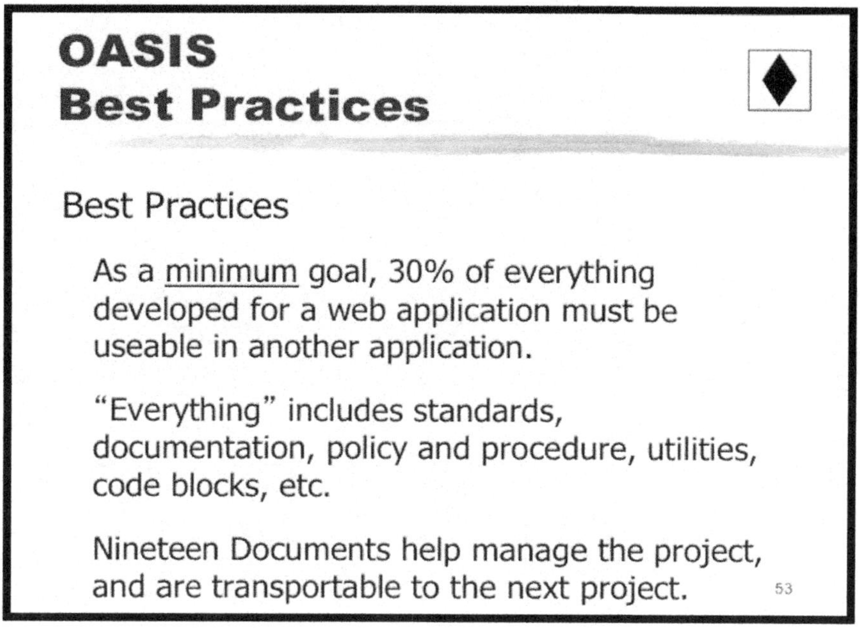

(2012 Note – 30% reusability seems outmoded today. In my opinion that is the greatest strength of the object oriented programming languages, OOP or OO. Bear in mind, however, that the level of design cost goes way up with OO use, and that using them puts you back in the days of assembler libraries and FORTRAN and COBOL – where a change to anything requires a recompilation of everything.)

My model is more tailored for folks who are moving toward a UNIX Client Server, Three Tier, Web application, than toward a mainframe data warehouse. The model still works, though, and if you have any feedback feel free to email me.

The starting point for this model, was a discussion with Christine Comaford. I recommend a visit to her web site (www.christine.com).

I recommend building your model on the cheap. Use MS Word to write the documents, save them as HTML to make a set of web pages. Some of them can be used interactively, for example, cut and paste the index crush, data drop, data reload and re-index code for a specific table.

Slide 54

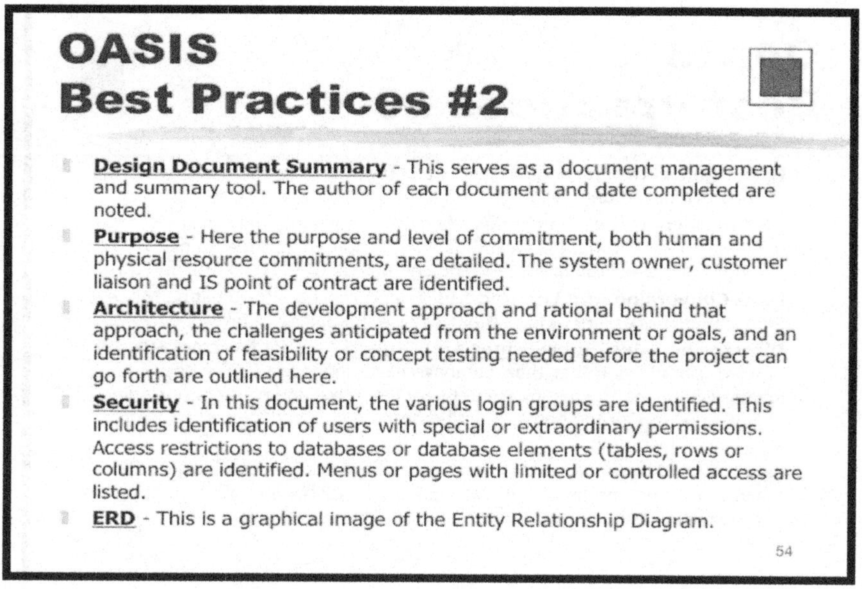

Documents 1 through 5

1 - Design Document Summary is a table of contents to the rest of the documents. Make it a clickable HTML page!

2 - Purpose, clearly lay out the who, what, when, where and why of the project. Leave the "how" for the rest of the model documents.

3 - Architecture - The physical and logical ... Again, I recommend that you do it on the cheap ... use a graphical tool, such as Visio, cut and paste the graphics into a Word document and save it as an HTML.

4 - Security - Mine is UNIX oriented, maps well to VMS too.

5 - ERD ... Same as Architecture above … Do it on the cheap whenever possible.

Slide 55

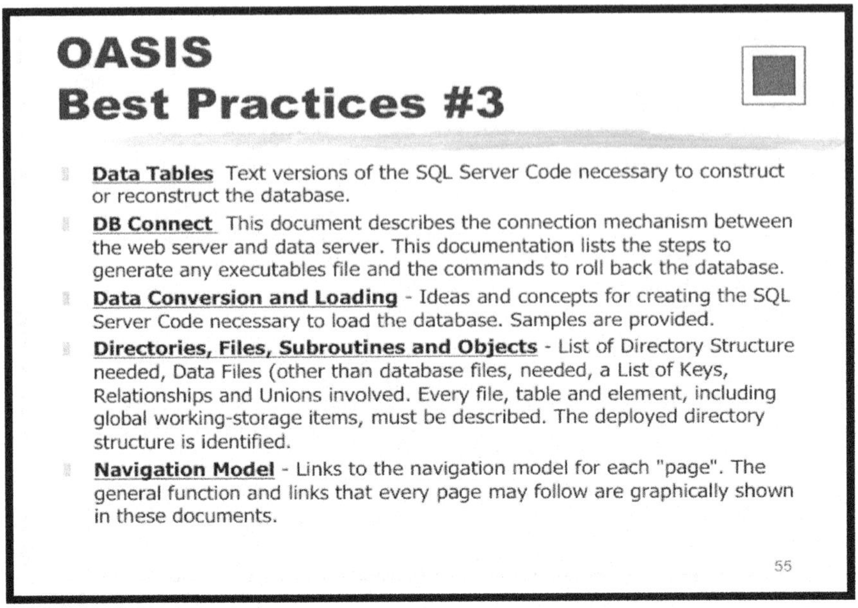

Documents 6 through 10

6 - Data Tables. Make them here and when your db gets trashed you can cut and paste the text to rebuild it. This is a key part of a cheap off site or business resumption plan.

7 - DB Connection - If you have to write a custom API and Server process, as we did, document it here. Put the code there. This also is a key part of your business resumption plan, just like the Data Tables.

8 - Data Conversion and Loading - Again, if you put the actual code you will use into a web document, the Perl scripts, VMS DCL commands, whatever, it will save you bunches when things go bad, or when you just need to reload test data.

9 - Directories - If you identify them here, when it comes to deployment or migration to another platform (or a downstream development team needs to borrow your graphics or code) all that's needed is to is a cut and paste.

10 - Navigation Model - How the user will get from point A to B. On Web applications this document has less downstream usefulness than on mainframe aps, but still good to document this piece of the puzzle

Slide 56

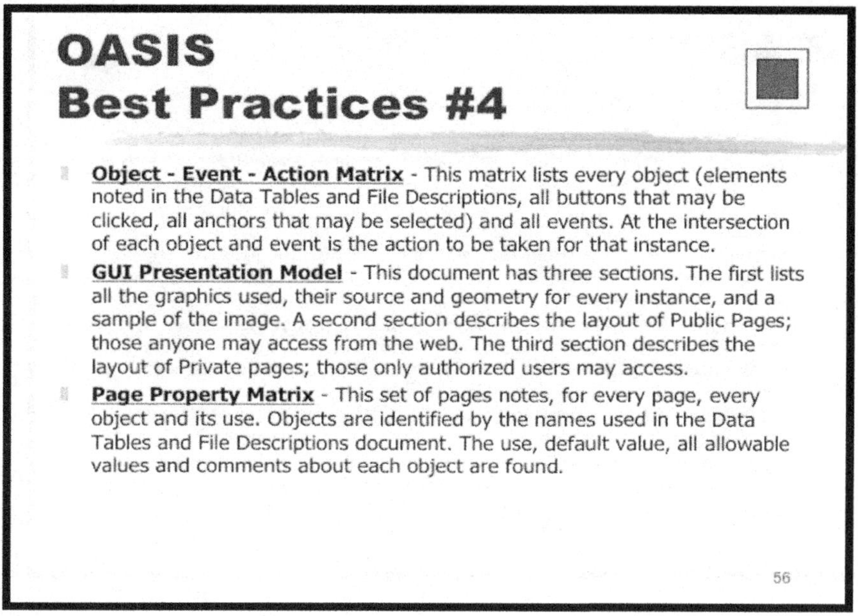

Documents 11, 12 and 13

11 - Object - Event - Action Matrix. This is an expensive document to produce and if you choose to drop one this is probably the one to hit. Basically, you're writing a roadmap for the maintenance team. If you like them, and / or you want them to like you, then develop this document.

12 - GUI Presentation Model - List all the graphics by their actual fully qualified pathname. List the preferred geometry (just in case you decide to use miniatures for navigation buttons later on). Why? So that when someone decides to change one of the gifs (an institutional icon) they can easily find which applications use it and are affected by their change.

13 - Page Property Matrix - Lists everything that's on each page. Why? Same as the GUI Presentation Model. If developers and maintainers can go to the web for cut and paste help in building or copying specifications and code … that reduces the institution's end cost!

Slide 57

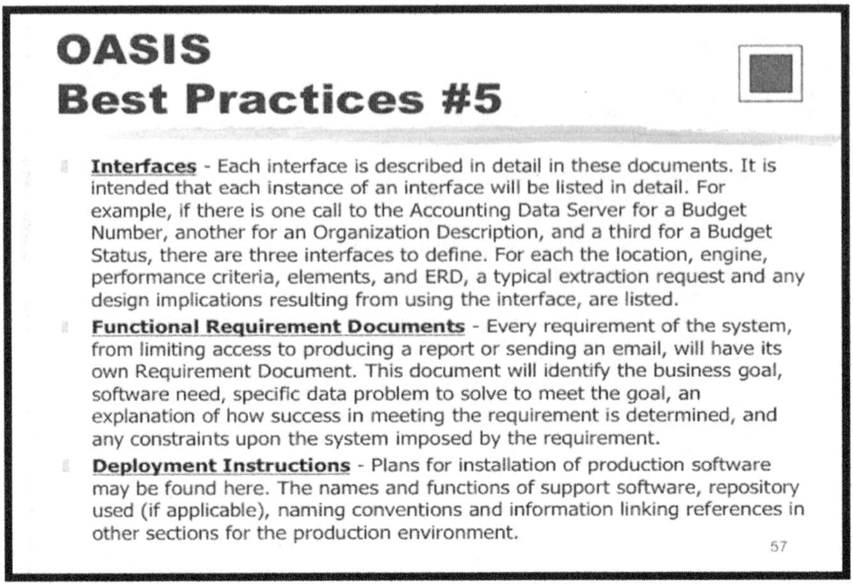

Documents 14 through 16

14 - Interfaces - Describe them all, data tables, ERD, foreign keys, even a sample SQL statement to get the data. You can cut and paste from here to your code, or vice versa, if you ever need to.

15 - Functional Requirements Documents - Everything that will be done has a distinct Requirement Document. From showing a menu, transferring to the Email Page, getting help, anything that the user community wants to have included must have a functional requirement document justifying that requirement. This is a throwback to the old COBOL type of design documents. It is costly up front, but remember, it is a "pay me now or pay me later" world.

16 - Deployment Instructions - We have four distinctly different environments; we wrote the deployment instructions once. Now all we do is cut and paste. Deployment for update or business resumption takes minutes and is done without fear.

Slide 58

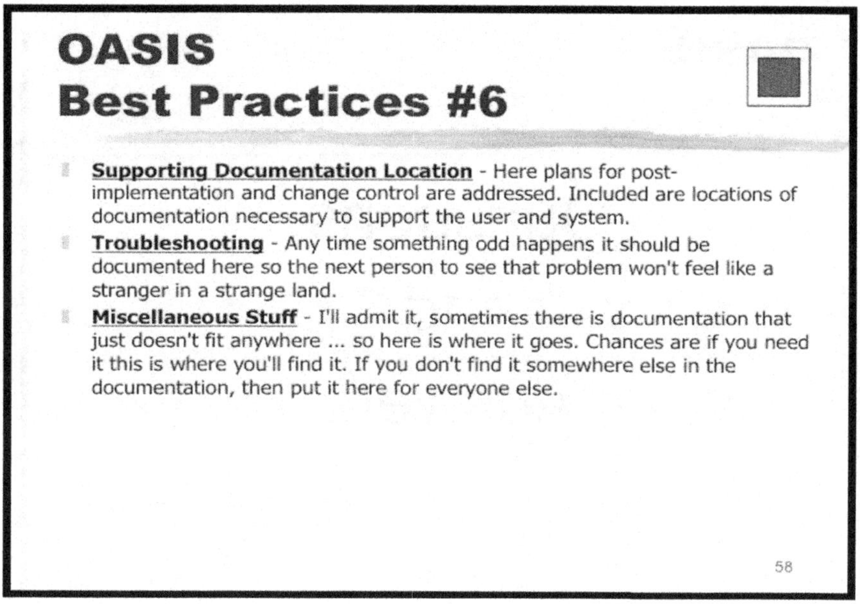

Last one ... Documents 17, 18 and 19

17 - Supporting Documentation Location - How many times have you asked, or been asked, "Where is the heck is the xxxx document". Put the location of it here (or better yet, put a hyperlink to it here) and you won't be asked again.

18 - Troubleshooting - Every time there is a reported problem you document it. This is a basic building block of professionalism.

19 - Miscellaneous Stuff - Points of contact, training schedules, on call lists, etc., etc.

Slide 60

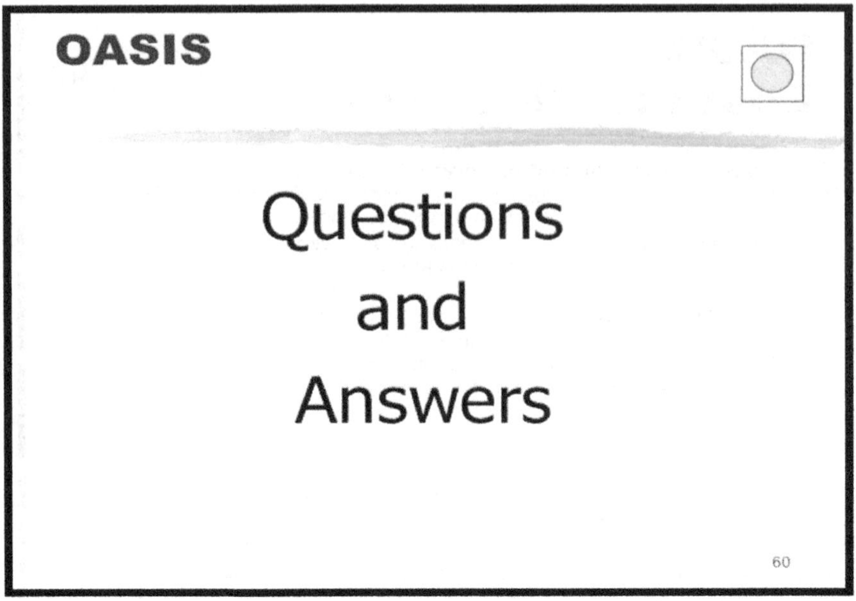

DONE.

Section 4 – (1999 WebDevShare) Performance Driven Design Issues in Web Development

In 1999, once again the WebDevShare conference at Indiana University invited me to come and present what the University of Washington was doing and where we would be taking our web-based systems.

I felt that, to a great extent, I had said all I could say about application and database sockets from a technical perspective. This conference I focused on what happens AFTER the beta application is pushed out to a user community. Topics such as:

- Performance (a short-form of the 1998 CAUSE presentation)
- Balancing, Compromises and Tradeoffs that had to be made
- Database Connections (extensions we'd implemented)

This again was a friendly audience. Many of the attendees I had spoken with at prior conferences. It was perhaps the most relaxed presentation I've ever given.

As with the 1998 CUASE presentation, there was no paper, just the annotated slides I've included here.

Slide 1

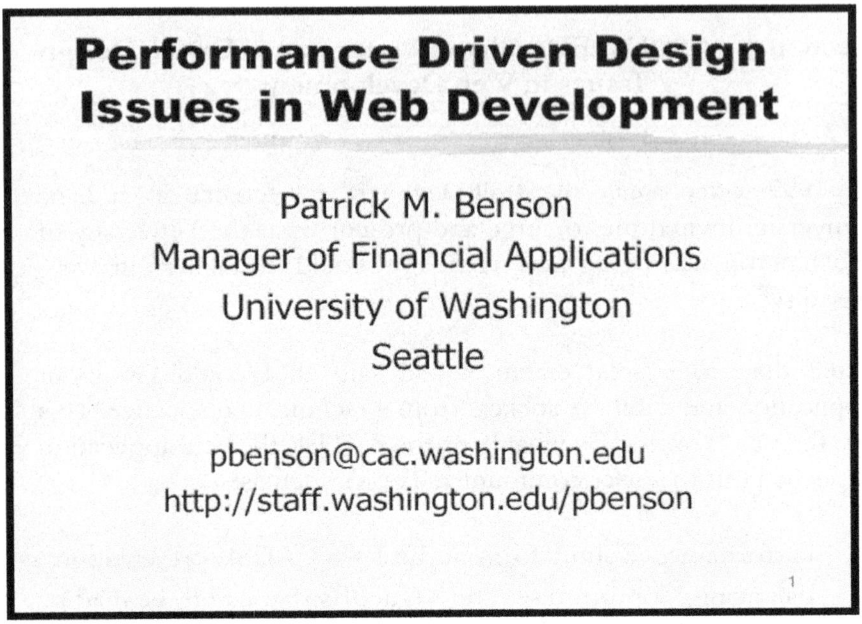

Thanks ______MIKE______. Good afternoon. Thanks for attending my presentation today.

This is Performance Driven Design Issues in Web Development. It is the outgrowth of work done by me and my staff, the University Services Renewal Project (USER) and other projects at the UW.

After the conference this presentation, complete with my notes, will be posted to my web site. The related papers and presentations from previous conferences I'll mention, along with a forms based Best Practices for Unix based web development, are there now.

I always answer email from educators and administrators, so feel free to send questions or suggestions.

A bit about myself before we get going. I've worked with computer hardware and software since 1969. Twelve years with the Air Force, two as a consultant with Cap Gemini DASD, two as a Data Process Manager with Ernst and Whinney. The last 14 years have been with the UW. I am responsible for development and support of all central financial systems.

I've been a promoter of replacing captive systems with web applications for years. My work with web implementation of the basic three tier architecture got me an invitation to address the first O'Reilly Perl Conference, last year's WebDevShare and Educause National Conference.

Chris Manley – Cornell morning session – There are parallels to our presentations – he is coming from the systems and server side while I am coming at it from the application side.

Slide 2

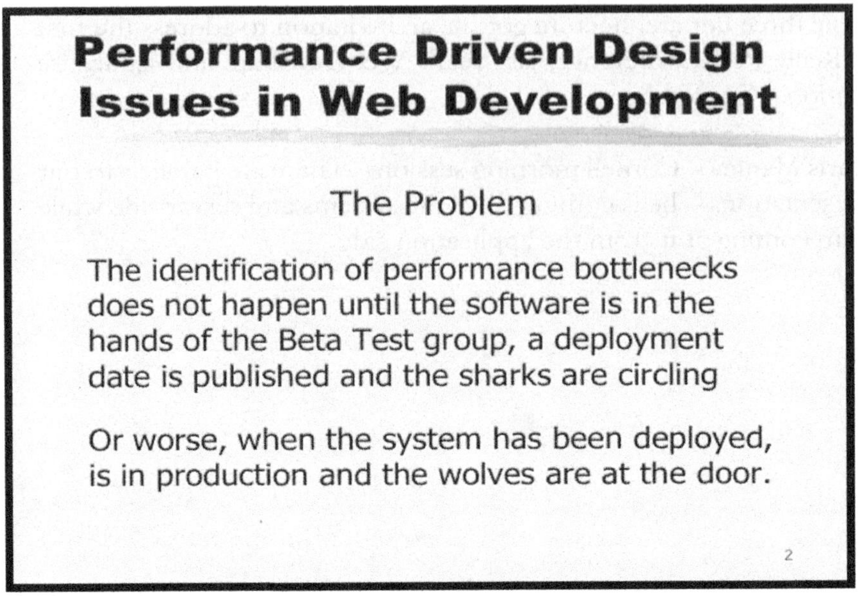

The web environment is difficult from an applications side because:

- The number of pieces necessary to build an application has grown with the web. No longer just allowed to consider one host and a private network.

- The tools to do end-to-end performance analysis just do not exist. I attended a focus group on this issue at the Miller Freeman Software Development Conference in April 99, and what came out is that everybody wants one, and would pay a pretty penny for one if it existed.

- The speed with which web applications can be developed fosters the mentality that you should rush an application to the users as soon as the Beta Group has had a look-see. This rush to deploy results in sub-optimal systems, degraded performance, clumsy code, difficult maintenance and a whole raft of issues that could have been caught if the tools existed, but they do not and we have to live with it.

- Everyone is left working out performance issues during Beta Testing or waiting until after implementation to see how it works under a production load and trying to fix problems as they come up.

The goals today are show you areas where we have experienced performance problems; to explain our solutions and show where designing for performance issue may be done up front to reduce, and if possible, to eliminate, some of the performance bottle-necks you'll face.

Slide 3

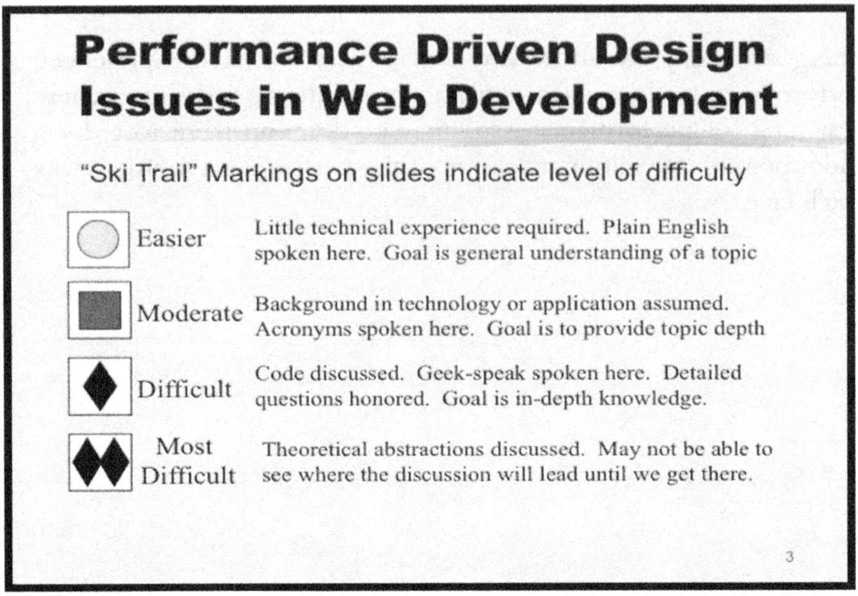

A couple of years ago I got into the habit of putting these ski trail level of difficulty markings on my slides. Sort of like movie ratings.

Let's you know when you can chat with your neighbors and when you should pay attention.

Most of the slides are Moderate or Difficult. There are three double diamonds to watch out for.

Slide 4

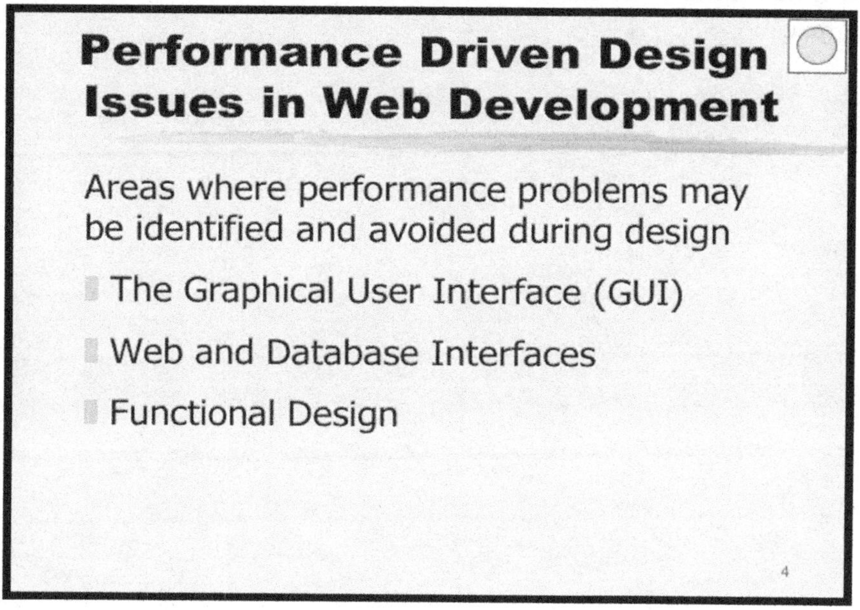

If you are prudent during design, you can mitigate many factors that will hurt overall performance. For the sake of this presentation, I've classified some of these considerations into three areas.

GUI - This is where the power of the web is most obvious. Although the GUI has less effect on overall response time that the other two items, we will go over ways the GUI can degrade or support performance. It can be the limiting factor of the application – most applications are limited by their desktop appearance and functionality.

The limiting factor of the GUI is the desktop hardware, software, configuration and use at any point in time.

Web and Database Interface. - I'll cover several ways to connect the two. The specific applications covered are three-tier, but I'll include comments about one and two-tier, and share experiences with a variety of vendors. The greatest performance challenge will be in the tuning of this area.

Functional Design - This includes showing how the server or server-farm, the user load and your application conflict. Also, areas where you can design for **throughput, not just speed**. There are many of what may be called "smaller" issues here, but the net effect is great.

Slide 5

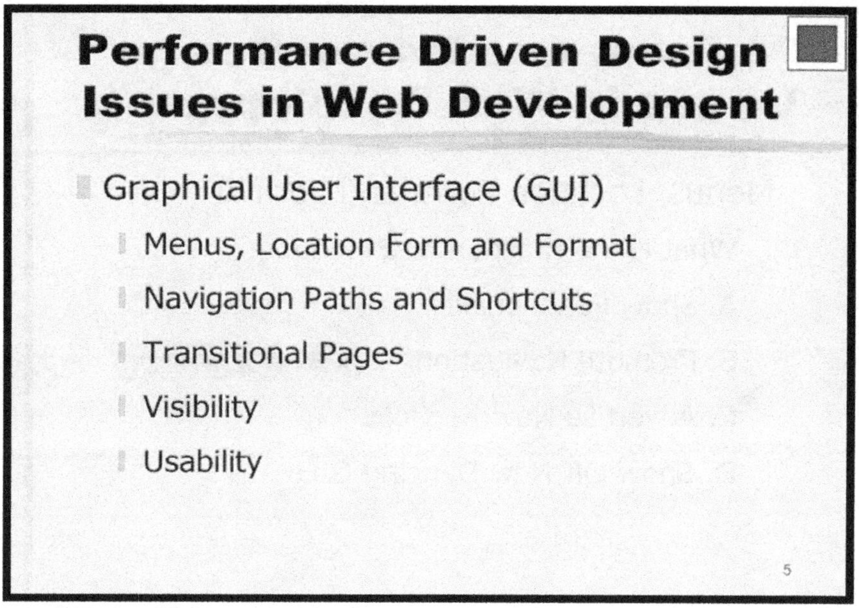

FIRST AREA - THE GUI

The web has considerable power to address issues that have dogged software development in the 24x80 world since day one. I'll be covering these five areas.

Most obvious is that the application programmers are freed from the restrictions of captive network and end-user display restrictions. Naturally, there is no such thing as a free lunch, and this freedom burdens applications with more of a need to be visually informative and directing. There is a pitfall to avoid. Beware of building pages, or parts of pages, that simply say, "Hey! Look at me! I'm talented, I'm cute!"

Slide 6

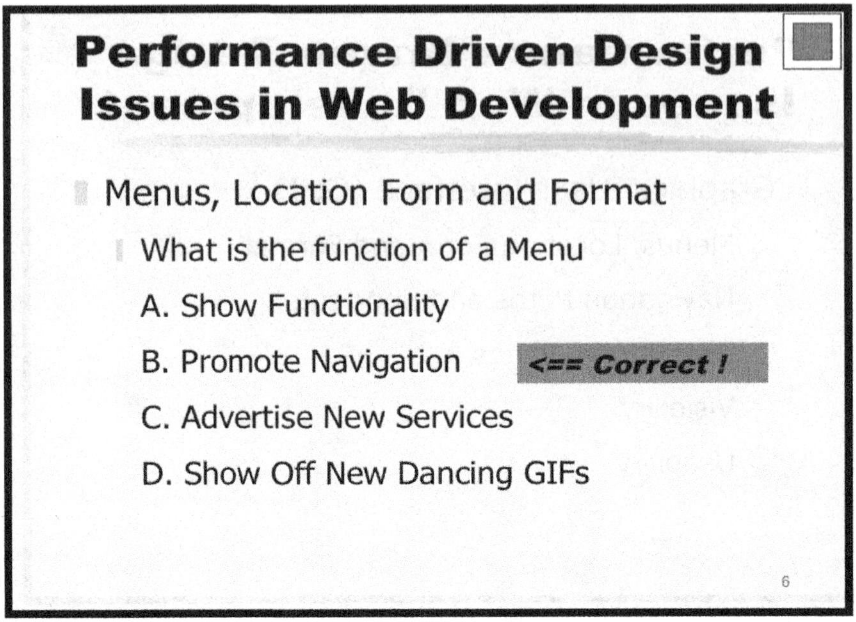

You don't have this page in your handouts. It came up as a result of some preliminary walk-throughs I did with the folks back in Seattle.

I think it is important to understand what function menus serve. You folks know that in multiple choice tests there is always one answer you can throw away, one that is sort of right and two that you have to choose between.

Most folks are tied up between A and B or B and C.

A - Showing Functionality is a training issue.
C - Advertising is better served through other means.
D - This is always wrong.

Slide 7

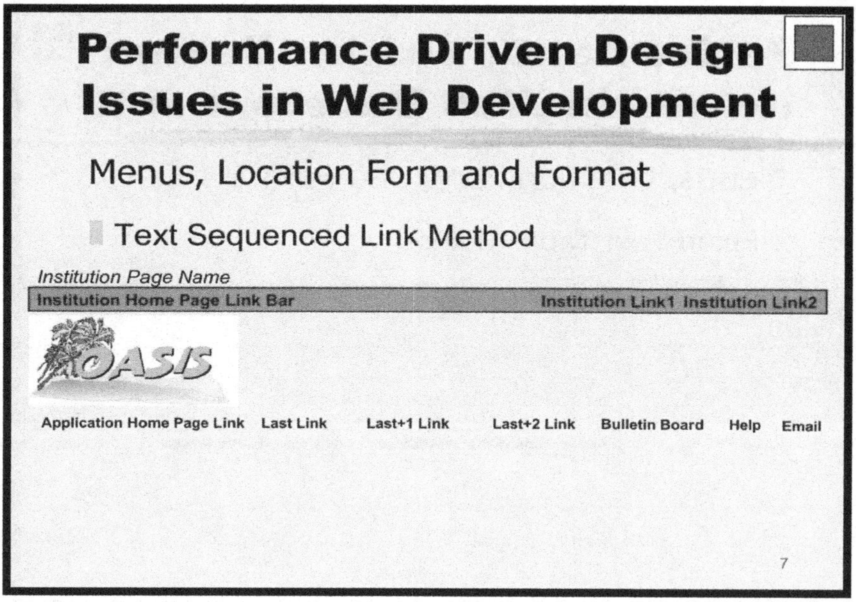

During development of the two applications, I'll discuss Fixed Assets and Timecard Entry, developers used **four menu structures**. There are others, but these four hit the essentials of them all.

This was our first cut. It tracked the last three pages a user had visited (within the system) in a list of three text boxes. We had disabled the Back button (via severe discouragement) fearing the cache versus database update problem.

We still use a form of this on the top of each page.

WEB VIEW.

Disabled Back buttons are on Jacob Neilsen's "Top Ten Mistakes" List.

We now allow full Back button functionality except where we've had to wrap the CGI in a "C" executable program to complete a SETUID command. We use it in our report generating functions to allow for both manager and user access to the report output

Slide 8

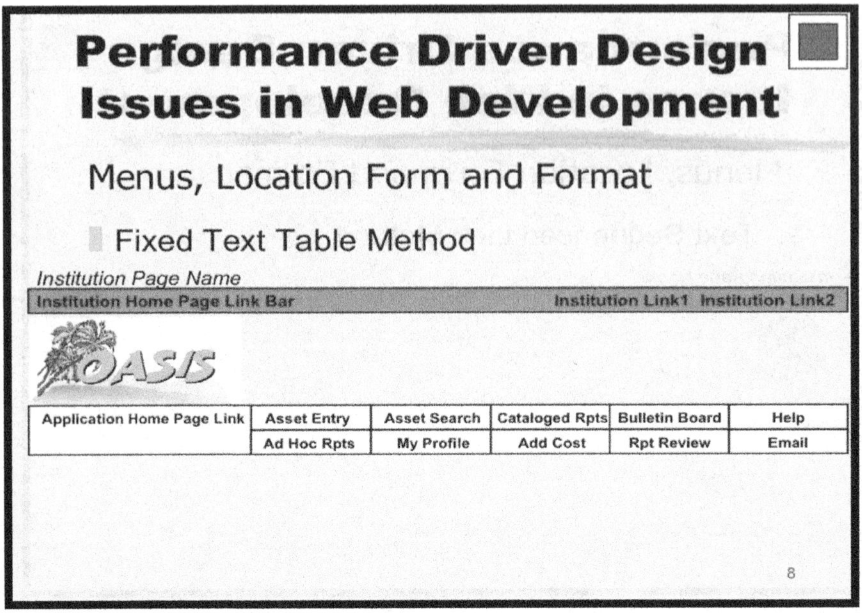

This method was preferred by programmers initially since we believed that the code to construct it would be the easiest to develop and fastest to run.

We built it to hold 8-10 of the most used anchors. Others were to be Bookmarked, memorized or gotten to via menus (Transitional Pages ... NO, NO)

Now I believe this technique should be used only when there are few destinations involved, eight (8) or fewer seems to be the limit.

Note that screen reading software has a difficult time reading this type of table code because of the variable column widths and row sizes. If Accessibility is an issue then you should consider other options.

Slide 9

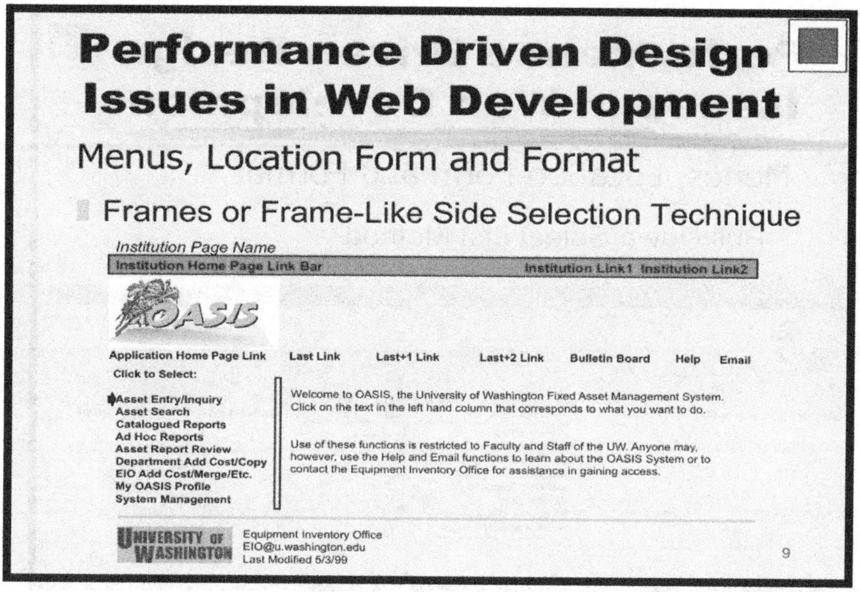

When we started this particular project, the Fixed Assets System, the use of frames was much more problematic than it is now. However, the speed of rendering and the fact that nearly all screen readers can render a table more or less intelligently now leads me to advocate the frame-looking table structure.

This is a Public Space Page - Will be discussed later.

The central part of this page is a single row table that is made up of another table and some other columns. There are actually 5 columns, one has 3 sub-columns.

Col 1 - A single cell, 175 pixels wide containing three columns
  1A - 6 pixels for a Javascript arrow
  1B - Anchor Title
  1C - 6 pixel blank gif for spacing
Col 2 - Five blank spaces <TD WIDTH="5"> </TD>
Col 3 - a 2 pixel gold bar with a height of 1 that expands vertically if needed
Col 4 - Five blank spaces <TD WIDTH="5"> </TD>
Col 5 - The descriptive text as one cell

Slide 10

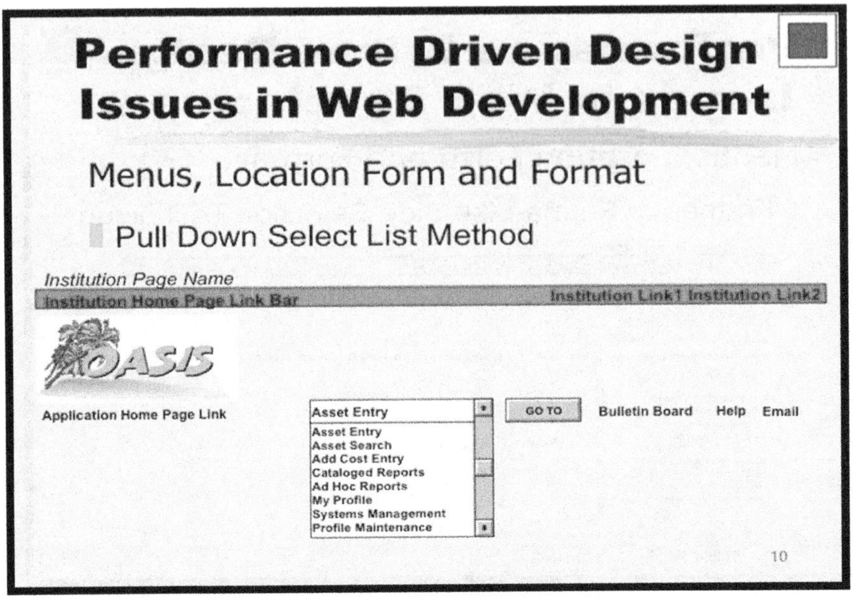

We settled on this is the approach for PRIVATE SPACE after working with the user group for some time. The entries in the drop down box are all in clear text, no gray optioning, and only appear if the user can actually go to them.

This is a Private Space Page - Will be discussed later.

We have only two user groups, those users who can access the Systems Management functions and those who cannot, so there are only two distinct drop-down menus. A single line of code selects one or the other based upon a test when we authenticate the user's permissions. (More on this later.)

We did try the gray out technique, but found that the code just was not worth it, and we had screen reader problems with it, too.

Greatest Benefit is that this maximizes the number of menu items available while using a minimum amount of real estate. Tailoring the list for user groups is a trivial

Slide 11

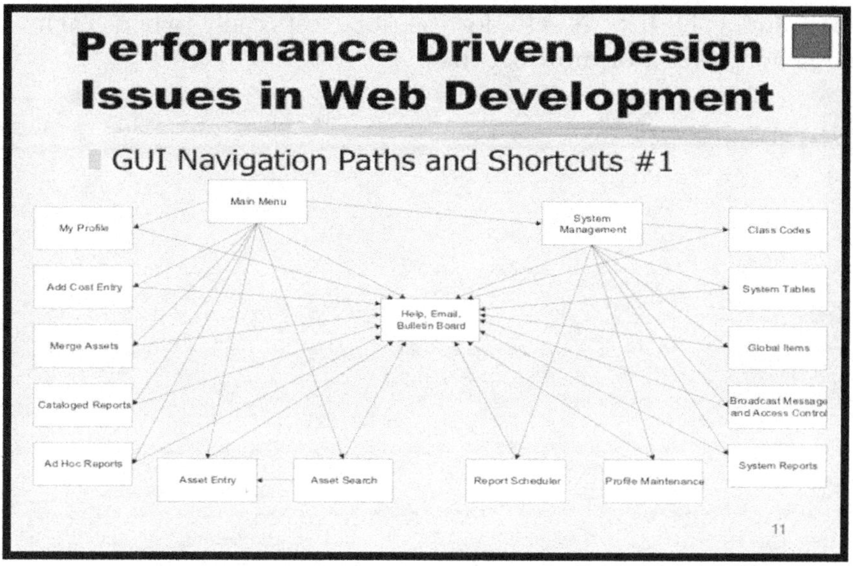

NEXT TOPIC - Navigation

This was the first cut at a Navigation Model (SEE THIS IN THE BEST PRACTICES MODEL) and it follows the logical arrangement of my Best Practices Model (DO NOT USE). Very hierarchical very 24x80. The strength of this model is that it can easily be drawn and explained. It just takes too many steps to the work done.

If the user is updating their profile to change the default printer before setting up and running an Ad Hoc Report. We had the Back Button disabled because of the local caching versus remote update conflict problem. Here are our first Cut Steps and Functions

Step 1 – Function: Main Menu to My Profile
Steps 2 thru 4 – Function: Review, Update and Review Profile Change
Step 5 – Function: My Profile to Main Menu
Step 6 – Function: Main Menu to Ad Hoc Report Page
Steps 7 thru11 – Function: Stage Report (will go into this a bit in a couple of screens)

11 Total Steps, with 7 Transitional pages, because of the Navigation Model. Remember, the goal of a menu is to promote navigation. This Model DOES NOT do the job, especially when each transaction takes 4 or more seconds.

Slide 12

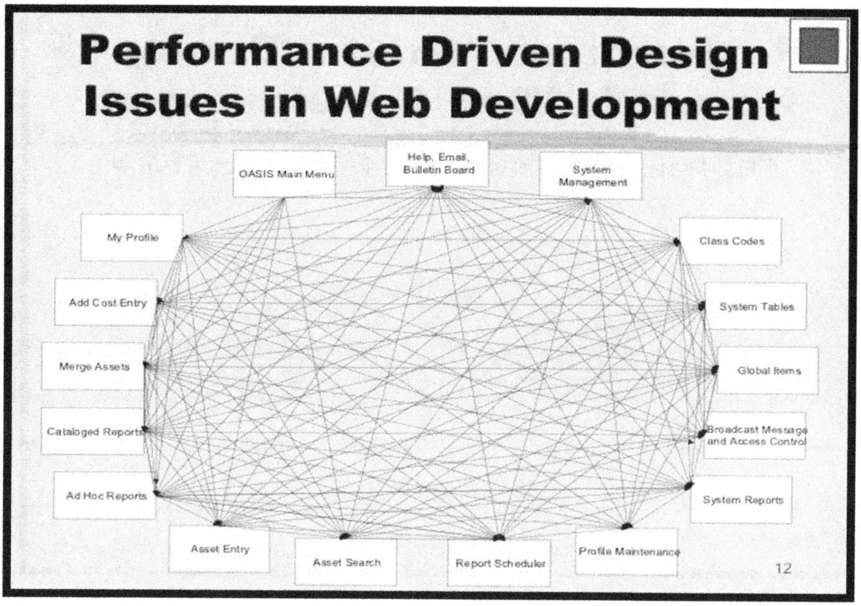

This is what the user wanted, and we gave it to them by adding the drop-down menu box described earlier.

If the user is updating their profile to change the default printer before setting up and running an Ad Hoc Report. We had the Back Button disabled because of the local caching versus remote update conflict problem. Here, the Steps and Functions are fewer:

Step 1 – Function: Main Menu to My Profile
Steps 2 and 3 – Function: Review, Update and Review Profile Change
Step 4 – Function: My Profile to Ad Hoc Report Page
Step 5 – Function: Stage Report (will go into this a bit in a couple of screens)

5 Total Steps, with 0 Transitional pages, because of the Navigation Model.

Slide 13

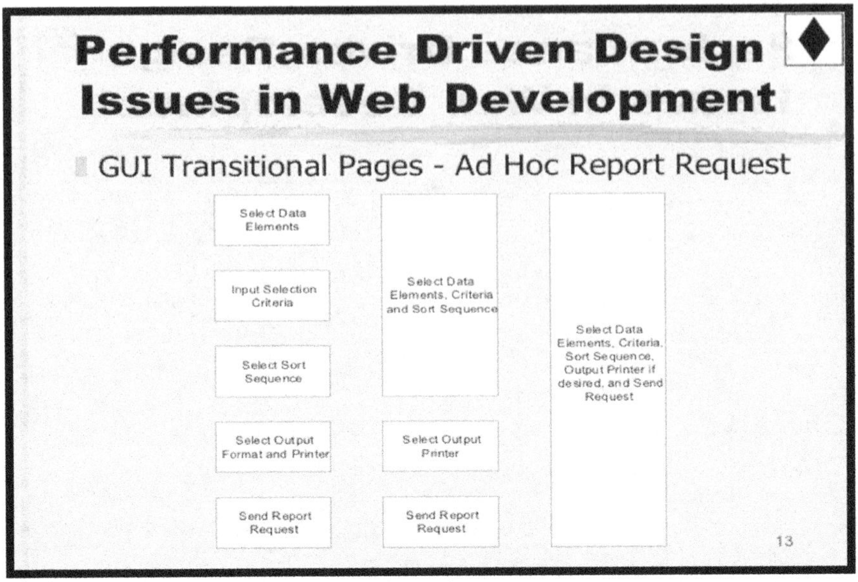

I've mentioned Transitional Pages a couple of times. These are those pages that get you from function to function without actually adding value. This is a brief discussion about implementation of the flow-of-control problem as it changes from a purely procedural to a visual-procedural problem. **To maximize performance, you must wring out all transitions … If a function doesn't absolutely need to be there then get rid of it!**

An example … This is the Ad Hoc Report Writer

As we first put it up, five steps to build a report. It looked good and led, I felt, the user through the process of constructing a report.

Middle phase … the users complained that there were too many steps so we merged the Selection, Criteria and Sort onto one page. I thought we were golden.

Where we are now. All on one page.

The number of clicks and keystrokes are about the same, but if you have 5 second response time, and this can be difficult to maintain in a web environment, then dropping the transitions saves a minimum of 20 seconds and more like 2 minutes with the mouse movements, screen reading, clicking, complaining about response time, etc. involved.

Chris Manley noted yesterday, and I am inclined to agree, that the page metaphor for design and display now may be inappropriate. It is blocks that may or may not exist on one visible "page" or "screen" or whatever.

Slide 14

(2012 Note – The graphic was larger and hid some of the text. I rescaled it from the original for this book.)

This should be old news ... every different user group requires a different design.

Public Space - Anyone from anywhere at any time. Clearly identified as yours

Private Space - Where actual work is done, must be self-initializing for bookmarks

User Space - Those pages in Public and Private space that users routinely hit

Manager Space - Pages that control access to User Space, set permissions, schedule jobs, control availability. Includes all Public and User but not necessarily all Private.

Developer Space - Everywhere. Keep the area here that is not in Manager Space as small as possible so the end user System Managers run the system. Backup, Restore, one-shots, etc., go here. Looks like the triangle

Standards - I've added Molly Holzschlag's article since the handout went to press. For the W3C Guidelines and Neilsen's work - see the URLs

Beware of colors, Red on Blue presentation at WWW6, "Everyone, Everywhere, Connected" during first keynote. My experience with Gordon and Bulletin Board colors. Revisit 6

months after deployment to see where the software has strayed from the straight and narrow.
Quote at WWW6 - "Your pages are so cluttered I cannot hear what you wrote."

Slide 15

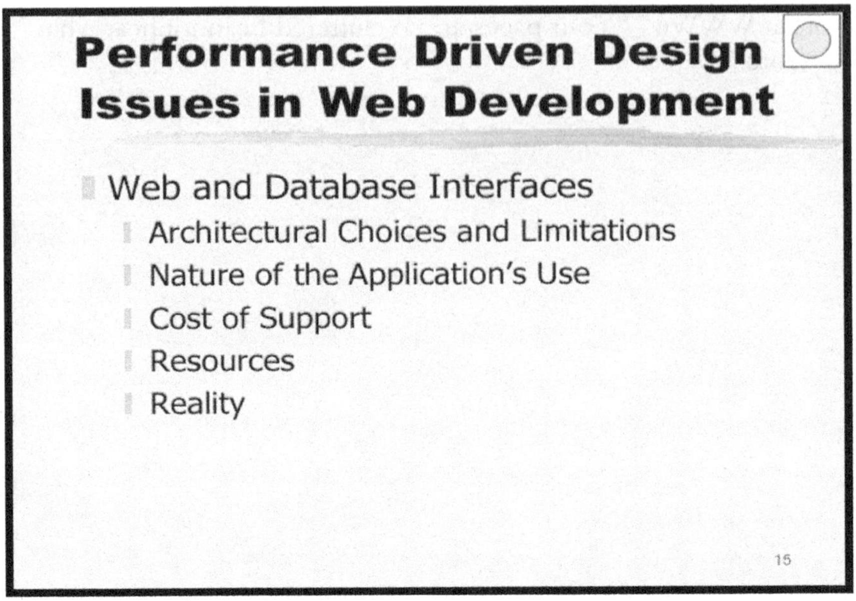

Next Subject ... In my experience, the greatest challenges to performance are in the Web and Database Interfaces.

The choices you have when selecting your architecture may be clear-cut; oftentimes management makes them for you. You may be limited to such-and-such equipment or software family. Your organization may be committed to supporting only one particular suite of software. Other times you have the flexibility to choose. Later we will discuss two distinctly different interfaces, one in open software another in vendor specific software.

Primarily, the choices should be based upon the following four (4) items: And ... again, Chris Manley's presentation this morning.

- The use of the application; is it a static information display system or a high volume data entry application? They have very different architectural needs.
- Your decisions about how much you want to be involved in the on-going support, and decisions that are made for you about what support the systems and operations staff can or will give you.

- There are physical considerations, hardware, software, human capabilities, networks, etc. that come into play in architectural design decisions.
- Finally, there are these two nasty question that's that come up, usually too late for you to do anything about it, "Can we do what they want done?" and "Should we do what they want done?"

Remember - Although wheat, arctic rye and basmati rice all are cereal grass, they are grown very differently. They may be the same type of product, but they are very different.

Slide 16

These are some issue to consider.

When making architectural choices, function follows form. A two-tier architecture has a very different form that a three-or-more-tier. And the Web to Database Interface may very well decide whether you use a two or three-tier architecture.

The nature of the application also is part of the decision mix. A predominantly static web application can make do with a simple interface and Web-Server default settings, where a data entry application carrying mission critical data (like payroll hours updates) must be robust and fast.

We'll hit these next. Some will be addressed directly, others as parts of other topics.

Slide 17

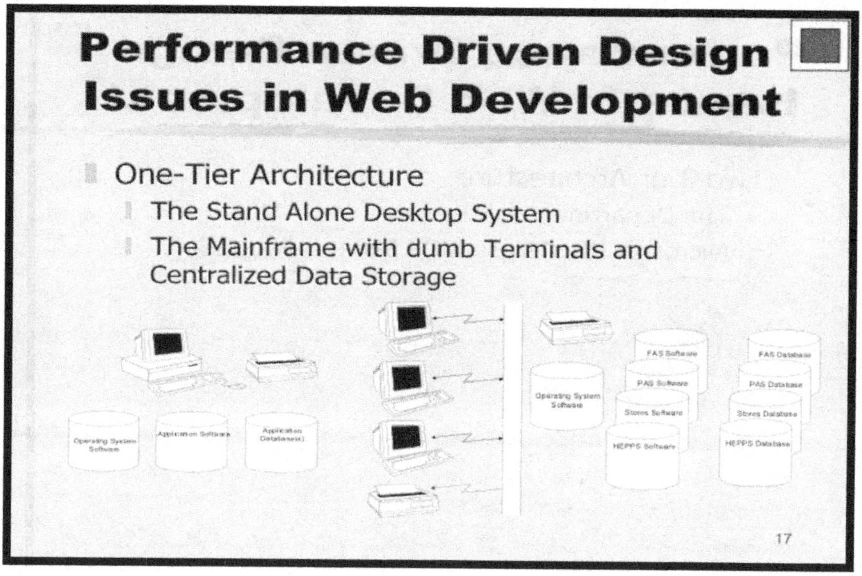

This architecture does not come into play in deployed web systems (development, yes). Unless you want to have a web system with one visitor … The Local Limited Web (LLW).

Slide 18

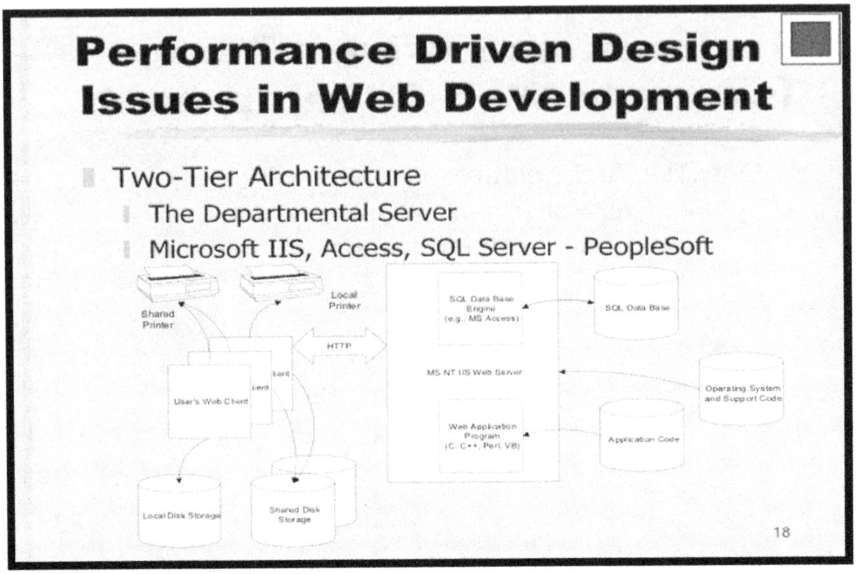

This is a changed slide from what is in your packet. It reflects another review of the PeopleSoft "PeopleTools 7.0", September 1997 (pages 7-10).

(2012 Note – This last week (June 4, 2012 – users are reporting the two-tier has finally been turned off – now that Oracle has purchased PeopleSoft and the general release number is 9.,1!!! I fought use of two-tier for five years at Northern Arizona University – just too many security and accuracy issues. BUT the customer proved they are always right, right until the crash!)

Advantages

- This is a good architecture for similar sized static pages, where the web server can use the standard or default memory paging algorithms to manage its space.
- Servicing is fast when content and presentation are closely coupled (static pages)
- Good ability to inform users when the database is not available (better messaging is generally available)
- Easier to troubleshoot problems since there are fewer components and connections to worry about.
- Deployment and maintenance may be easier.

Disadvantages

- Limited number of users or limited functionality (memory paging), cannot mix and match static and dynamic pages - **EXPLAIN**
- Hardware may be tuned for Network or Database activities ... not both. This may be the source of Insert response time problems with PeopleSoft
- Personally, I have a security concern with a two tier system. When, NOT IF, your web server is compromised so is your data.

A Thick-Client can be either a two or three-tier. The number of network transitions determines it.

Slide 19

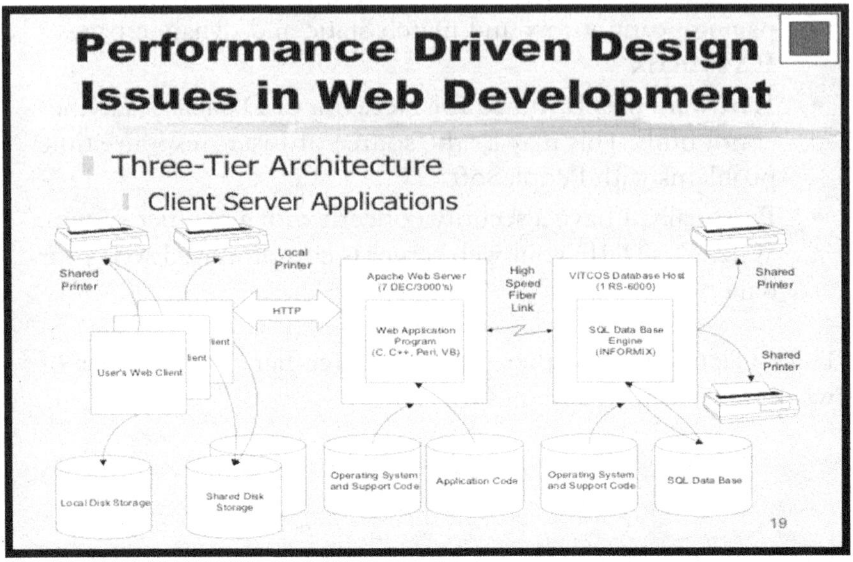

This is the industrial-strength work-horse of these three architectures.

OASIS is an anomaly – it is a mature web application – is it now a "legacy" application?

This is an old graphic. The box names and counts are those used for the Fixed Assets System I've mentioned.

Advantages

- Better security.
- Better optimization possibilities since the web server can be optimized for web traffic and LDAP, while the data server can be optimized for database access.
- Better use of resources
- Supports larger, more vendor independent databases.

Disadvantages

- Response time is not as fast as a two-tier when the database must be accessed since additional network calls must be made and data passed.

- Depending upon the level of interconnection between the web and data server there will be an additional support exposure.

Slide 20

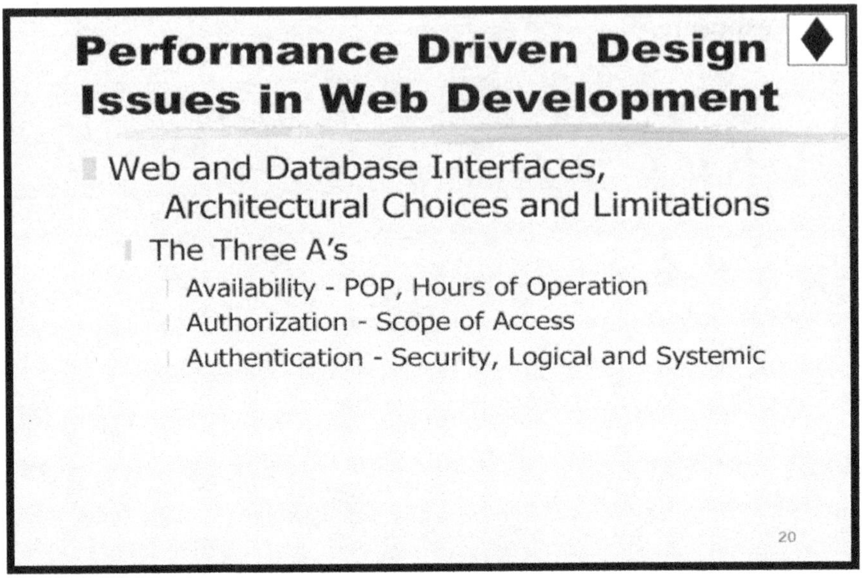

During design, it is absolutely essential you know these three things, and have user acceptance of them.

1. **Availability** - Presumes that the application will tell users when it is not available. If some limited operation is available, the appropriate messages will be generated. When you do not control the Pont of Presence, you user community must accept that there are times availability really is "beyond your control". Everyone must understand that the interface of a 24x365 system will be different that a 5x12x52.
2. **Authorization** - How do you control data that may be seen? We use a system specific authorizations with PIPE logic. "You can see anything and may update anything we say you may, unless we say you can't." See me after the session for an explanation of how to do multiple overlapping include and exclude of budgets or organization codes.
3. **Authentication** - includes LDAP access and Kerberos technology impacts. Who is allowed access and from where. If you restrict access based upon POP, the folks at home with DSL lines may have a problem. If you restrict upon status in a personnel file (e.g., faculty or staff, but not students) then how do you support guests, like external auditors? How do you

verify, in a stateless world, that the user coming in is the user who came in last time with that id? Do you really trust cookies?

Example - We use both POP and personnel file status to control access. Shortly, 3 days to be exact, after deployment the user discovered that the external State Auditor's Office in the Capitol, 70 miles away, could not be put into our personnel system.

Slide 21

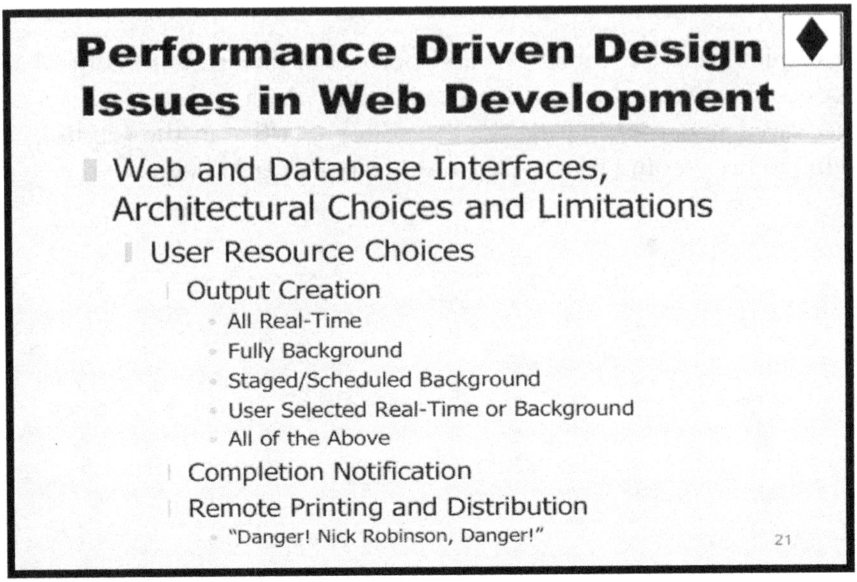

The web's power allows you to give substantial control over what data users wish to see, both in the form and format, and when they can see it, too. The software controls the "Who", and can be written to give full "What, When Where and How" control. The "Why" sometimes will remain a total mystery.

Five Choices for creating output

Fastest, but requires many dbms access licenses (give an overview of understanding of current Oracle, Sybase and Informix policies)

.**Slower** but gets the results in a timely manner. (Put job requests in a file that is interrogated on a cyclic basis by a cron job or Maestro type product.)

Predictable, and preferred where central printing facilities are used.

Politically Correct, but users all their work is of utmost importance and will always ask for Real-Time processing (See 1 above). Again, this answer is usually wrong. Here it is out due to support costs.

We use a combination of **#1** (Asset Search, 7-14 rows), **#2** (Ad Hoc Reporter, 70-10,000+ rows) and **#3** (Cataloged Reports, 10-1,000,000+ rows).

Completion Notification ... Email based upon user's My Profile information and entered parameters - allows the user to "Tell Bill when his data is ready."

Remote printing… UW and MIT both facing severe problems. Duplex printing,3-hole right-side and top-of-page spacing, reprinting and rerouting problems. **MANY OPEN ISSUES HERE!**

Slide 22

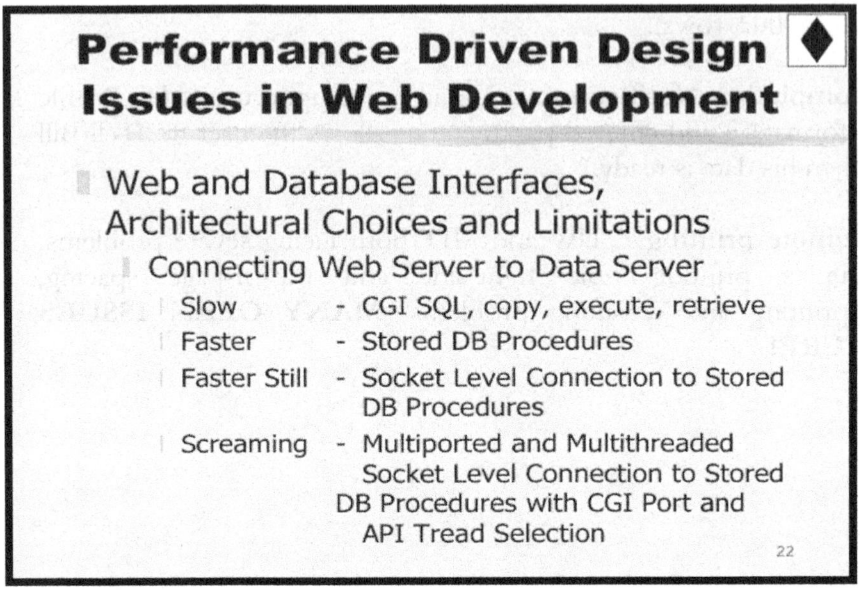

We faced the greatest performance challenges in this area.

SLOW - Good for prototyping. In UNIX this is the "rcp, rsh, cat -e-v" described in my Perl Paper and here at last year's WebDevShare.

FASTER - Good for low volume transactions. Personnel Masterfile updates. Will result in a license used for each concurrent user. Incurs overhead of bringing up the dbms engine on each request.

FASTER STILL - Socket level connection can be written to keep a persistent connection open on the Data Server. All transactions to the socket are seen as coming from one user, so cuts license requirements. NOTE - Vendors are raising questions about this and looking for ways to charger for each potential web client …(How they will do this is undefined). A single thread impacts response times as transactions are queued. There is a sample of a single-port, single-thread Database Server API in last year's WebDevShare paper.

SCREAMING - Socket level connection keeps persistent Database Server connections open and supports multiple users. Will use up to (#ports)x(#threads) licenses. CGI directs "fast" transactions (few rows returned) to one port and "slow" (many rows) ones to another. Data Server API controls threads.

Slide 23

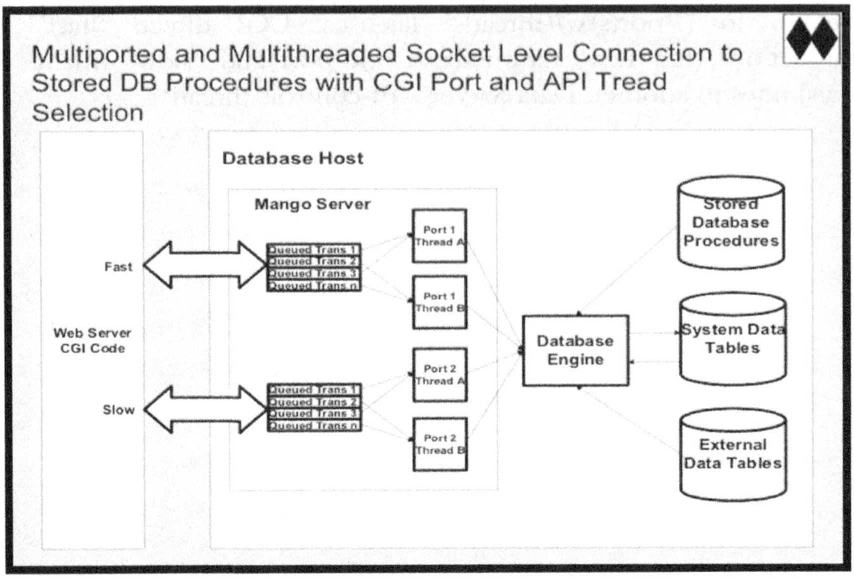

Here is a DOUBLE DIAMOND – A Full-Sized version is in the packet.

(2012 Note – A full-page version of this graphic is included as SLIDE 23 at the end of this section.)

The Web CGI prepares the parameters and calling strings necessary, then forwards the request to the appropriate port (socket). By convention, one port is for fast, low volume transactions (look up an asset, the related expenditures, notes and history, 7-15 records typically but can go as high as 400) and the other is for slow, high volume ones (look up all assets in Building 532, 750 of the 7-15 noted above).

The Socket is connected to the Mango Server, maintaining a persistent connection for a fixed period of time, typically 5 minutes or less. Each instance of the Mango can be configured for a different number of threads, two each are shown here. The threads, if all are open, are seen as concurrent users and "use" one of available licenses. Will use up to (#ports)x(#threads) licenses. The process is not linked to the user, just open for transactions from the web user (who is not NOBODY). It is easy to monitor the number of ports and treads used, so tweaking is easy.

Requests are serviced by applying the supplied parameters into precompiled stored database procedures and piping the results back through the open socket to the Web Server. There the returned string is parsed, formatted and sent to the desktop web Browser Client for display.

Although end-to-end (User mouse click to end of receipt) takes 4-8 seconds, the times through the database access code (from call to parse) run from far less than 1 second (a 1 row profile check) to about 2.5 seconds (400 row sorted return).

Slide 24

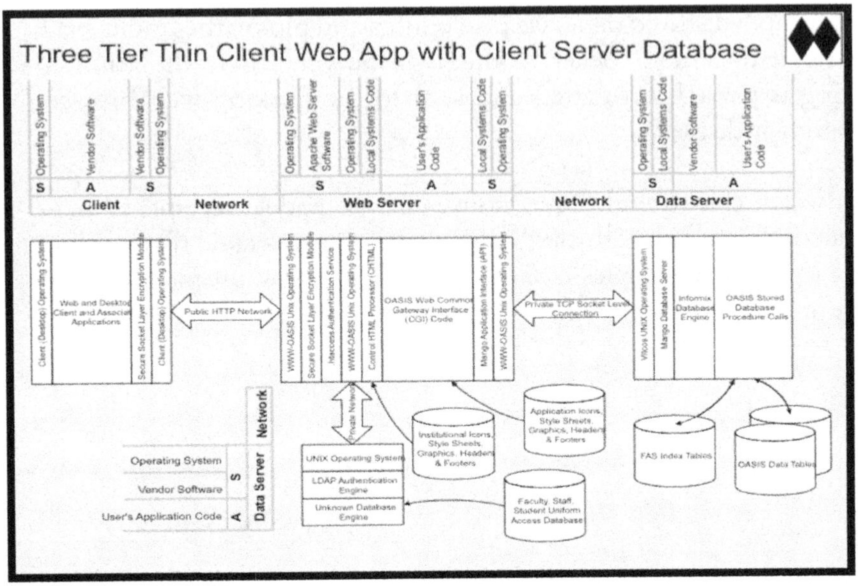

Here is a DOUBLE DIAMOND – **A Full-sized copy is in the conference packet -** Typo "Application"

(2012 Note – A full-page version of this graphic is included as SLIDE 24 at the end of this section.)

Here is the big picture of the fixed assets system, **an open software code project.** All the parts are not included, this is only the direct web portion (Maestro, remote printing, systems management are not included).

This picture violates nearly every rule for PowerPoint slides, but it has been such a good tool I included it.

This is a typical three-tier application with distinct Web and Database Servers. It is dominated by locally developed code, and is vendor independent (e.g., swapped from Informix to NT SQL Server in 2 days - did not scale so was abandoned).

Four types of information.

- Long Bar - Distribution of physical resources - Client, Servers and Network

- S's and A's - Shows areas of responsibility - Systems and Applications
- Top Vertical Text Boxes - Indicate who provides the that part of the system
- In-Line Text Boxes - Describe the various pieces of code and hardware that are used in the order that a transaction would normally use them - Useful for understanding the interaction within and among systems.

Slide 25

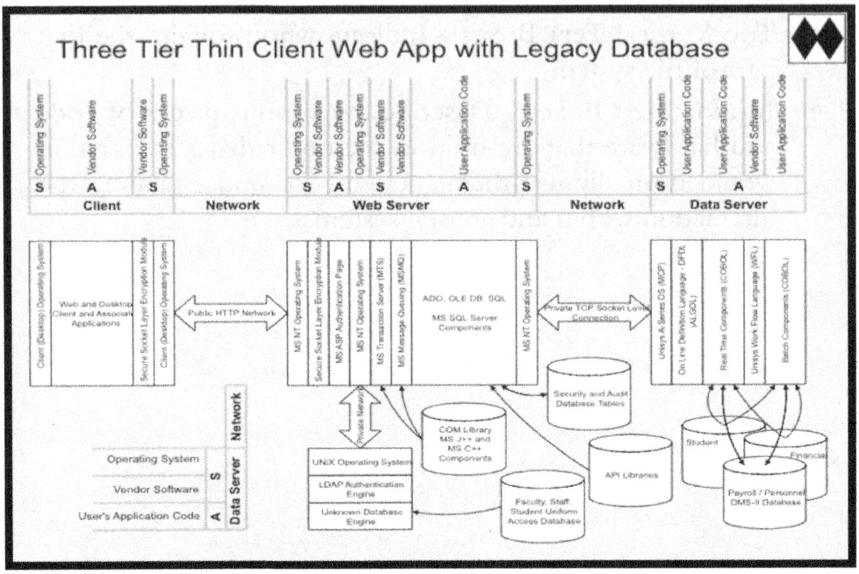

Here is a DOUBLE DIAMOND – **A Full-sized copy is in the conference packet -** Typo "Application"

(2012 Note – A full-page version of this graphic is included as SLIDE 25 at the end of this section.)

Here is the big picture of the payroll timecard processing system, a vendor specific project. This was used as part of a long-term strategy to reduce development and support costs.

This is a typical three-tier application with a legacy database, in this case Unisys DMS-II. This dbms is used in banking because it is exceptionally resilient and robust.

Although is resembles the last slide, this system is dominated by vendor code. Problem area in the application are in the ADO area. It is heavily used, touchy and comparatively poorly documented.

Again, there are four types of information.

- Long Bar - Distribution of physical resources - Client, Servers and Network
- S's and A's - Shows areas of responsibility - Systems and Applications

- Top Vertical Text Boxes - Indicate who provides the that part of the system
- In-Line Text Boxes - Describe the various pieces of code and hardware that are used in the order that a transaction would normally use them - Useful for understanding the interaction within and among systems.

Slide 26

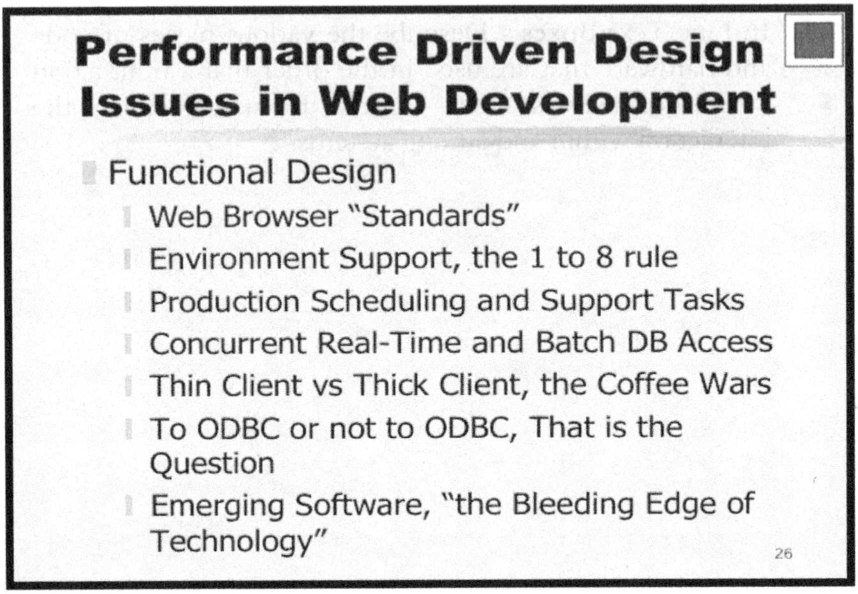

NEXT SUBJECT

Many things outside the application developer's span of control affect the Functional Design. These items are sometimes considered "the small stuff".

These are issues that have a foot in both the GUI and Interface Architecture. We'll hit them next.

Slide 27

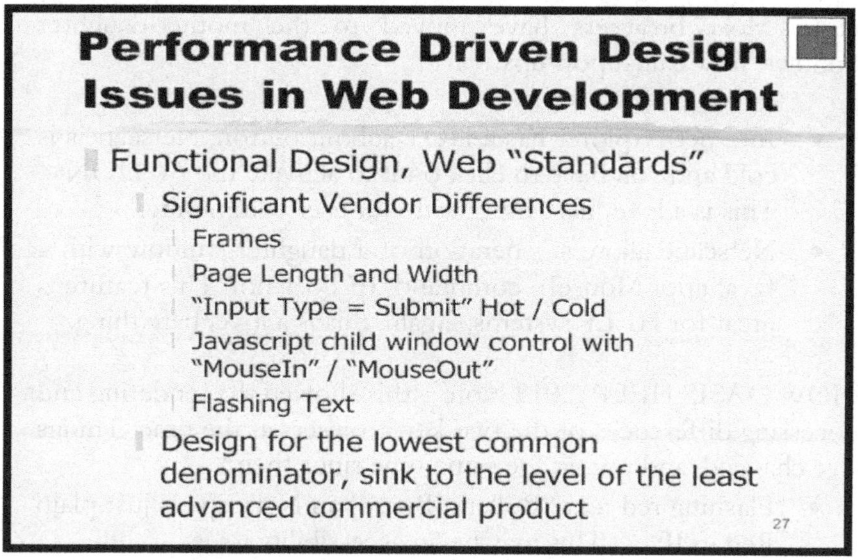

Frames render differently and will always affect performance. Avoid them in production systems with moderate or high data entry volumes. Prohibit where accessibility is an issue (as address earlier). Always good in fully static environments.

VENDOR DIFFERENCES

Some administrators want the entire dynamic output to fit on a single screen. This is not do-able since the user can easily resize the window or change the font to defeat your program settings. Think beyond the 24x80 world. We have an asset that can display down over 400 lines and out 125 columns. And it renders from submit to first light in about 10 seconds.

Again, and I won't beat this dead horse again, Chris Manley's opinion that a "pate" is an improper metaphor for web output must be considered.

(2012 Note –Time and technology have proven Chris absolutely correct! The idea that 25% of the visible panel should be reserved for static information such as corporate headers and footers was wrong then and it is wrong now.)

WEB VIEW (2012 Note – These comments had to do with the impact of pressing the RETURN button when the browser was active. Most browsers have moved to the mother-daughter windows, now called pop-ups.)

- Internet Explorer has a HOT submit button, Netscape's is cold and you have to click on it to activate the ACTION=. This is a love/hate thing with our user community.
- Netscape allow s generation of a daughter window with a JavaScript MouseIn command, IE does not. This feature is great for HELP systems. Again, this is a love/hate thing.

SHOW OASIS HELP (2012 Note – this showed the rendering and processing differences of the two key browsers at the time. Things have changed, and not, at the same time since then.)

- Flashing red text "Bulletin Board" in Netscape is just plain Red in IE … This may be an accessibility issue.

Designing for the Lowest Common Denominator is unfortunate, but it has kept us out of trouble.

STRIVE FOR 30% REUSABILITY

(2012 Note – yow! We were easily satisfied back then.)

Slide 28

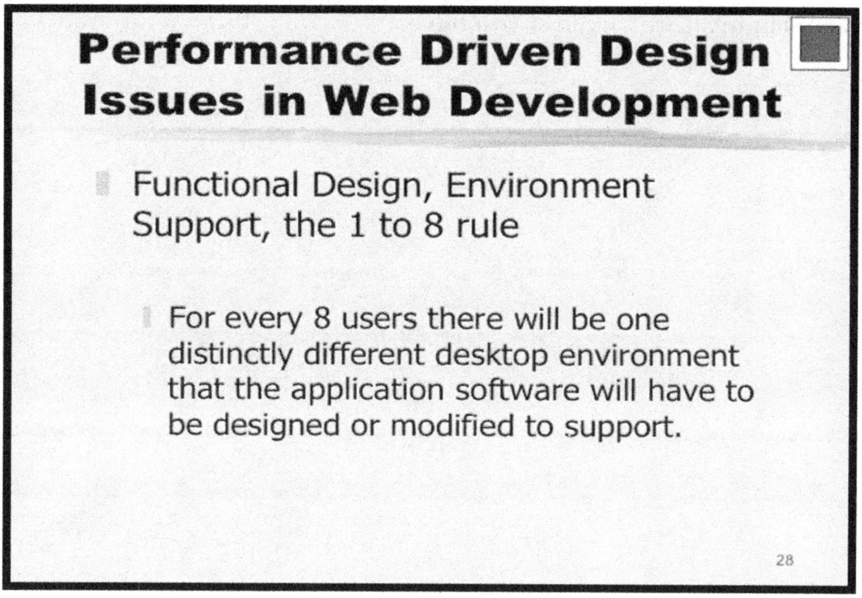

This is a rule developed after observing several applications at the UW, MIT and Boeing. Oracle rep says at Princeton (100% pure Microsoft) they found 126 different browser variations.

Differences:

- User physical challenges … color sensitivity, manual dexterity, language issues, work shifts and color selections (For example, this screen in a dark place at night may make a good night light)
- Desktop platform … an 80386 may run your Java just like that Mac G4 rocket ship down the hall, it will just be really SSSSSSLLLLLLOOOOOOWWWWWW.
- OS Choice … can you spell Linux
- OS Version
- Browser Manufacturer (also homegrown systems, especially a problem colleges with Schools of Computer Science)
- Browser Versions (Netscape 4.05 and 4.05a render trailing nulls in tables differently)

The lesson is to design so you do not have to control the desktop, as if you did not have the ability to enforce desktop standards by draconian measures, even if you have.

Slide 29

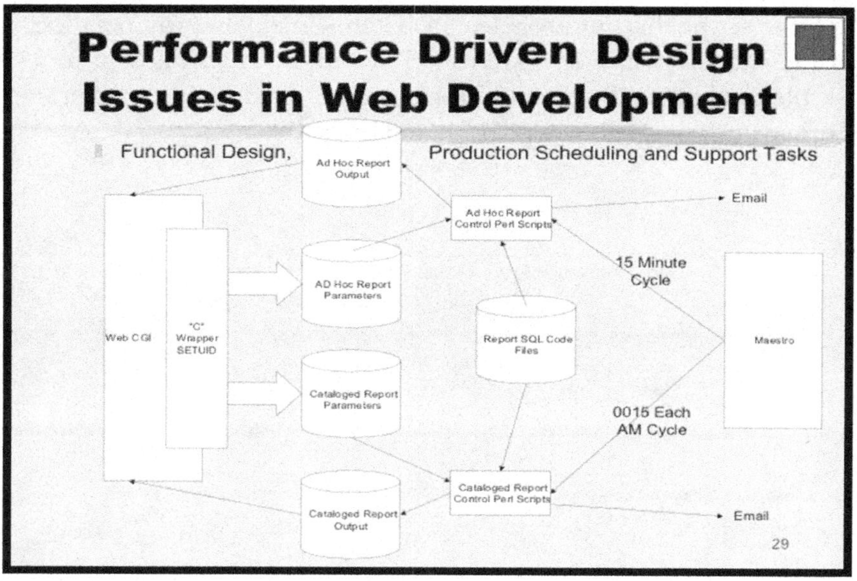

One issue that arises is, "just who will assure my jobs are run?"

We use a common product enterprise wide for scheduling and control of UNIX hosted jobs. Maestro from Tivoli.

"C" Wrapper is a security issue. It keeps user NOBODY out of the way.

Every 15 minutes, Monday to Sunday, Maestro starts a Perl script on our fixed assets host that interrogates the contents of the Ad Hoc Report Parameter File. If there are jobs to run, they are (also Perl scripts). The output is written (generally to disk) and email sent to the user of origin and/or an address designated.

(2012 Note – Maestro is a registered trademark)

(2012 Note – At this point I went live and showed how an ad hoc job ran ... and had a backup of one I'd run before the conference just in case. I remember showing the process timer, waiting for the email while I spoke, and then showing the report. Worked like a champ.)

Every morning at 0015, Monday to Saturday, Maestro runs a different script that interrogates all batch schedules. Any pending jobs, regardless of the day, are run. The output, if any, is sent to a disk file (and generally to print, too), and an email sent to the user of origin and/or an address designated.

Slide 30

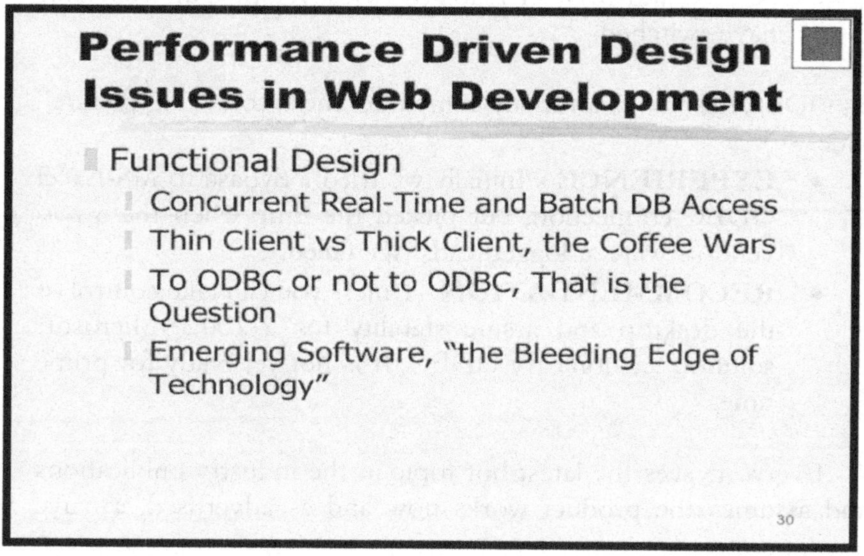

For these 4 topics I'm going to give you a set of **EXPERIENCES** and **RECOMMENDATIONS**.

1 - Our goal was to give users concurrent real-time and batch database updates, true 24x7 operation, in the Private Space.

- **EXPERIENCE** - Severe problems with web server response due to the size and volume of user report requests. The typical symptom is throughput lockup.
- **RECOMMENDATION** - Take your system folk's recommendation on optimum Web Server configuration and double it. Add an additional sever box for redundancy.

2 - I showed two applications earlier.

- **EXPERIENCE** - The attempts at a true thick client stalled because we could not take control of the desktop environment. J++ was to be used and significant dollars were invested, this was a dead product that seems to be coming back from the grave. Java is popular because it has Sun's Marketing Division pushing it but loading all the classes necessary for operation takes too much time (OO purists will disagree but the fact is that few not-for-profits have the dollars to entice OO gurus to come work for them).

- **RECOMMENDATION** - Perl is as fast as "C" and "C++" and MUCH FASTER to develop. Our web folks have switched.

3 - ODBC ties you to a vendor, remember the second "big-picture" slide.

- **EXPERIENCE** - Initially we tried a Sybase to MS-Excel ODBC connection, but picked the time when these two vendors were at loggerheads. We failed.
- **RECOMMENDATION** - Unless you can take control of the desktop and assure stability for a 100% Microsoft solution … don't try ODBC. It is not yet ready for prime time.

4 - Everyone sees the latest hot topic in the industry publications and assumes the product works now and as advertised, a naïve assumption.

- **EXPERIENCE** - We had a department that went around IS and got permission to invest substantially to build a data warehouse for all Financial System transactions. It was intended for 3-7 local users and written in MS-Access. It seemed logical to their management based upon tech reports and died when the first month's 750,000 transaction hit it.
- **RECOMMENDATION** - Leave the bleeding edge to the vendors and experimental groups. Nothing is stable enough for mission critical applications until 2-3 years after initial release.

SLIDE 23 Full-Page Version

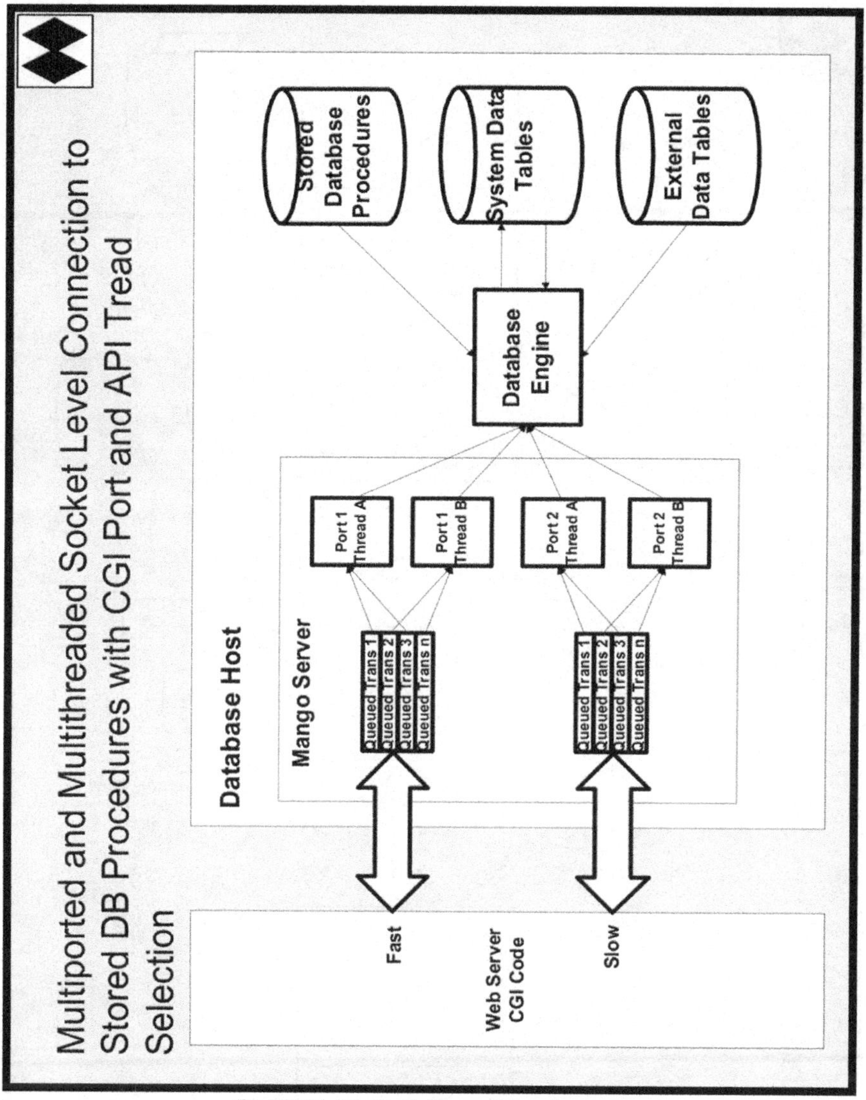

SLIDE 23 Full-Page Version

(2012 Note – Added for clarity)

SLIDE 24 and SLIDE 25 Full-Page Version

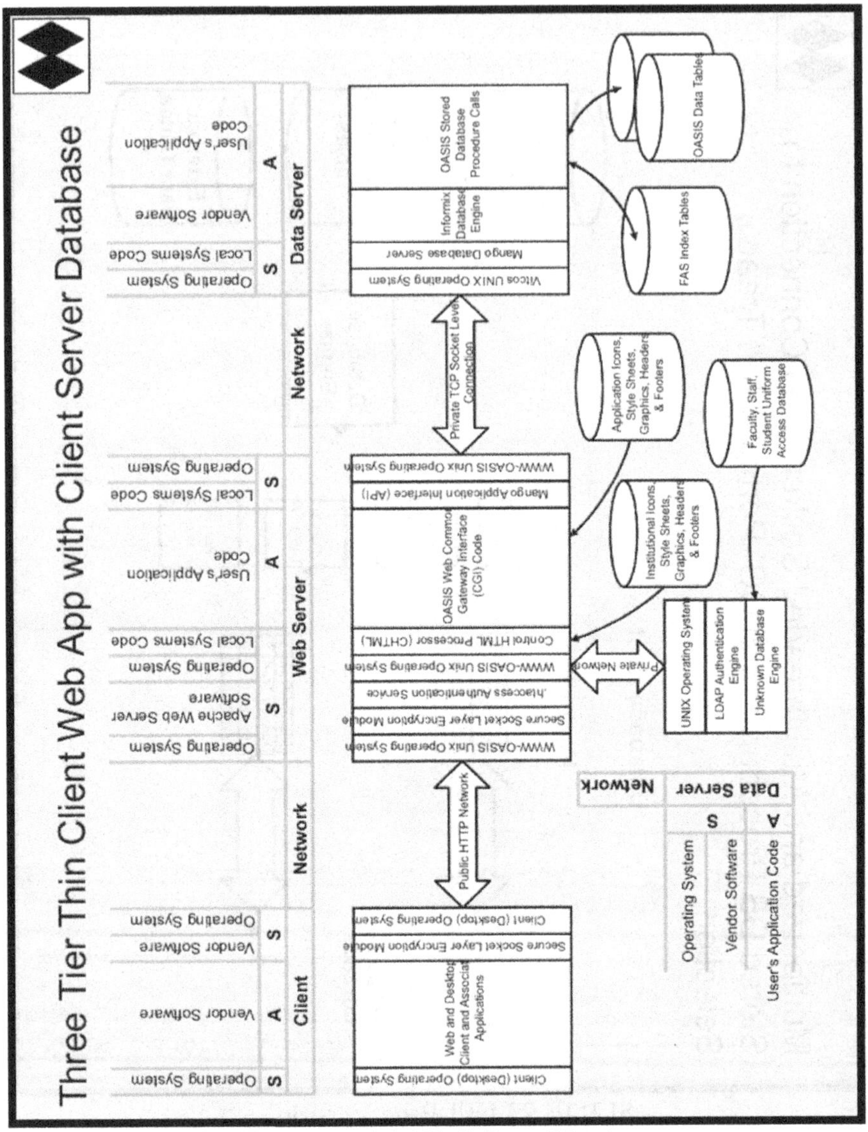

SLIDE 24 and 25 Full-Page Version

Slide 31

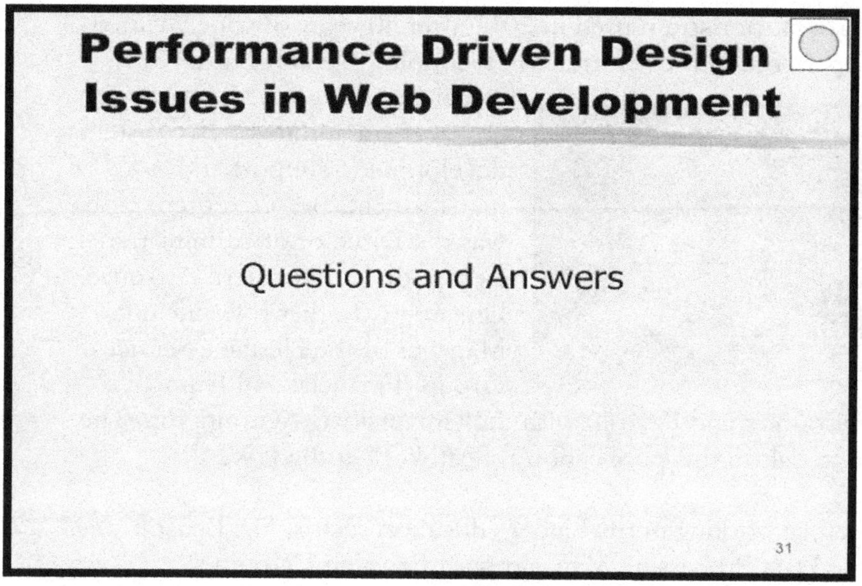

DONE

ABOUT THE AUTHOR

Patrick Benson retired in 2011 after 40 years of widely varied experience in the information technology sector. During this career he worked in all phases of government administrative systems development, support and management. Before retirement he was the Director of Administrative Computing at Northern Arizona University. Earlier roles include Manager of the Heritage Services Group (Financial and Human Resources and Payroll) with the University of Washington. The materials in this publication reflect work at the UW.

Before working in the higher education sector, Mr. Benson was the Data Processing Manager with Ernst and Whinney Telecommunications Group. Patrick also spent 12 years with the USAF working on and teaching fighter aircraft weapons control systems, and programming military intelligence applications and database management systems.

Since retirement Mr. Benson has engaged a life-long dream of writing. In 2011 his play "*Hearing*" received an Honorable Mention in the 80th Annual *Writer's Digest* Writing Competition.

Patrick and Shirley Benson, his wife of 50 years, enjoy living in Flagstaff - especially visiting and hiking the front and backcountry areas of Arizona's Canyon Country; the Grand, Oak Creek, Walnut and Sycamore are favorites.

For More Information or Contact Patrick M. Benson

For technical publications and presentations at various national and regional conferences, please refer to my papers at web pages currently linked from http://sites.google.com/site/patrickmbenson/. For other conference notes you should refer to the EDUCAUSE, CAUSE, RMAIR and O'Reilly Perl Conference sites, or contact me directly.

Mr. Benson may be contacted via his preferred and permanent email address, pbenson@uw.edu (and thanks to the UW for that!), or via commercial email accounts at patrickmbenson@gmail.com or patrickmbenson@hotmail.com.
(2020 Note – Added those commercial email addresses.)

Made in the USA
Monee, IL
04 November 2026

67382859R10167